Unl⌀ck

Second Edition

5

Listening, Speaking & Critical Thinking

STUDENT'S BOOK WITH DIGITAL PACK

Jessica Williams and Sabina Ostrowska
with Chris Sowton, Jennifer Farmer,
Christina Cavage and Laurie Frazier

CAMBRIDGE
UNIVERSITY PRESS

Shaftesbury Road, Cambridge CB2 8EA, United Kingdom

One Liberty Plaza, 20th Floor, New York, NY 10006, USA

477 Williamstown Road, Port Melbourne, VIC 3207, Australia

314–321, 3rd Floor, Plot 3, Splendor Forum, Jasola District Centre,
New Delhi – 110025, India

103 Penang Road, #05–06/07, Visioncrest Commercial, Singapore 238467

Cambridge University Press & Assessment is a department of the University of Cambridge.

We share the University's mission to contribute to society through the pursuit of
education, learning and research at the highest international levels of excellence.

www.cambridge.org
Information on this title: www.cambridge.org/9781009031493

First published 2019
Second Edition update published 2021

20 19 18 17 16 15 14 13 12 11 10 9 8 7 6 5 4 3

Printed in Malaysia by Vivar Printing

A catalogue record for this publication is available from the British Library

ISBN 978-1-009-03149-3 Listening, Speaking and Critical Thinking Student's Book with Digital Pack 5
ISBN 978-1-009-03137-0 Listening, Speaking and Critical Thinking Student's eBook with Digital Pack 5

CONTENTS

MAP OF THE BOOK

UNIT	VIDEO	LISTENING	VOCABULARY	
1 CONSERVATION Listening 1: A lecture about sustainable agriculture (Ecology/Environmental science) Listening 2: A panel discussion about climate change (International development/Ecology)	Saving Indonesia's birds of paradise one village at a time	**Key listening skills:** Listening to introductions Identifying rhetorical questions as signposts Understanding key vocabulary Using your knowledge Listening for main ideas Taking notes on detail Summarizing Synthesizing **Pronunciation for listening:** Intonation of complete and incomplete ideas	Language for assigning blame and responsibility	
2 DESIGN Listening 1: A presentation on 3-D printing (Design/Manufacturing) Listening 2: A student presentation about planned obsolescence (Manufacturing/Marketing)	Designer bikes become showcase for social status	**Key listening skills:** Using a table to take notes on main ideas and detail Reviewing and organizing notes Using your knowledge Understanding key vocabulary Predicting content using visuals Taking notes on main ideas and detail Summarizing Synthesizing **Pronunciation for listening:** Word stress	Using cause-and-effect phrases	
3 PRIVACY Listening 1: A moderated forum on individual privacy and law enforcement (Law/Ethics) Listening 2: A public presentation about internet security and privacy (Information technology/Marketing)	Internet security expert on latest ransomware attack	**Key listening skills:** Listening for facts and supporting information Listening for opinion Using your knowledge Understanding key vocabulary Making inferences Taking notes on main ideas and detail Synthesizing **Pronunciation for listening:** Sentence stress	Collocations (the internet and the law)	
4 BUSINESS Listening 1: A lecture about disruptive innovation (Business) Listening 2: An overview of the business model of a US non-profit organization (Management)	Ugandan tech start-up caters to local markets	**Key listening skills:** Listening for definitions Understanding figurative language Identifying figurative language Understanding key vocabulary Using your knowledge Taking notes on main ideas and detail Making inferences Synthesizing **Pronunciation for listening:** Pausing and thought groups	Academic alternatives	
5 PSYCHOLOGY Listening 1: A planning session for a group presentation on the psychology of first impressions (Psychology) Listening 2: A lecture on navigation techniques and the brain (Psychology/Neurology)	New virtual reality game helping to fight against dementia	**Key listening skills:** Listening for generalizations and summaries Listening for dependency relationships Using your knowledge Understanding key vocabulary Taking notes on main ideas and detail Summarizing Making inferences Synthesizing **Pronunciation for listening:** Emphasis	Academic word families	

GRAMMAR	CRITICAL THINKING	SPEAKING
Parallel structure in comparisons	Analyzing issues	**_Preparation for speaking:_** Challenging other points of view **_Pronunciation for speaking:_** Intonation of complete and incomplete ideas **_Speaking task:_** Have an informal debate about the mission of national parks.
Degree expressions	Evaluating pros and cons	**_Preparation for speaking:_** Acknowledging other arguments **_Pronunciation for speaking:_** Stress in compound nouns and noun phrases **_Speaking task:_** Give a group presentation about a product designed for obsolescence.
Subject-verb agreement with quantifiers	Eliciting information via surveys Analyzing data	**_Preparation for speaking:_** Presenting survey data Presenting conclusions from research **_Pronunciation for speaking:_** Question intonation **_Speaking task:_** Give a presentation of the data you have gathered from a survey and your conclusions.
Emphasizing and contrasting	Persuading your audience in a business presentation	**_Preparation for speaking:_** Mission statements Crafting a pitch **_Speaking task:_** Make a pitch for investment or donations to get a new venture started.
Noun clauses with *wh-*words and *if/whether*	Synthesizing information from multiple sources	**_Preparation for speaking:_** Talking about research Incorporating visual support **_Speaking task:_** Give a group presentation with visual support about research on an aspect of human behaviour.

UNIT	VIDEO	LISTENING	VOCABULARY	
6 CAREERS Listening 1: A presentation by a careers advisor for Computer science students (Education/Human resources) Listening 2: A workshop about job interview skills (Business/Education/Human resources)	'100k opportunities' job fair in Chicago	*Key listening skill:* Making inferences Using your knowledge Understanding key vocabulary Listening for main ideas Taking notes on detail Synthesizing *Pronunciation for listening:* Reduction of auxiliary verbs	Emphatic expressions of belief and certainty	
7 HEALTH SCIENCES Listening 1: A talk about the possible causes of increased asthma rates (Health sciences/Medicine) Listening 2: A community meeting about water quality (Environmental management/Politics)	Water pollution in West Virginia	*Key listening skills:* Making unstructured notes as you listen Identifying persuasive appeals Using your knowledge Predicting content using visuals Understanding key vocabulary Taking notes on main ideas and detail Summarizing Taking notes on detail Synthesizing *Pronunciation for listening:* Contrastive stress	Adjectives of strong disapproval	
8 COLLABORATION Listening 1: A training session on group dynamics and the 'bad apple' effect (Business/Sociology/Human resources) Listening 2: A class discussion about two systems for decision making (Business/Politics/Law/Ethics)	Lufthansa signs cooperation deal with Etihad	*Key listening skill:* Using anecdotes and proverbs to illustrate larger ideas Using your knowledge Understanding key vocabulary Summarizing Taking notes on detail Making inferences Taking notes on main ideas Synthesizing *Pronunciation for listening:* Connected speech: linking words with vowels	Dependent prepositions	
9 TECHNOLOGY Listening 1: A lecture about the adoption cycle of new technology (Sociology/Business/Technology/Marketing) Listening 2: A university seminar about the impact of AI on human employment (Computer science: Artificial intelligence/Ethics)	First anthropomimetic robot	*Key listening skills:* Listening for examples Supporting speculation Understanding key vocabulary Predicting content using visuals Listening for main ideas Listening for detail Synthesizing *Pronunciation for listening:* Connected speech: elision	Negative prefixes	
10 LANGUAGE Listening 1: A university seminar about machine translation (Linguistics/Computer Science) Listening 2: A research interview with a non-native English teacher (Education)	Language diversity	*Key listening skill:* Noting down follow-up questions Understanding key vocabulary Using your knowledge Listening for main ideas Making inferences Taking notes on main ideas and detail Synthesizing *Pronunciation for listening:* Connected speech: linking	Phrasal verbs about communication	

GRAMMAR	CRITICAL THINKING	SPEAKING
Degree expressions with *so ... that; such a ... that*	Understanding job descriptions	***Preparation for speaking:*** Body language Presenting yourself in a job interview ***Speaking task:*** Participate in a mock job interview.
Establishing cohesion with *so* and *such*	Understanding motivation	***Preparation for speaking:*** Inclusive language ***Pronunciation for speaking:*** Emphasis for emotional appeal ***Speaking task:*** Participate in a meeting to discuss whether a fast-food restaurant should open at a local commercial complex.
Wh- clefts	Evaluating options	***Preparation for speaking:*** Steps for consensus building Collaborative language: suggestion and concession ***Speaking task:*** Participate in a consensus-building decision-making task to decide on future food service operations at your college or university.
Hypothetical future	Providing supporting detail	***Preparation for speaking:*** Leaving and returning to the topic Asking for clarification and confirmation ***Pronunciation for speaking:*** Assimilation in connected speech ***Speaking task:*** Take part in an informal discussion about artificial intelligence.
Complex gerunds and infinitives	Asking appropriate and productive questions	***Preparation for speaking:*** Interrupting and handling questions ***Pronunciation for speaking:*** Intonation when interrupting ***Speaking task:*** Conduct an in-depth semi-structured interview about learning English.

YOUR GUIDE TO UNLOCK

Unlock your academic potential

Unlock Second Edition is a six-level, academic-light English course created to build the skills and language students need for their studies (CEFR Pre-A1 to C1). It develops students' ability to think critically in an academic context right from the start of their language learning. Every level has 100% new inspiring video on a range of academic topics.

Confidence in teaching.
Joy in learning.

Better Learning WITH UNLOCK SECOND EDITION

Better Learning is our simple approach where insights we've gained from research have helped shape content that drives results. We've listened to teachers all around the world and made changes so that *Unlock* Second Edition better supports students along the way to academic success.

CRITICAL THINKING

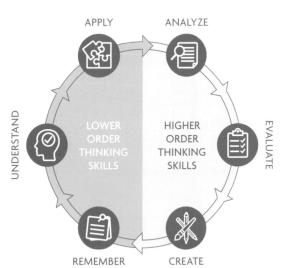

Critical thinking in *Unlock* Second Edition ...

- is **informed** by a range of academic research from Bloom in the 1950s, to Krathwohl and Anderson in the 2000s, to more recent considerations relating to 21st Century Skills
- has a **refined** syllabus with a better mix of higher- and lower-order critical thinking skills
- is **measurable**, with objectives and self-evaluation so students can track their critical thinking progress
- is **transparent** so teachers and students know when and why they're developing critical thinking skills
- is **supported** with professional development material for teachers so teachers can teach with confidence

... so that students have the best possible chance of academic success.

INSIGHT

Most classroom time is currently spent on developing lower-order critical thinking skills. Students need to be able to use higher-order critical thinking skills too.

CONTENT

Unlock Second Edition includes the right mix of lower- and higher-order thinking skills development in every unit, with clear learning objectives.

RESULTS

Students are better prepared for their academic studies and have the confidence to apply the critical thinking skills they have developed.

DIGITAL CLASSROOM MATERIAL

The *Unlock* Second Edition Digital Classroom Material ...

- offers extra, **motivating** practice in speaking, critical thinking and language
- provides a **convenient** bank of language and skills reference informed by our exclusive Corpus research ⊙
- is easily **accessible** and **navigable** from students' mobile phones
- is fully **integrated** into every unit
- provides Unlock-**specific** activities to extend the lesson whenever you see this symbol ▯

... so that students can easily get the right, extra practice they need, when they need it.

INSIGHT

The digital classroom material is most effective when it's an integral, well-timed part of a lesson.

CONTENT

Every unit of *Unlock* Second Edition is enhanced with bespoke digital classroom material to extend the skills and language students are learning in the book. The symbol ▯ shows when to use the material.

RESULTS

Students are motivated by having relevant extension material on their mobile phones to maximize their language learning. Teachers are reassured that the material adds real language-learning value to their lessons.

RESEARCH

We have gained deeper insights to inform *Unlock* Second Edition by ...

- carrying out **extensive market research** with teachers and students to fully understand their needs throughout the course's development
- consulting **academic research** into critical thinking
- refining our vocabulary syllabus using our **exclusive Corpus research** ⊙

... so that you can be assured of the quality of *Unlock* Second Edition.

INSIGHT

- Consultation with global Advisory Panel
- Comprehensive reviews of material
- Face-to-face interviews and Skype™ calls
- Classroom observations

CONTENT

- Improved critical thinking
- 100% new video and video lessons
- Clearer contexts for language presentation and practice
- Text-by-text glossaries
- Digital workbook with more robust content
- Comprehensive teacher support

RESULTS

"Thank you for all the effort you've put into developing Unlock Second Edition. As far as I can see, I think the new edition is more academic and more appealing to young adults."

Burçin Gönülsen,
Işık Üniversity, Turkey

HOW *UNLOCK* WORKS

Unlock your knowledge
Encourages discussion around the themes of the unit with inspiration from interesting questions and striking images.

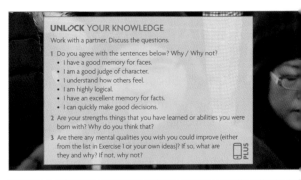

UNLOCK YOUR KNOWLEDGE
Work with a partner. Discuss the questions.

1 Do you agree with the sentences below? Why / Why not?
- I have a good memory for faces.
- I am a good judge of character.
- I understand how others feel.
- I am highly logical.
- I have an excellent memory for facts.
- I can quickly make good decisions.
2 Are your strengths things that you have learned or abilities you were born with? Why do you think that?
3 Are there any mental qualities you wish you could improve (either from the list in Exercise 1 or your own ideas)? If so, what are they and why? If not, why not?

Watch and listen
Features an engaging and motivating video which generates interest in the topic and develops listening skills.

WATCH AND LISTEN

ACTIVATING YOUR KNOWLEDGE

PREPARING TO WATCH
1 Complete the sentences with your own ideas. Work in a small group and compare your ideas.
  1 Dementia is a medical condition which affects _____ .
  2 _____ is a common symptom of dementia.

LISTENING

Listening 1
Provides information about the topic and practises pre-listening, while-listening and post-listening skills. This section may also include a focus on pronunciation which will further enhance listening comprehension.

LISTENING

LISTENING 1

USING YOUR KNOWLEDGE

PREPARING TO LISTEN
1 You are going to listen to a group of students discussing an assignment on the topic of first impressions. Before you listen, answer the questions then discuss your answers in small groups.
  1 How important are these elements when you meet somebody for the first time? Rank them in order from 1 (most important) to 8 (least important). Discuss the reasons for your ranking.

___ eye contact	___ attractiveness	___ voice
___ clothing	___ facial expression	___ handshake
___ greeting	___ clean and tidy	

Language development
Practises the vocabulary and grammar from Listening 1 and pre-teaches the vocabulary and grammar for Listening 2.

⊘ LANGUAGE DEVELOPMENT

NOUN CLAUSES WITH *WH-* WORDS AND *IF/WHETHER*

We often introduce issues with *wh-* noun clauses. These clauses begin with *what, who, which, when, how, why, whether* or *if* and occur most frequently as the object of a sentence. These clauses present questions within a larger sentence.
Let's talk about **what we found in our readings** and then plan the presentation.
The authors of the study discussed **how useful this will be in computer-generated graphics in games and films**.
Participants had to decide **if they thought they'd like the person in the picture**, on a scale of one to four.

Listening 2
Presents a second listening text on the topic, often in a different format, and serves as a model for the speaking task.

LISTENING 2

PREPARING TO LISTEN
1 You are going to listen to a lecture on how the brain makes and uses mental maps. Before you listen, work with a partner. Look at the diagram of the brain. Read the description of the parts and then label the diagram.

USIN
KNO

1 ___   2 ___

SPEAKING

Critical thinking

Develops the lower- and higher-order thinking skills required for the speaking task.

Preparation for speaking

Presents and practises functional language, pronunciation and speaking strategies for the speaking task.

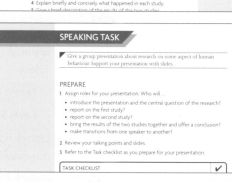

Speaking task

Uses the skills and language learned throughout the unit to support students in producing a presentational or interactional speaking task. This is the unit's main learning objective.

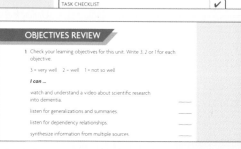

Objectives review

Allows learners to evaluate how well they have mastered the skills covered in the unit.

Wordlist

Lists the key vocabulary from the unit. The most frequent words used at this level in an academic context are highlighted. ⊙

Unlock offers 56 hours per Student's Book, which is extendable to 90 hours with the Digital Pack, and other additional activities in the Teacher's Manual and Development Pack.

Unlock is a paired-skills course with two separate Student's Books per level. For levels 1–5 (CEFR A1 – C1), these are **Reading, Writing and Critical Thinking** and **Listening, Speaking and Critical Thinking**. They share the same unit topics so you have access to a wide range of material at each level. Each Student's Book provides access to the Digital Pack.

Unlock Basic has been developed for pre-A1 learners. **Unlock Basic Skills** integrates reading, writing, listening, speaking and critical thinking in one book to provide students with an effective and manageable learning experience. **Unlock Basic Literacy** develops and builds confidence in literacy. The *Basic* books also share the same unit topics and so can be used together or separately, and **Unlock Basic Literacy** can be used for self-study.

Student components

Resource	Description	Access

Student's Books	• Levels 1–5 come with the Digital Pack (Digital Workbook, Digital Classroom Material, downloadable audio and video)
	  – Levels 1–4 (8 units)
	  – Level 5 (10 units)
	• *Unlock Basic Skills* comes with downloadable audio and video (11 units)
	• *Unlock Basic Literacy* comes with downloadable audio (11 units)
		• The Digital Pack (Digital Workbook, Digital Classroom Material, downloadable audio and video) is accessed on our **learning platform** via the unique code inside the front cover of the Student's Book
		• The audio and video are downloadable from the Student's Resources section on the **learning platform**

Digital Workbook	• Levels 1–5 only • Extension activities to further practise the language and skills learned • All-new vocabulary activities in the Digital Workbook practise the target vocabulary in new contexts	• The Digital Workbook is on our **learning platform** and is accessed via the unique code inside the front cover of the Student's Book
Digital Classroom Material	• Levels 1–5 only • Extra practice in speaking, critical thinking and language	• Please go to **cambridgeone.org** to access the digital classroom material. • Students use the same login details as for the **learning platform**, and then they are logged in for a year
Video	• Levels 1–5 and *Unlock Basic Skills* only • All the video from the course	• The video is downloadable from the Student's Resources section on the **learning platform**
Audio	• All the audio from the course	• The audio is downloadable from the Student's Resources section on the **learning platform**

Teacher components

Resource	Description	Access
Teacher's Manual and Development Pack	• One manual covers Levels 1–5 • It contains flexible lesson plans, lesson objectives, additional activities and common learner errors as well as professional development for teachers, *Developing critical thinking skills in your students* • It comes with downloadable audio and video, vocabulary worksheets and peer-to-peer teacher training worksheets	• The audio, video and worksheets are downloadable from the Teacher Resources section on the **learning platform**
Presentation Plus	• Software for interactive whiteboards so you can present the pages of the Student's Books and easily play audio and video, and check answers	• Presentation Plus is available from the Teacher Resources section on our **learning platform**

LEARNING OBJECTIVES	IN THIS UNIT YOU WILL ...
Watch and listen	watch and understand a video about endangered birds in Indonesia.
Listening skills	listen to introductions; identify rhetorical questions as signposts.
Critical thinking	analyze issues.
Grammar	use parallel structure in comparisons.
Speaking skill	challenge other points of view.
Speaking task	have an informal debate.

UNL⌾CK YOUR KNOWLEDGE

Work with a partner. Discuss the questions.

1 How is human activity changing the world? Are these changes for the better or for the worse?

2 Is it possible for humans to live in harmony with nature, or does any type of human activity upset the balance of nature?

3 Are there any places on Earth that should be off-limits to humans? If so, where?

WATCH AND LISTEN

PREPARING TO WATCH

ACTIVATING YOUR KNOWLEDGE

1 Work with a partner. Discuss the questions.

1 Which species of wild animals are popular in your country? Why?
2 Do you know of any popular species of wild animal which are endangered? Why has that species become endangered?
3 What are some ways that humans can protect endangered species?

PREDICTING CONTENT USING VISUALS

2 You are going to watch a video about an endangered species of bird of paradise. Before you watch, look at the pictures and discuss the questions with your partner.

1 What part of the world do you think this species of bird of paradise comes from? What kind of habitat does it live in?
2 What do you think is happening in the third picture? What other threats might there be to this species' survival?
3 What kind of action do you think environmentalists are taking to protect the species?

GLOSSARY

destructive (adj) causing damage

logging (n) the activity of cutting down trees in order to use their wood

plantation (n) a large farm, especially in a hot part of the world, on which a particular type of crop is grown

treasure (v) to take great care of something because you love it or consider it very valuable

illicit (adj) illegal

smuggle (v) to take things into or out of a place secretly and often illegally

WHILE WATCHING

UNDERSTANDING MAIN IDEAS

3 ▶ Watch the video. Which statement best summarizes the main idea?

a There are many ways that humans are causing *cendrawasih* numbers to fall, but only one hope for saving them.
b The *cendrawasih* were once seriously endangered, but numbers are recovering thanks to local conservation efforts.
c Illegal human activities are damaging the *cendrawasih's* habitat and in future it is likely that they will only be seen in books and zoos.

4 ▶ Watch again. Write *T* (true) or *F* (false) next to the statements below. Correct the false statements.

_____ 1 The *cendrawasih* bird of paradise is commonly seen in the Indonesian jungle.

_____ 2 The forest where the *cendrawasih* lives is being destroyed by people.

_____ 3 The *cendrawasih* is the only species of bird of paradise found in Indonesia.

_____ 4 It is illegal to catch and sell tropical birds to people in other countries.

_____ 5 The forest where the *cendrawasih* live is not protected by law.

_____ 6 Tourism by birdwatchers is another threat to the *cendrawasih*.

5 ▶ Watch again. Complete the student notes with one word in each gap.

Threats to the cendrawasih	Conservation
1_____ in danger because of 2_____ human activities: • Illegal 3_____ • Conversion from rainforest to 4_____ plantations Sales of birds of paradise are 5_____ but birds are often illegally 6_____ abroad.	Papua has 1/3 of Indonesia's 7_____ rainforests. Environmentalists want to: • save the bird's habitat • improve the local 8_____ . Birdwatchers = jobs for local people • women cook • men provide 9_____

DISCUSSION

6 Work in a small group. Discuss the questions.

1 Why do you think that the *cendrawasih* is 'treasured' in Papua?

2 Why is improving local economies often important for environmentalists?

3 Would you like to work on a project to help endangered species? If so, where in the world and which species? If not, why not?

4 What do you think are the main challenges for environmentalists who want to protect endangered species in the rainforests?

5 Do you think that it is more important to protect some endangered species than others? Why / Why not?

LISTENING

LISTENING 1

PREPARING TO LISTEN

1 Read the sentences. Write the words in bold (1–8) next to their definitions (a–h) below.

1 Even after years of farming, the soil remains **fertile** and produces successful crops every year.
2 Technology has allowed farmers to get much higher **yields** from their crops than in the past.
3 About 10 percent of the global population suffers from serious hunger and, without help, many will die of **starvation**.
4 Dark green, leafy vegetables are full of important **nutrients** that are difficult to obtain from other sources.
5 In warm tropical climates, both flowers and insects are **abundant**.
6 We need to find a **viable** alternative to traditional agriculture, which isn't sustainable.
7 The shift in population from the countryside to cities has resulted in the **conversion** of a great deal of farmland into suburbs.
8 Before you plant the trees, you need to dig a deep hole and then **loosen** the soil all around it so the roots have plenty of room.

a _loosen_ (v) to make something less firm or tight
b _abundant_ (adj) more than enough; existing in large amounts
c _conversion_ (n) the process of changing from one thing to another
d _starvation_ (n) death or terrible suffering due to a lack of food
e _yields_ (n) the amount that is produced of something, such as a crop
f _viable_ (adj) able to succeed
g _fertile_ (adj) rich; able to produce good-quality crops
h _nutrients_ (n) substances that a plant or animal needs to live and grow

USING YOUR
KNOWLEDGE

2 You are going to listen to a lecture on whether sustainable agriculture is a viable option. Before you listen, work with a partner and complete the tasks.

1 What do you think the term *sustainable agriculture* means?
2 Read the statements below and try to work out the meanings of the terms in italics. Use a dictionary or look online to check your ideas.

If fields are not designed well, wind and rain can cause *erosion* of the soil. The top layer of soil may completely disappear.

erosion: ~~the process of the~~ the gradual destruction of the

rock
soil

One way to improve the *retention* of nutrients in the soil is to *diversify* crops. For example, a farmer can grow different crops in a particular field every year, instead of only corn or wheat year after year.

retention: _the continuet pesit ion, cna or control of th_

diversify: _diversity_

employee

plants, species

Listening to introductions

The introduction to a lecture can provide valuable information. Speakers often give a preview of what they plan to talk about (the *topic*) and the order in which they will discuss the points (the *structure*).

WHILE LISTENING

3 🔊 1.1 Listen to the introduction to the lecture. Circle all the correct answers to each question.

1 What details about high-yield agriculture are presented?
   a the need for chemical fertilizers
   b the use of irrigation systems to bring water to the crops
   c the use of heavy equipment
   d the use of pesticides to kill insects
   e an increase in wheat production
   f reduced labour requirements

2 What have been the benefits of the green revolution?
   a high crop yields   c more food for more people
   b better soil   d conservation of resources

3 What do you think the speaker will discuss next?
   a more benefits of intensive agriculture
   b the negative impact of intensive agriculture
   c how we can improve agricultural practices
   d who deserves credit for the green revolution

Identifying rhetorical questions as signposts

A rhetorical question is a question form that is used to make a point, rather than to get an answer. It is usually followed by important information. The speaker may expand on a point, provide an explanation or reason, or give examples. Speakers often use rhetorical questions to introduce their opinion about some piece of information they are presenting. Using rhetorical questions is somewhat less direct than expressing the same idea in a statement.

4 🔊 1.2 Read the questions and then listen to the rest of the lecture. Answer the questions. Write the main ideas.

1 So what is intensive farming, and what happens when we farm intensively? Intensive farming involves _huge one crop year after_ year
The advantage is _labour_ .
The disadvantage is _damage soil_ .

2 What are the most important resources in agriculture?
water, soil

3 Now, what are some other advantages of practices like crop rotation and the use of cover crops? _improve quality of soil_
reduce pest, need pesticide, reduce erosion

4 So why doesn't everybody in the world just switch to sustainable practices? _not no revenue , labour cost_
better crops , yield

5 🔊 1.2 Listen again and complete the student's notes.

I. Soil

  1 Original quality of the soil declines because _____

  2 To replace lost nutrients, farmers use _cover crop_

  3 Three alternative approaches: _____

  4 Another problem with soil quality is _we_

  5 Causes: _erosion,_

II. Water

  6 Agriculture uses _70_ % _of the_ world

  7 The two main sources of water: _rain, underground_

  8 Two approaches to conserving water / reducing erosion:
  _____ ; _reforestation soil no is_
  terms

POST-LISTENING

6 Circle the statement (a–c) that best matches the speaker's opinion on each topic (1–4).

1 Intensive farming
   a It has been a huge success. With future technological advances, we can make it even more successful.
   b It has been beneficial, but it is not worth the environmental cost.
   c It has been very successful, but it's time to consider its pros and cons.

2 Farming that specializes in one crop
  a It is very efficient.
  b It is not sustainable.
  c It is not very practical.
3 Water
  a Agriculture uses too much water.
  b Agricultural use of water is likely to increase.
  c Rain will never provide enough water for agriculture.
4 Sustainable farming
  a It is a better option than conventional farming.
  b It is just as practical as conventional farming.
  c It will replace conventional farming.

PRONUNCIATION FOR LISTENING

Intonation of complete and incomplete ideas

It is important to listen not just to *what* speakers say, but *how* they say it. Intonation is the pitch, or rise and fall, of the voice, and changes in intonation can change meaning. In English, intonation that falls to a low level shows that an idea is complete. Intonation that rises or intonation that falls only very slightly can show that an idea is incomplete and that the speaker intends to say more.

7 🔊 1.3 Listen. Are the speaker's ideas complete (C) or incomplete (I)?

  1 I want to talk about some issues _____
  2 Let's start by talking about natural resources _____
  3 I'm a professor of Agricultural Science now _____
  4 These farmers are using animal waste _____
  5 They're also rotating crops _____
  6 Diversifying crops can reduce the number of pests _____
  7 It's hard to talk about soil _____
  8 This practice is *not* sustainable _____

DISCUSSION

8 Work with a partner. Discuss the questions.

  1 Would you be willing to pay more for food if it were grown using sustainable agricultural practices? Why / Why not?
  2 All over the world, people have been leaving their farming communities and moving to cities. What impact might this have on sustainable agriculture?

PARALLEL STRUCTURE IN COMPARISONS

When using comparisons in explanations and arguments, it is important to make sure that the items being compared are parallel. They should follow the same grammatical pattern to be clear.

Be can be omitted in the second item compared:
Chemical fertilizers **are** <u>more expensive than</u> organic fertilizers **(are)**.

However, comparisons with other verbs need a verb after *than* to be clear:
Chemical fertilizers **have caused** <u>more damage than</u> erosion **has caused**.
Today, farmers **grow** <u>more wheat than</u> they **grew** in the past.

To avoid repetition, substitute the main verb with the correct form of the auxiliary *do* or omit the main verb if there is already an auxiliary:
Today, farmers **grow** <u>more wheat than</u> they **did** in the past.
Today, farmers **grow** <u>more wheat than</u> they **used to**.
Chemical fertilizers **have caused** <u>more damage than</u> erosion **has**.
Chemical fertilizers **have caused** <u>more damage than</u> erosion **ever could**.

Comparisons of nouns inside a prepositional phrase require repetition or substitution of the full noun phrase to be clear:
~~The costs of sustainable agriculture are higher than conventional agriculture.~~
The costs of sustainable agriculture are higher than **the costs of** conventional agriculture.
The costs of sustainable agriculture are higher than **those of** conventional agriculture.

1 Rewrite the non-parallel sentences so that they are clear.

1 Wind causes more coastal flooding than rain. _____

_____

2 Some people say farmers should not grow almonds because they need more water than wheat and other grains. _____

3 The cost of labour in organic farming is higher than traditional farming techniques. _____

4 Farms take up a greater percentage of the land in Turkey than Saudi Arabia. _____

_____

2 Write three comparison sentences using the information in the table below. Make sure each sentence has parallel structure. Compare your sentences with a partner.

Wheat farms in China produce more than those in India do.

wheat production in metric tons			
	2012	2013	2014
European Union	134.5	143.3	157.2
China	125.6	121.7	126.2
India	94.9	93.5	94.5
United States	61.8	60	55.4

Source: Wikipedia/FAOSTAT

1 _____

_____

2 _____

_____

3 _____

_____

3 Write three sentences comparing past agricultural practices in your country to how farming is done today.

1 _____

_____

2 _____

_____

3 _____

_____

LANGUAGE FOR ASSIGNING BLAME AND RESPONSIBILITY

Here are some common expressions that can be used to assign the credit, responsibility or blame for something when making an argument.

attribute credit	He is **credited with** solving the problem. We **have him to thank for** solving the problem.
accept credit	The CEO **took credit for** the innovations.
attribute blame or responsibility	**Responsibility falls (squarely) on the shoulders of** the company. Who is **to blame / responsible** for damage to the environment caused by these emissions? And how should we **hold** these countries **accountable / to account**. The regulators **pointed the finger at** the company.
accept blame or responsibility	It's the governments and citizens of the developed world who need to **step up (and accept responsibility** for the health of the environment). The company **faced up to their responsibilities**.
avoid blame or responsibility	The company attempted to **shirk the blame / their responsibilities**. The company attempted to **sidestep responsibility** (for the problem).

4 Complete the sentences below using expressions from the Explanation box. Write one word in the correct form in each gap.

1 People often _____ _____ _____ at the government for environmental problems, but we are all _____ _____ for the situation.

2 The responsibility for the loss of habitat _____ _____ _____ _____ of mining companies who profit from the extraction of resources.

3 The company is _____ _____ increasing the popularity of organic foods across the nation.

4 The company can't _____ _____ _____ forever. At some point, they will be _____ _____ _____ by the regulators.

5 If you are in a position of leadership, you need to be prepared to

_____ _____ _____ _____ _____

for unpopular policies and decisions.

6 The CEO _____ _____ for the success of the project, despite the fact that others had done the actual work.

LISTENING 2

PREPARING TO LISTEN

1 You are going to listen to a panel discussion on the topic of assigning responsibility for climate change. Before you listen, work with a partner. Look at the graph and answer the questions.

> This graph compares the carbon emissions of countries in the OECD (Organization for Economic Co-operation and Development) with non-OECD countries. OECD members are the countries of North America and Europe, as well as Australia, Chile, Israel, Japan, Mexico, New Zealand and Korea.

1 Why should we be concerned about CO_2 emissions?
2 What change does the graph show around the year 2007?
3 What does it suggest for the future?
4 What do you think non-OECD countries could do to reduce their emissions?

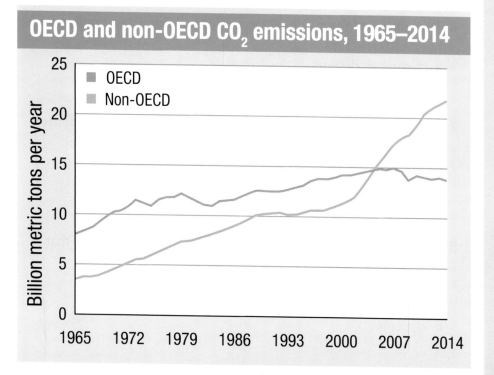

OECD and non-OECD CO_2 emissions, 1965–2014

- OECD
- Non-OECD

(y-axis: Billion metric tons per year, 0 to 25)
(x-axis: 1965, 1972, 1979, 1986, 1993, 2000, 2007, 2014)

Source: BP Statistical Review of World Energy

2 Read the sentences and choose the best definition for the words in bold.

1 These new environmental policies place an unnecessary **burden** on the population, and especially on the poor.

  a a process that takes a lot of time

  b a difficult or unpleasant responsibility

  c a major delay

2 The World Health Organization has been working to **combat** diseases caused by air and water pollution.

  a to decrease

  b to research into

  c to try to stop

3 Medical centres that use dangerous chemicals must have a plan to **dispose of** them properly.

  a to throw away

  b to label and store

  c to manage and protect

4 The death of hundreds of babies caused by dangerous chemicals in their milk has been described as **shameful** by the official enquiry.

  a morally wrong

  b guilty

  c misunderstood

5 Destruction of the forest has **accelerated** since the government relaxed the laws on logging.

  a to become more difficult

  b to happen more quickly

  c to enter a new stage

6 They **diverted** the money intended for building a new stadium to help the disaster victims.

  a to earn; to deserve

  b to maintain for a long time

  c to use something for a different purpose

7 The chemical company has offered two journalists **unprecedented** access to hundreds of internal documents. It has rarely, if ever, allowed anything like this before.

  a without any restrictions; completely open

  b having never happened in the past

  c unlikely, unpredictable

8 The government has threatened **sanctions** against countries that pose a threat to global environmental health.

  a punishments

  b laws

  c agreements

PLUS

3 🔊 1.4 Listen to the announcement about a forthcoming panel discussion. Answer the questions. Compare your answers with a partner.

1 How many participants do you think will be in the discussion? Will the participants present similar or different views?
2 What is the topic?
   a which countries are responsible for climate change and how they should be held accountable
   b a scientific explanation of climate change and which countries are the worst impacted
   c a look into the future of the planet if climate change is not immediately addressed
3 What are 'CO$_2$ and other greenhouse gases'?
   a gases produced by rainforests that combat global warming
   b gases in the atmosphere that protect Earth from the sun's energy
   c gases produced by human activity that contribute to global warming
4 The speaker asks if we should use *boycotts* or other *economic sanctions* to punish countries whose emission levels are too high. What do the terms in italics mean?
5 Do you think boycotts and economic sanctions are a successful tool in promoting environmentally-friendly policies?

WHILE LISTENING

4 🔊 1.5 Listen to the panel discussion. Match the people to their ideas about climate change and global responsibility (a–d).

Grace Chin (StepUp) _____
Russell Sanchez (Fair Share) _____
Dara Staples (Citizens for Global Justice) _____
Vijay Gupta (Fund for the Environmental Future) _____

a All countries have to cut emissions immediately.
b Developed countries should be the first to change their practices.
c Practices in developing countries which drive climate change should be punished.
d Developing countries need help to pursue environmentally responsible development.

LISTENING FOR
MAIN IDEAS

5 🔊 1.5 Listen again. Take notes on details each speaker uses to support their position.

I Grace Chin

Developing countries should not be held responsible for controlling climate change.

II Russell Sanchez

Developing countries should be forced to help control climate change.

III Dara Staples

Developed countries need to change their practices in the developing world.

IV Vijay Gupta

All countries need to take action against climate change now.

6 Use your notes in Exercise 5 to answer the questions.

SUMMARIZING

1 Why does Grace Chin think that developing countries should not be held responsible for climate change?

_____

_____

2 Why does Russell Sanchez disagree with Grace Chin?

_____

_____

3 What changes does Dara want to see from developed countries?

_____

_____

4 Why does Vijay want immediate action from all countries?

_____

_____

POST-LISTENING

7 Work with a partner. What opinion does each rhetorical question express? Explain each opinion in statement form, in your own words.

1 So shouldn't the United States and other developed nations be the ones making changes, even if those changes *are* expensive?

_____

2 Why not organize a global boycott of any products whose manufacture causes significant negative environmental effects?

_____

3 How useful will economic development and resource extraction be to the people of Bangladesh then (when it is under water)?

_____

4 What good is pointing fingers and blaming one another?

_____

DISCUSSION

8 Work in small groups. Use ideas from Listening 1 and Listening 2 to answer the following questions.

SYNTHESIZING

1 Which figure do you think is more important: per capita emissions or total emissions?

2 If a country has to choose between allocating resources to economic development or to environmental issues, which is the better course of action? Why?

3 Which of the speakers' positions to do you support? Why?

SPEAKING

CRITICAL THINKING

At the end of this unit, you are going to do the speaking task below.

> Have an informal debate about the mission of national parks. Is their primary purpose to protect the natural world from human activity, or to provide a natural area where people can enjoy responsible interaction with nature? Is it possible to accomplish both these goals?

SKILLS

Analyzing issues

Before you can take a stand, it is important to have some background information and to define the issues you want to address. You can then evaluate each piece of relevant information to determine if it is relevant and whether it supports your argument.

 **REMEMBER**

1 Work in small groups. Discuss the questions.

1 Many nations have national parks, historically important or beautiful wild spaces that the government protects from development. Think about a national park – a place you have visited or would like to visit. Where is it? What did you do and see there? What do you remember most about your visit? Or, why would you like to visit it?

2 Why do you think national parks were established?

3 Why do you think governments choose particular places to become national parks?

ANALYZE

2 Read about some of the issues that national parks need to address today. Consider the potential problems and write some possible consequences if the issues are not resolved.

Neighbours

Parks do not exist in isolation. They are often surrounded by residential areas, as well as commercial, agricultural and industrial development. The wild species that live in a park do not recognize the park's boundaries, often moving in and out of it. Local human populations may threaten wild species by hunting them as game, to sell as pets or for exotic trophies and medicines.

Possible consequences:

_____

_____

Non-human visitors

Wild places like national parks are very attractive to all kinds of species, including those from other parts of the country or other parts of the world. They often arrive in the park with human visitors. These 'invasive species', including insects, plants and fish, pose a serious threat to a park's native species and its ecosystem.

Possible consequences:

_____

_____

Climate change

All over the world, weather conditions are getting more extreme every year. Parks in coastal and upland areas are experiencing accelerated soil erosion. Wetland parks are flooded to greater depths. In other parks, increased temperatures are causing rivers and streams to dry up.

Possible consequences:

_____

_____

Popularity

The ever-growing popularity of national parks is placing increasing pressure on their ecosystems. Visitors to national parks need roads and services. What happens when the visitors' needs and desires conflict with those of the natural inhabitants?

Possible consequences:

_____

_____

Natural resources

National parks are often rich in natural resources, both on and under the land. These resources include trees, oil, gas and minerals. There is great pressure on the parks to allow private companies to extract these resources.

Possible consequences:

_____

_____

3 Work in small groups. Discuss the questions.

1 Which issues affect national parks in your part of the world or a park you know well?
2 Which of the issues facing national parks do you think represents the biggest challenge?
3 Which are the most important issues to resolve?

 UNDERSTAND

4 ◀》 1.6 Listen to a park ranger talking about the situation in Grand Canyon National Park in the United States. Then work in small groups and discuss the questions.

1 Which of the issues from Exercise 2 does the ranger mention in his description of Grand Canyon National Park?
2 In what ways is the Grand Canyon fulfilling the two potential missions of a national park?
mission A: National parks should protect the natural world from human activity.
mission B: National parks should encourage responsible human interaction with the natural world.

 EVALUATE

5 Work in small groups. Discuss each potential mission of national parks. Take notes on all the arguments for and against each mission.

mission A	
points in favour (for)	points opposed (against)

mission B	
points in favour (for)	points opposed (against)

6 What do you think the mission, or missions of national parks should be? Take notes on your position below. Consider the most important arguments that support your position.

My position: _____

_____

PREPARATION FOR SPEAKING

CHALLENGING OTHER POINTS OF VIEW

When discussing important issues, people often want to challenge an opinion or point of view presented by somebody else. It is important to be able to express your views clearly, yet remain polite. There are many ways to do this.

Not necessarily.
That doesn't follow.
Actually, ...
On the contrary, ...
That's not (necessarily)
true / the case.

That would be fine, except ...
That may be true, but ...
That might be the case if ...
I'm afraid that's not really the point.
I would agree with you if ...

1 Complete the conversation below with the phrases from the box.

> **a** Not necessarily   **b** I'm afraid that's not really the point
> **c** Actually   **d** I would agree with you if

Steve: You're poisoning the groundwater by using those pesticides in your garden.
Mia: (1)_____ . If you use pesticides carefully, they're totally safe. At least, that's what I've read.
Steve: (2)_____ there is no way to use these products safely. They should not be used under any circumstances.
Mia: (3)_____ there were any other options, but nothing works as well against the insects that ruin my flowers and vegetables.
Steve: (4)_____ . What does it matter if they work really well in your garden? It's irresponsible.

2 🔊 1.7 Compare your answers in Exercise 1 with a partner. Then listen to the conversation to check your answers. Notice the intonation that the speakers use to signpost complete or incomplete ideas after the phrases for challenging other points of view. Review the Explanation box on page 21.

3 With a partner, discuss the environmental benefits of changing to a plant-based diet using some of the other words and phrases from the Explanation box.

 PLUS

PRONUNCIATION FOR SPEAKING

4 With your partner, read and then continue the conversation in Exercise 1 using some of the other words and phrases from the Explanation box. Use the appropriate intonation for complete and incomplete ideas.

SPEAKING TASK

> Have an informal debate about the mission of national parks. Is their primary purpose to protect the natural world from human activity, or to provide a natural area where people can enjoy responsible interaction with nature? Is it possible to accomplish both these goals?

PREPARE

1 Work in small groups with students who share your point of view.

2 Review your notes in Critical thinking, Exercises 5 and 6 on page 32. Write a statement that presents your point of view. Share your statements for feedback. Revise your arguments if needed.

3 Anticipate opposing points of view by preparing a list of arguments that you think the other side will make. Discuss how best to argue against these points.

4 Refer to the Task checklist as you prepare for your debate.

TASK CHECKLIST	✔
Present a statement of your point of view.	
Offer supporting points for your position.	
Ensure that any comparisons you make are parallel.	
Use expressions of blame and responsibility where appropriate.	
Challenge other points of view with appropriate expressions.	

PRACTISE

5 Practise responding to the list of arguments you made in Exercise 3 in your group.

DISCUSS

6 Join a group of students who support a different point of view. Have your debate. One student from each side should begin with an opening statement. Then, open the floor for a discussion of the topic. Each student should contribute the following:

- at least one statement arguing for your point of view
- at least one statement arguing against another point of view

OBJECTIVES REVIEW

1 Check your learning objectives for this unit. Write *3, 2* or *1* for each objective.

3 = very well   2 = well   1 = not so well

I can ...

watch and understand a video about endangered birds in Indonesia.   _____

listen to introductions.   _____

identify rhetorical questions as signposts.   _____

analyze issues.   _____

use parallel structure in comparisons.   _____

challenge other points of view.   _____

have an informal debate.   _____

2 Use the *Unlock* Digital Workbook for more practice with this unit's learning objectives.

UNLOCK ONLINE

WORDLIST

abundant (adj) ⊙
accelerate (v)
be to blame for (v phr)
be responsible for (v phr)
burden (n) ⊙
combat (v) ⊙
conversion (n) ⊙
credit somebody with (phr v)
dispose of (phr v)
divert (v)
face up to (responsibilities) (phr v)
(responsibility) fall (squarely)

on the shoulders of (v phr, idiom)
fertile (adj) ⊙
have somebody to thank for (v phr)
hold somebody accountable / to account (v phr)
loosen (v)
nutrients (n pl) ⊙
point the finger at (v phr, idiom)

sanctions (n pl) ⊙
shameful (adj)
shirk the blame / your responsibilities (v phr)
sidestep responsibility (v phr)
starvation (n)
step up (and do something) (phr v)
take credit for (v phr)
unprecedented (adj)
viable (adj) ⊙
yield (n) ⊙

⊙ = high-frequency words in the Cambridge Academic Corpus

LEARNING OBJECTIVES

	IN THIS UNIT YOU WILL ...
Watch and listen	watch and understand a video about designer bikes in France and Japan.
Listening skills	use a table to take notes on main ideas and detail; review and organize notes.
Critical thinking	evaluate pros and cons.
Grammar	use degree expressions.
Speaking skill	acknowledge other arguments.
Speaking task	give a group presentation.

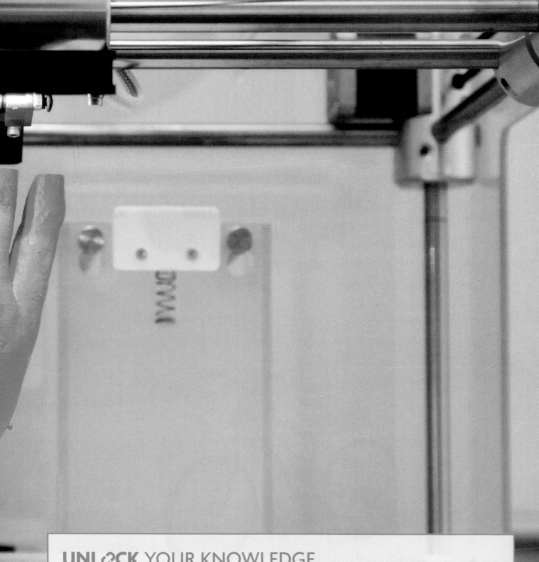

UNLOCK YOUR KNOWLEDGE

Work with a partner. Discuss the questions.

1 What is happening in this picture? Do you think this is the most important technological advance of recent years? Why / Why not?

2 Do you think that the products we use every day are better now than in the past? Is there any way in which products in the past were superior?

3 What types of shopping (clothes, shoes, electronics, household items, etc.) would you avoid doing if you could? How much extra would you be willing to pay to avoid it or them?

PLUS

PREPARING TO WATCH

1 You are going to watch a video about bicycle design. Before you watch, circle the statements you think are true about cycling in your country. Explain your answers to a partner.

1 Cycling is more popular today than it used to be.
2 Cycling is a fashionable way to travel.
3 Cycling is the best way to get around a city.
4 People care what their bicycles look like.
5 There are too many different bicycle designs to choose from.

2 Look at the diagram and discuss the question with your partner.

How could a designer make each part of a bicycle special or luxurious?

seat
handlebars
saddlebags
frame
water bottle
chain
pedals

GLOSSARY

fashion statement (n) something that you own or wear in order to attract attention and show other people the type of person you are

classic (adj) having a simple, traditional style that is always fashionable

gap in the market (n) an opportunity for a product or service that does not already exist

personalize (v) to make something suitable for a particular person

accessory (n) something added to a machine or to clothing that has a useful or decorative purpose

status (n) the amount of respect, admiration, or importance given to a person, organization, or object

WHILE WATCHING

3 ▶ Watch the video. Number the main ideas in the order you hear them.

_____ A Japanese designer has started making luxury bicycles instead of boats.

_____ Hermès have launched two designer bicycles.

_____ Hermès' designer bikes are extremely popular.

_____ People are using bicycles to show how much money they have.

_____ Shops in Paris sell a variety of expensive cycling products.

UNDERSTANDING MAIN IDEAS

4 ▶ Watch again. Complete the sentences.

1 Hermès started making designer bicycles because there was a
_____ .

2 The Japanese artisan thinks it is the first time that the whole world
_____ .

3 Paris shops are increasing their sales by
_____ .

4 These days bicycles are becoming a showcase for
_____ .

UNDERSTANDING DETAIL

5 ▶ Watch again. Answer the questions.

1 What are the special features of Hermès' 'Le Flâneur Sportif'?
_____

2 How much does Hermès' 'Le Flâneur Sportif' cost?
_____

3 How much do some designer bikes cost in Tokyo?
_____

4 What material does the Japanese artisan make bicycles from?
_____

5 What examples are given of cycling accessories sold in Paris?
_____

DISCUSSION

6 Work in a small group. Discuss the questions.

1 What kind of people do you think buy the designer bicycles you saw in the video? Why?

2 What other kinds of cycling accessories do you think that cycling shops sell? How might they be made luxurious or personalized?

3 Do you think that the bicycles you saw in the video would sell well where you live? Why / Why not?

4 Think of another type of product that people use to show off their wealth. What are the features of an expensive model of this type of product?

5 Are status symbols important to you? If so, which one(s) would you like to have? Why? If not, why not?

LISTENING

LISTENING 1

PREPARING TO LISTEN

1 You are going to listen to a presentation on current and future uses for 3-D printing. Before you listen, work with a partner. Discuss which of the items in the photos you think were produced by a 3-D printer. Then discuss the questions below.

1 All these items were made with a 3-D printer. Does that surprise you? Why / Why not?
2 What kind of objects cannot be created with a 3-D printer today?

2 Read the definitions. Use the correct forms of the words in bold to complete the sentences below.

> **customize** (v) to make or change something to fit a user's needs
> **downside** (n) disadvantage
> **drastically** (adv) severely; with very noticeable effect
> **fabric** (n) cloth; material for making clothing
> **foundation** (n) the thing on which other things are based
> **junk** (n) things of no use or value
> **mass production** (n) the process of producing large numbers of one thing in a factory
> **rejection** (n) the failure of the body to accept a new body part that has been put in during surgery

1 When computers go out of date, they become _____ that has to be thrown away.
2 You can _____ the software so that it only includes the functions that you need.
3 Early 3-D fashions used a flexible plastic instead of the _____ you find most clothing is made of.
4 With a 3-D printer, I can print just about everything. The _____, however, is that it is much more expensive than a traditional printer.

5 The maths skills that you acquire in secondary school provide a
_____ for the more advanced work you do at university.

6 Kidney transplants have a very high success rate these days; the
chances of _____ during the first year are only seven percent.

7 The market for compact disc players dropped _____ in the early
years of the 21st century, as the public switched to MP3 players, and
later to streaming.

8 The _____ of cars began in the early twentieth century. Prior to
that, cars had been produced to order.

USING YOUR
KNOWLEDGE

3 Work with a partner. Look at the diagram of a supply chain. Discuss what
happens at each stage.

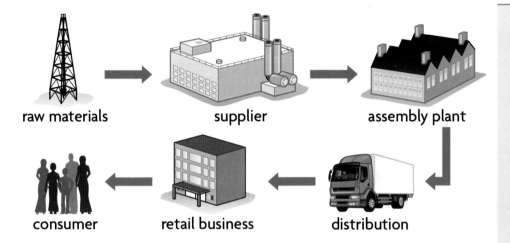

raw materials supplier assembly plant

consumer retail business distribution

WHILE LISTENING

LISTENING FOR
MAIN IDEAS

4 🔊 2.1 Listen to the presentation. Circle the best summary of each main
idea in the presentation.

1 a Replacement body parts are routinely printed.
 b Methods of printing replacement body parts are in development.

2 a Fashion designers are using 3-D printing in their collections.
 b 3-D printing is widely used in the production of fashion items.

3 a Mass production will be more profitable with 3-D printing.
 b Manufacturing small quantities could be profitable with 3-D printing.

4 a 3-D printing will totally change the manufacturing process.
 b 3-D printing will benefit everybody who works in manufacturing.

5 a We do not know if 3-D printing will increase or decrease waste.
 b 3-D printing will reduce the amount we throw away.

SKILLS

Using a table to take notes on main ideas and detail

When a speaker makes the structure of upcoming information clear, it can be helpful to use the same structure as you take notes. Using a table to capture this structure helps you separate the main ideas from the detail. This makes it easier to review and study your notes later. Listen for signposts like numbers (e.g. *There are two ... .*), and phrases that indicate that a main idea is coming (e.g. *the most important ... .*). Don't try to write down everything you hear. You want your table to provide an outline of the talk, not everything the speaker said.

TAKING NOTES
ON MAIN IDEAS
AND DETAIL

5 🔊 2.2 Listen to an excerpt from the presentation and complete the table.

AM (Additive Manufacturing) disrupts two elements of manufacturing:

(1)_____	(2)_____
parts made as a single piece (3)_____ stronger (4)_____ – reduced fuel consumption = cost savings	won't need (5)_____ or (6)_____ fabricated on demand reduce (7)_____ short supply chains

LISTENING
FOR DETAIL

6 🔊 2.1 Listen to the presentation again. Write *T* (true), *F* (false) or *DNS* (does not say) next to the statements. Then correct the false statements.

_____ 1 3-D printing is a very new technology.

_____

_____ 2 3-D printing can create body tissue which is a perfect match for the patient.

_____

_____ 3 Clothing is printed using natural fibres, like cotton.

_____

_____ 4 Most 3-D fashions will probably be printed in developing countries.

_____

_____ 5 There has been a lot of opposition to 3-D printing from manufacturers.

_____

_____ 6 One man printed several parts of an aeroplane and assembled them himself.

_____

_____ 7 3-D printing will reduce the need for companies to hold items in stock.

_____

_____ 8 3-D printing may help criminals to escape from prison.

_____

7 🔊 2.1 Listen again. Take more detailed notes on the presentation.

POST-LISTENING

Reviewing and organizing your notes

After a lecture, while the information is still fresh in your mind, rewrite your notes in an outline structure. This helps you understand the main ideas and details of the lecture. Doing this can also help you reflect critically on the content of the lecture, which is difficult to do while you are listening.

8 🔊 2.1 Use your answers from Exercises 4–7 to make a set of notes. Start by listing the main ideas (1, 2, 3, etc.) and supporting details for each main idea (a, b, c, etc.). Leave space to add more details. Listen to the presentation again. Check that your notes are accurate and add more detail if necessary.

> 1. Methods of printing replacement body parts are in development.
>   a. can create body tissue ...
>   b.
>
>
> 2.
>   a.
>   b.
> 3.

9 Work with a partner. Complete the tasks.

1 Use your notes from Exercise 8 to recap the talk on 3-D printing. Include only the main points and important details. Present it aloud to your partner.

2 As you listen to your partner's presentation, write down any important details that your partner included that you missed. Add them to your notes.

3 Whose recap do you think was more accurate and complete? Does the order of main points make a difference? Were the details presented with the relevant main points?

SKILLS

Word stress

In words with more than one syllable, one syllable is stressed more than the others. A stressed syllable is generally longer, louder, and higher in pitch than an unstressed syllable.

<u>down</u>-side (n) ad-<u>vance</u> (v) con-<u>sum</u>-er (n)

Although stress is sometimes difficult to predict, there are some rules. For example, always stress the syllable that comes directly before these suffixes: *-ical, -ion, -ity, -logy.*

tech-no-<u>log</u>-i-cal   cog-<u>ni</u>-tion   poss-i-<u>bil</u>-i-ty   tech-<u>no</u>-lo-gy

10 Underline the stressed syllables in the words below.

1	a	tech-no-lo-gy	b	pro-cess	c	ob-ject (n)
2	a	com-pu-ter	b	soft-ware	c	sce-nar-i-os
3	a	dra-ma-tic	b	bi-o-med-i-cal	c	re-search (n)
4	a	at-tracts	b	pos-si-bil-i-ty	c	cus-tom-iz-ing
5	a	pro-duc-tion	b	fa-cil-i-ties	c	in-dus-try
6	a	el-e-ments	b	foun-da-tion	c	man-u-fac-tur-ing
7	a	en-tre-pre-neur	b	fac-to-ries	c	as-sem-bled

11 🔊 2.3 Listen to the excerpts from the talk to check your answers in Exercise 10.

DISCUSSION

12 Work with a partner. Discuss the questions.

1 The speaker mentions the disruptive power of AM several times. What do you think the long-term consequences might be for the clothing industry? For example, what would happen if all clothing could be printed at home?

2 Use your imagination to think of an application for 3-D printing that was not discussed by the speaker. Share your ideas with another pair of students or the class.

PLUS

⊙ LANGUAGE DEVELOPMENT

USING CAUSE-AND-EFFECT PHRASES

To express a cause using a phrase

What's more, **by printing it as one piece**, he created a part that was five times stronger than the original part and 83% lighter.

What's more, he created a part that was five times stronger than the original part and 83% lighter **by printing it as one piece**.

Notice that, although the subject is not expressed in the cause-and-effect phrase, you can infer it. Such phrases can only be used if the inferred subject is the same as the subject of the whole sentence – in this case, *he printed it as one piece*.

To express an effect using a phrase

The blouses appear on shelves the following week, **encouraging the trend**.

This is a reduction of a non-defining relative 'comment' clause:

The blouses appear on shelves the following week, **which encourages the trend**.

VOCABULARY

1 Complete the sentences with a phrase that explains the cause.

1 _____ , manufacturers ensure that consumers buy new items on a regular basis.

2 _____ , clothing companies encourage people to buy new clothes more often.

3 _____ , the team completed the project just before the deadline.

4 _____ , they were able to find a better design for the product.

5 _____ , manufacturers can print small quantities and keep costs low.

PLUS

2 Rewrite each non-defining relative clause as a phrase expressing the effect.

1 Clothing can be made very cheaply today, which makes it psychologically easier to throw things away.

_____

2 AM makes it easier to complete all production steps in one place, which leaves assembly plants in developing countries out of the process.

_____

3 AM even has the potential to be used to print human organs, which gives hope to those on transplant waiting lists.

_____

3 Complete the sentences with a phrase that expresses an effect. Use your own ideas.

1 Clothing companies respond immediately to consumer preferences,

_____ .

2 Thousands of people throw away their mobile phones every year,

_____ .

3 Many resourceful consumers have made their own repairs independently,

_____ .

4 The cost of consumer electronics has dropped significantly,

_____ .

4 Write three sentences using phrases for cause and/or effect about a situation in your own life. The sentences can be on any topic.

By working on my essay last weekend, I was able to hand it in on time.

_____ .

_____ .

_____ .

DEGREE EXPRESSIONS

GRAMMAR

Sometimes you need to measure the amount or degree of something against a standard. When the amount or degree does not match the standard, use the adverb *too* + an adjective or adverb for the degree and the *to* + infinitive form of the verb for the standard.

The cost of printing is **too high to make** *this practical.*
                      degree   standard

When the amount or degree does match the standard, use an adjective, adverb, or verb + *enough* for the degree and the *to* + infinitive form of the verb for the standard.

The costs **have fallen enough to make** *these scenarios more than a dream.*
            degree   standard

5 Complete the degree expressions in the sentences with your own ideas.

1 My phone is too old _____ .
2 Some consumer electronics are cheap enough _____ .
3 _____ to be used with the latest software.
4 _____ are not comfortable enough to wear all day long.
5 Some video games are too complicated _____ .

PREPARING TO LISTEN

1 Read the sentences. Write the words in bold next to their definitions below.

1 The protests were seen as an angry public **backlash** against the disposal of obsolete electronics in developing countries.
2 **Innovation** in product design was the main reason for Apple's success.
3 The employees **resent** the fact that their boss gets the latest technology while they have to make do with out-of-date computers.
4 Computer hackers are very good at finding ways to **circumvent** security protocols.
5 The company has **devised** a system to keep track of all their customers and the purchases they make.
6 The government has **issued** new guidelines regarding the disposal of computers and other electronics.
7 The biggest **obstacle** to our success is a lack of funds to market our products.
8 We only have a **finite** amount of money, so we need to spend it wisely.

a _____ (v) to feel angry because you have been forced to accept something that you do not like
b _____ (v) to say or send out something official
c _____ (n) the development of new products, designs, or ideas
d _____ (v) to find a way of avoiding something, especially a law or rule
e _____ (v) to create a plan or system using intelligence and creativity
f _____ (n) a strong negative reaction among a group of people
g _____ (adj) limited; set and fixed
h _____ (n) something that prevents progress

PLUS

2 You are going to listen to a presentation about planned obsolescence. Before you listen, work with a partner. Answer the questions.

1 What is in the photo?
2 How did all these devices end up here?
3 What are the possible consequences if this continues?

3 How often do you replace these items? Complete the table about yourself and an older friend or family member. Add one more item to the table. Then compare tables with a partner and answer the questions below.

item	me	older friend or family member
mobile phone		
computer		
shoes/boots		
jeans		
car		

1 Why do you replace these items as often as you do?

_____

_____

2 Do you ever repair items to make them last longer? Why / Why not?

_____

_____

3 Do you think you replace these items more or less often than other people replace them?

_____

_____

4 Do you think it is environmentally responsible to replace the items as often as you do?

_____

_____

WHILE LISTENING

LISTENING FOR MAIN IDEAS

4 2.4 Listen to the presentation. Circle the topics that are mentioned in the listening.

a the history of planned obsolescence
b an explanation of the concept of planned obsolescence
c consumer responses to planned obsolescence
d planned obsolescence in electronics
e consumer efforts to combat planned obsolescence
f fast fashion

5 ◀)) 2.4 Listen again and note the main ideas each speaker discusses. Leave space in your notes for details.

TAKING NOTES ON MAIN IDEAS AND DETAIL

> 1. Planned obsolescence is a deliberate policy to create products
>   with a finite and usually short lifespan.
>   a) Detail:
>   b) Detail:

6 ◀)) 2.4 Listen to the presentation again. Add supporting details for each main idea in your notes.

7 Work with a partner. Complete the tasks.

SUMMARIZING

1 Use your notes to create a brief recap of the presentation on planned obsolescence. Include the main points and important details. Present it aloud to your partner.

2 As you listen to your partner's presentation, write down any important details that they included that you missed. Add them to your notes.

3 Whose presentation do you think was more accurate or effective? Does the order of main points make a difference? Were the details presented with the relevant main points?

POST-LISTENING

8 Circle the best description of the attitude of the speakers in Listening 2 to planned obsolescence (PO). Explain your answer to a partner.

a strongly supportive of the advantages of PO
b mostly objective, but generally supportive of PO
c objective and neutral – not supporting either side
d mostly objective, mildly negative attitude towards PO
e strongly negative attitude toward PO

DISCUSSION

9 Work in your group. Read the facts about the clothing industry in the United Kingdom. Then answer the questions below.

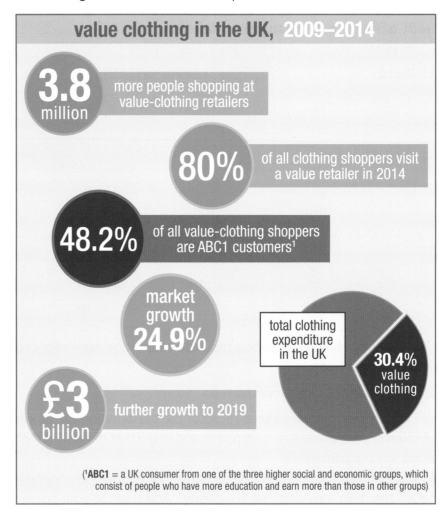

value clothing in the UK, 2009–2014

3.8 million more people shopping at value-clothing retailers

80% of all clothing shoppers visit a value retailer in 2014

48.2% of all value-clothing shoppers are ABC1 customers[1]

market growth 24.9%

total clothing expenditure in the UK — **30.4%** value clothing

£3 billion further growth to 2019

([1]**ABC1** = a UK consumer from one of the three higher social and economic groups, which consist of people who have more education and earn more than those in other groups)

1 What do you think *value clothing* is?
2 Who is shopping differently in the UK? In what way? What impact has this had on the value clothing market?
3 How do these facts support the information in the presentation?
4 Do any of the facts surprise you? Explain your answer.
5 Think of some implications of this phenomenon for the United Kingdom, for the rest of the world, and for the environment.

SYNTHESIZING

10 Work with a partner. Use ideas from Listening 1 and Listening 2 to answer the following questions.

1 Look back at the table you completed in Exercise 3 on page 48. Do you think your behaviour will ever change in any way? If so, when and why? If not, why not?
2 Review Listening 1. What impact do you think AM will have on planned obsolescence in general and fast fashion in particular?

SPEAKING

CRITICAL THINKING

At the end of this unit, you are going to do the speaking task below.

> Give a group presentation about a product that you believe was designed for obsolescence. Discuss the reasons, both positive and negative, why it was designed in this way.

Evaluating pros and cons

Few situations are black and white. Most require you to decide what is good and what is bad about something – the 'pros and cons'. Remember, the pros and cons may not be the same for everyone involved in the situation. An advantage for one group may be a disadvantage for another. You will need to evaluate all the information and then make your own argument.

ANALYZE

1 Work in small groups. Complete the tasks.

  1 Read this list of consumer products and add one or two more. Discuss the extent to which each product is designed for planned obsolescence. Take notes.

video games	cars	running shoes
games consoles	software	_____
ink cartridges	textbooks	_____

Video games are made for specific consoles – new games often aren't available on the old consoles.

  2 For each product, come up with at least one negative aspect and one positive or neutral aspect of its short lifespan.
  The graphics and gameplay just keep getting better and better.

  3 For each product, discuss how (or if) it could be made to last longer.

2 Look at this list of reasons that consumers purchase goods and services. Add more reasons to the list. What are some examples of products that people buy for each reason? Take notes. Then share your ideas in your group.

  • They have no choice. They need it.
  • It is really useful. It makes their lives easier.
  • It represents their aspirations. People they admire have it.
  • It's new and cool.
  • It's good value.
  • The company that makes it has a good reputation.
  • It has some specific attractive quality (e.g. colour for sports shoes).

3 Work in your group. There are many different planned obsolescence strategies that a company may use to encourage consumers to continue buying new products from them, instead of buying other companies' products or not buying a new product at all. Read the strategies (a–d) below. Then complete the tasks (1–3).

1 Identify a product that would fit each strategy as a way of encouraging future purchases.
2 Discuss whether you think each is an effective strategy. Explain why.
3 How might each strategy *backfire*, that is, how could it go wrong?

> **a** Design a product to fail after a short period of time.

> **b** Stop supporting old products, in other words, stop providing updates and service.

> **c** Make different accessories and related products that will only function with your company's products. (They won't work with other companies' products.)

> **d** Every few years, introduce new, better and more exciting versions of your products.

4 Work in your group. Make a table like the one below. Choose two or three products that you have been considering for the speaking task. For each product, decide if obsolescence is, or could be …

scenario 1: entirely for the benefit of the producer – purely to increase revenue.
scenario 2: a plan to increase revenue, but also of some benefit to the consumer.
scenario 3: a side effect rather than an intentional act.
Note: For some instances of obsolescence, multiple scenarios are possible.

product/feature	scenario 1	scenario 2	scenario 3
Mobile phone: Consumers cannot access/replace battery. Battery has a limited lifespan.	Consumers will have to buy a new phone when the battery stops working. They have no choice.	Consumers will need to replace frequently. (good for company) Keeps costs down. (good for consumers)	The design allows for a more attractive product. The inaccessible battery is smaller and lighter than a replaceable battery.

5 Work in your group. Decide which product you will talk about in your presentation. Discuss the questions and take notes.

- How will you describe the product?
- Why and how was it designed for obsolescence?
- What are the pros and cons of its obsolescence?
- Who benefits from its obsolescence? Who does not benefit?
- Why do consumers continue to buy this product?

PREPARATION FOR SPEAKING

PRONUNCIATION FOR SPEAKING

Stress in compound nouns and noun phrases

In compound nouns, the stress is usually on the first word in the compound.
so̲ftware   u̲pgrade   di̲shwasher

Syllable stress still applies within each word.
depa̲rtment store   tra̲ining centre

In adjective + noun phrases, both words are stressed equally, and syllable stress still applies within each word.
pla̲nned obso̲lescence   so̲cial me̲dia

1 🔊 2.5 Circle the stressed words and underline the stressed syllables in these compound nouns and noun phrases. Then listen and check your answers.

1 clothing industry	2 complex devices	3 backlash
4 design policy	5 digital locks	6 fast fashion
7 finite lifespan	8 runway	9 tech sector

2 🔊 2.6 Work with a partner. Practise saying these compound nouns using the correct stress patterns. Listen to check your work.

1 dishwasher	2 video game	3 games console
4 textbook	5 ink cartridges	6 gym shoes

3 Work with a partner. Use the words in Exercise 2 in sentences and add an adjective. Make any changes to the stress pattern that are necessary.

*My parents have just bought an **energy-efficient dishwasher**.*

ACKNOWLEDGING OTHER ARGUMENTS

When you are assessing the pros and cons of a situation, it is useful to step back and examine other perspectives. It is important to understand opposing arguments. You may still favour one side, but you can also concede the merit of other perspectives.

Several phrases are commonly used to express this even-handed approach:
On the one hand, … on the other hand, …
Granted, … , but …
Many people think that … , some others say that …
There are two sides to / ways of looking at this question/issue/situation:
That said, …
Having said that, …

Expressions of concession follow several patterns:
position A + concession expression + position B
Planned obsolescence clearly benefits manufacturers; **that said,** it can also be seen as providing some consumer benefits.

concession introduction + position A + position B
There are two different ways of looking at planned obsolescence: either it is for the exclusive benefit of manufacturers, or it can be seen as beneficial to both buyers and sellers.

concession introduction + position A + concession expression + position B
Granted, planned obsolescence is a huge benefit to manufacturers, **but** consumers also benefit from the constant variety of new products on the market.

4 Use the phrases below (a–e) to complete the sentences.

1 There are two ways to look at increased industrialization: either _____, or it has a negative impact on the environment.
2 On the one hand, _____, on the other hand _____ .
3 Granted _____, but companies like Enviroserve are taking the lead in solving it.
4 Technology has improved our lives in many ways. That said, _____ .

a e-waste (old electronics) has become a big problem in the Middle East
b we want more and more features on our devices
c it brings essential economic development and an expanded job market
d it's become more and more difficult to operate them
e it creates problems, like the growing mountain of e-waste

PLUS

5 Write three sentences about planned obsolescence that address both sides of the issue.

1 position A + concession expression + position B

_____

_____

2 concession introduction + position A + position B

_____

_____

3 concession introduction + position A + concession expression + position B

_____

_____

6 Work with a partner. Check each other's sentences in Exercise 4. Make any necessary corrections based on your partner's feedback.

SPEAKING TASK

Give a group presentation about a product that you believe was designed for obsolescence. Discuss the reasons, both positive and negative, why it was designed in this way.

PREPARE

1 Work in a small group with the same students you worked with in the Critical thinking section on pages 51–52. Follow the steps below and on page 56 to prepare your presentation.

step 1: Assign roles
Decide on roles for your presentation: Who will:
- explain the concept of planned obsolescence?

  _____

- introduce the product?

  _____

- explain its obsolescence?

  _____

- explain the pros and cons?

  _____

- explain who benefits from its obsolescence and who does not?

  _____

Think about how to make transitions from one speaker to another. For example, one speaker could briefly introduce the next speaker.

step 2: Review
Review all your notes in the Critical thinking section as well as the phrases and expressions you will need to make your presentation.

step 3: Prepare notes

Prepare some talking points, but do not write out what you will say. If you read from your notes, you will not sound natural.

_____

_____

_____

_____

_____

_____

_____

_____

_____

_____

_____

2 Refer to the Task checklist as you prepare for your presentation.

TASK CHECKLIST	✔
Briefly explain the concept of planned obsolescence.	
Introduce the product.	
Explain the pros and cons of planned obsolescence for this product.	
Discuss who is affected by the planned obsolescence and whether these effects are positive or negative.	
Acknowledge other points of view with appropriate expressions.	
Make smooth transitions between speakers.	
Use correct word and syllable stress with compound nouns and noun phrases.	

PRACTISE

3 Practise your parts of the presentation in your group. Give other students feedback on their parts of the presentation and consider the feedback they give you. Make any necessary changes to your notes in Exercise 1.

PRESENT

4 Give your presentation.

OBJECTIVES REVIEW

1 Check your learning objectives for this unit. Write *3*, *2* or *1* for each objective.

3 = very well   2 = well   1 = not so well

I can ...

watch and understand a video about designer
bikes in France and Japan.   _____

use a table to take notes on main ideas and detail.   _____

review and organize notes.   _____

evaluate pros and cons.   _____

use cause-and-effect phrases.   _____

use degree expressions.   _____

acknowledge other arguments.   _____

give a group presentation.   _____

2 Use the *Unlock* Digital Workbook for more practice with this unit's
learning objectives.

WORDLIST		
backlash (n)	fabric (n) ⊙	mass production (n)
circumvent (v)	finite (adj) ⊙	obstacle (n) ⊙
customize (v)	foundation (n) ⊙	rejection (n) ⊙
devise (v)	innovation (n) ⊙	resent (v)
downside (n)	issue (v) ⊙	
drastically (adv)	junk (n)	

⊙ = high-frequency words in the Cambridge Academic Corpus

UNL⦾CK YOUR KNOWLEDGE

Work with a partner. Discuss the questions.

1 What two types of technology can you see in this photograph? What are they being used for?

2 What information could be collected about the person in this photo because of their use of this technology?

3 How much data is stored about you on the devices you carry with you? What, if any, steps do you take to protect your personal data? Why?

PLUS

PREPARING TO WATCH

1 Work with a partner. Discuss the questions.

1 What is a computer virus? How does a computer become infected with a virus?

2 Have you ever had a virus on your computer? What problems did it cause?

3 What can you do to make your computer less vulnerable to viruses?

4 Look at the glossary definition of *ransomware*. Would you pay money if your computer was attacked by ransomware? Why / Why not?

2 You are going to watch a video about a ransomware attack. Before you watch, look at the pictures and discuss the questions with your partner.

1 What country or countries do you think have been affected by the attack?

2 What types of organizations do you think have been targeted?

3 Who do you think is trying to deal with the problem?

GLOSSARY

malicious (adj) intended to cause damage to a computer system, or to steal private information from a computer system

code (n) a sequence of numbers, letters and symbols which form the instructions for a computer program

ransomware (n) software designed by criminals to prevent computer users from getting access to their own computer system or files unless they pay money

potent (adj) very effective

terminal (n) a piece of equipment consisting of a keyboard and screen, used for communicating with the part of a computer system that deals with information, for example, one PC or laptop connected to a computer network

wreak havoc (verb phrase) to cause confusion and lack of order, especially that which causes damage or trouble

WHILE WATCHING

3 ▶ Watch the video. Choose the best option to complete the main idea.

The new ransomware …

a is only likely to affect businesses in the Ukraine.

b can infect networks more easily than previous viruses.

c has attacked computers protected by Kaspersky's anti-virus software.

UNDERSTANDING MAIN IDEAS

4 ▶ Watch again. Answer the questions. *100 000*

1 What kind of company is Kaspersky? _____

2 What have they called the new virus? *ransom*

3 How many computers may be infected? *100 000*

4 How serious is the virus compared to the WannaCry virus? _____

5 How many infected computers does it take to infect a network? *1*

6 Where have the ransom demands been appearing? *...... Ukraine*

UNDERSTANDING DETAIL

5 ▶ Watch again. Choose the best answer (a, b or c) to explain the meaning of words and phrases in bold in the sentences (1–4).

1 It's more **virulent** than the WannaCry attack last month.

a complicated   b infectious   c famous

2 It certainly wreaked havoc and Ukraine has **borne the brunt**.

a taken the blame   b caused the problem   c been the worst affected

3 The ransom demand's been **popping up on** bank machines …

a appearing on   b shutting down   c taking over

4 … computer users **wrestle with** the latest threat.

a recover from   b fear   c try to deal with

WORKING OUT MEANING FROM CONTEXT

DISCUSSION

6 Work in a small group. Discuss the questions.

1 Why do the criminals who design ransomware target large organizations? What problems can they create for these organizations?

2 Do you think that large organizations ever pay the ransoms? Why / Why not?

3 Why is it difficult for large organizations to protect all of their computers?

4 Imagine you work for a global corporation and have been put in charge of improving network security. What steps could you take?

LISTENING

LISTENING 1

PREPARING TO LISTEN

1 You are going to listen to a moderated public forum about privacy issues in modern society. Before you listen, work in small groups. Discuss the questions.

1 Do you think that mobile devices are useful to criminals? Why / Why not?

2 Can the police use information from mobile devices to solve crimes? How and when do they get access to the information?

2 Read the sentences and choose the best definition for the words in bold.

1 This law was passed **in the interest of** protecting public safety online.
   a as one option for
   b for the purpose of
   c to limit the cost of

2 The court requires a **legitimate** reason for requesting information about private citizens.
   a allowed by law
   b adequate
   c medical

3 The manager was **compelled** to resign because his actions had led to a huge loss of customers' financial information.
   a to force someone to do something
   b to beg someone to do something
   c to advise someone to do something

4 Our website has **encryption** software that protects customer data from identity theft.
   a the process of stealing data through cookies in the computer code
   b the process of destroying dangerous data instantly
   c the process of protecting data by changing it into code

5 Independent online retailers depend on the security of internet transactions for their **livelihood**.
   a entertainment
   b the money people need to live on
   c a place to do business

6 The police are required to obtain a **warrant** before they make an arrest or search inside someone's home or business.
   a an official copy of an important document
   b specific training for the police and military
   c an official document that allows the police to take action

7 The interviews with detectives who solve crimes involving identity theft gave viewers an **insight** into the threats that exist online.
   a new understanding of a complicated problem or situation
   b useful tips or recommendations
   c photos, videos and other visual information

8 You can buy the cheaper security software, but the **trade-off** is that it will probably not work as well as the more expensive products.
   a a close relationship
   b a situation in which one thing increases the value of the other
   c a situation in which you accept something bad in order to have something good

3 🔊 3.1 Listen to the introduction. Then complete the tasks.

1 What issue will be discussed?
   a recent criminal invasions of privacy by the media
   b the compromise between privacy and protecting the public from crime
   c serious crimes which have been solved using surveillance

2 What will you be listening to?
   a a conversation among acquaintances
   b a debate between experts
   c a radio discussion with ordinary people

3 Complete the two questions that will be discussed.
   a Should tech companies have to give information about the activities of _____ to the police?
   b Should tech companies have to help law enforcement agencies _br eakin to_ the devices of private individuals?

4 Predict one point of view or opinion that you think will definitely be presented.

   _____

   _____

WHILE LISTENING

4 3.2 Listen to the forum. In the *answer* column, write Y (yes), N (no),
or ? (not stated) for each question (Q1 and Q2).

speaker	answer	notes	type of support
Joel	Q1 Yes Q2 No		
Lauren	Q1 No Q2 No		
Dave	Q1 Yes Q2 Yes		
Karina	Q1 Yes Q2 No		
Tony	Q1 Yes Q2 No		
Min	Q1 Yes Q2 No		

Listening for facts and supporting information

When speakers express their point of view, they are really talking about their beliefs and opinions. They often support their views with facts. These may include references to scientific research, information in published reports, expert statements, statistics, laws and personal experience.

5 🔊 3.2 Listen again. In the *notes* column in the table in Exercise 4, take notes on the support each speaker gives for their position. Then in the *type of support* column, describe the type of support the speaker offers (e.g. *opinion only, facts – the law, facts – personal experience*).

TAKING NOTES
ON DETAIL

POST-LISTENING

6 Choose the best answer (a–c) to complete the explanations.

MAKING INFERENCES

1 Joel says, 'We need to keep one step ahead of serious criminals.'
   He means police should ...
   a come up with new ways to fight crime.
   b use the same technology as the criminals.
   c maintain a position in which they are winning the fight against crime.

2 Joel says that asking tech companies to break into devices would be 'crossing the line.' He means it would be ...
   a justified.
   b unacceptable.
   c open to debate.

3 Lauren starts her response to the second question by saying, 'Don't get me started.' She means she ...
   a doesn't want to talk about it now or in the future.
   b has strong feelings and could talk about it for a long time.
   c doesn't need any help from the interviewer to state her ideas.

PRONUNCIATION FOR LISTENING

SKILLS

Sentence stress

English sentences follow a rhythm of stressed and unstressed words. Stress helps listeners focus on the important words in a sentence.

The stressed syllables in stressed words are generally louder, longer and higher in pitch than unstressed syllables. Stressed words are often content words, such as nouns, adjectives, adverbs and main verbs. Negative auxiliary verbs, e.g. *don't* are usually also stressed.

Unstressed words are often grammar or function words, such as articles, pronouns, prepositions and auxiliary verbs.

7 ◀ 3.3 Listen and underline the stressed syllables in each sentence. The number of stressed syllables is given in brackets for the first two sentences. Listen again and check your answers.

1 We'll take questions and comments from listeners at the end of the programme. (6)
2 Joel, should companies have to hand over information about their customers? (5)
3 Law enforcement is made more difficult without access to this kind of information.
4 I think the majority of these agencies have their own experts.
5 Without evidence from surveillance that's admissible in court, we don't have a hope of putting them away.
6 The information on that phone doesn't belong to the tech company; it belongs to a private individual.
7 That might be true if we were talking about the physical world – like unlocking the door to your apartment.

DISCUSSION

8 Work with a partner. Discuss the questions.

1 Which of the speakers in Listening 1 do you agree with? Why?
2 Will any of the information change how you store personal information? What will you do differently?
3 What kind of crime do you think police need information from private devices to solve? How would they have got this information before the invention of mobile technology?

⊙ LANGUAGE DEVELOPMENT

SUBJECT-VERB AGREEMENT WITH QUANTIFIERS

Many quantifiers (e.g. *some*, *many*, *all*) appear in expressions with *of* and definite nouns and noun phrases.

<u>All of the computers in our network</u> need protection.

Other quantifiers with *of* appear with both definite and indefinite noun phrases. These include:

fractions	percentages	other expressions of quantity
half of	*fifty percent*	*a/the majority of*
a quarter of	*25% of*	*a number of*

<u>The majority of people</u> just don't understand.

In sentences, the verb agrees with the noun phrase.

<u>Half of the people surveyed</u> weren't sure which antivirus software they used.
<u>Some of our customers' data</u> was hacked.

Expressions of quantity can also be used as pronouns. The noun phrase that the expression refers to must be inferred. The verb agrees with the inferred noun phrase.

<u>75% believe</u> all of their data is encrypted, but **<u>most is</u>** not.
(Inferred phrases: 75% of the people surveyed, most of their data)

---

1 Complete the sentences with the correct form of the verb in brackets.

1 The majority of online retailers _____ (offer) a secure form of payment.
2 Some of the cookies _____ (be) stored outside of the browser.
3 Half of the information that you read online _____ (contain) factual errors.
4 Most of your online activity _____ (be) visible to cybercriminals.

PLUS

2 Choose the correct forms of the verbs to complete the sentences.

1 Most gave this app positive reviews, but a minority *say / says* it takes too long to load.
2 The survey indicates that 35%, or about one-third, *prefer / prefers* to shop for special occasion gifts at a shopping centre or department store, rather than online.
3 We had about 70 members, but a number *has / have* left.
4 It took hours to fix my PC! Part of that time was spent upgrading it, but most *was / were* taken up with deleting adware.
5 A few users make up very strong passwords, but most *choose / chooses* a password that is easy for criminals to guess.

COLLOCATIONS

3 Complete the paragraph using the collocations for online activity in the box in the correct form. There are two collocations you do not need to use.

> clear (your) cookies   surf the internet / the web / the net
> enable/disable cookies   secure network
> search engine   search terms

> Whenever you provide private information online, or even if you are just (1)_____ , you should make sure you are using a (2)_____ . If you don't want any personal information to be stored, you should use a (3)_____ that allows you to browse anonymously. And you should always (4)_____ after you have finished working online.

4 Complete the paragraph using the collocations relating to law and order in the correct form. Use a dictionary if needed. There are two collocations you do not need to use.

> combat crime   identity theft   public safety
> law-abiding   law enforcement   organized crime

> I am a (1) _____ citizen and I spend a lot of time online.
> I believe that the majority of people who do business online are honest and they obey the law. However, an increasing number of cyber criminals and identity thieves are now active on the internet.
> (2) _____ officials need to do a better job of (3) _____ that occurs online and ensuring (4) _____ .

PLUS

LISTENING 2

PREPARING TO LISTEN

1 You are going to listen to a presentation about internet security and privacy. Before you listen, think about what kinds of activities you do online. Complete the survey. Then compare your answers with a partner.

USING YOUR KNOWLEDGE

activity	occasionally	regularly
shop; check prices and products		
read news, features or blogs		
comment on websites, blogs or online forums		
check social media		
send and receive messages, images or videos		
do research		
watch videos		
upload content (e.g. videos to YouTube)		
play games		
manage your finances		
take care of healthcare-related needs or business		

2 Work with a partner. Discuss the questions.

1 When you engage in the online activities in Exercise 1, what kind of information is stored online (for example, your search history, passwords, address, etc.)?

2 Do you actively control what gets stored? How?

3 Do you always click 'agree' or 'yes' when a website asks for permission? Why / Why not?

4 What is *identity theft*? Has this ever happened to you or somebody you know?

3 Read the sentences. Write the words in bold (1–8) next to their definitions below (a–h).

1 Tariq had worked in internet security for more than fifteen years when he decided it was time to **move on**. He changed to a position in finance.

2 We can **personalize** our products to meet the security needs of your company.

3 Detectives are using email messages to find somebody who stole five million dollars. They have **traced** the messages to a computer on a Caribbean island.

4 I prefer to do my work **offline**, where there are no security issues.

5 You can **disable** the camera feature on your computer if you don't want people to see you.

6 This website is **targeted** at young women between 15 and 20.

7 Many **retailers** have shifted most of their business online, where costs are lower.

8 The government is **taking steps** to protect the security of its records.

a _____ (v) to begin to act towards achieving a particular goal
b _____ (v) to start a new activity
c _____ (v) to stop something from working
d _____ (v) to direct something at somebody
e _____ (n) a business that sells to the public
f _____ (v) to make something suitable for a particular person
g _____ (adv) not connected to the internet
h _____ (v) to find the origin of something

WHILE LISTENING

4 🔊 3.4 Draw a table like the one below. Listen to the presentation and complete the table with notes on main ideas and details.

main ideas	details

5 🔊 3.4 Listen again. Listen for the key terms and write a definition or explanation of each term.

1 behavioural targeting: _____

2 cookie: _____

3 third-party cookie: _____

4 secure cookie: _____

5 surfing incognito: _____

6 flash cookies: _____

7 web beacon: _____

POST-LISTENING

Listening for opinion

Informational presentations consist mostly of facts. However, even primarily objective presentations may include a presenter's opinions and beliefs. It is useful to annotate your notes to show which information is factual and which represents an opinion. Signposts of speaker opinion include the following:

expressions of belief	expressions of certainty		
I think/believe …	probably	maybe	no doubt
In my view/opinion, …	likely	clearly	surely
Let's be honest, …	evaluative expressions		
suggestions or inferences	These are the best / most valuable …		
You / This / We all should …			

6 Work with a partner. Are these statements facts (F), opinions (O) or neither (N)?

1 You're reading an online newspaper or blog, and then, bam! An advert for that lens you want appears on your screen. _____

2 Companies track your browsing activity and use it to send you advertisements that target you specifically. _____

3 The primary tool that companies use to track and remember you is the 'cookie'. _____

4 So cookies are clearly useful. _____

5 Every time you visit another site that has advertisements from the same company, the cookies can be traced back to you. _____

6 I think more sites will probably move to secure cookies in the future, but for now, only about half of all websites use secure cookies. _____

7 Maybe you're thinking you should stop using the internet altogether! _____

8 You should say 'no' if you don't want that company to store information about you. _____

7 Update your notes in Exercise 4 with the key terms in Exercise 5. Review all of the details you have written in your table. Add any missing main ideas to your notes. Compare your notes with a partner.

8 Circle all the answers that are correct according to the information in the presentation. More than one answer may be correct.

1 Retail businesses target customers by …
   a tracking consumer behaviour and preferences.
   b creating special advertisements.
   c sending cookies to potential customers' accounts.
2 Cookies store information about …
   a financial records.
   b consumers and their browsing behaviour.
   c consumer purchases.
3 Identity theft may occur when …
   a a third-party cookie is created.
   b a non-secure cookie is transmitted.
   c a flash cookie is stored.
4 You can prevent online retailers from building a profile about you by …
   a browsing incognito.
   b disabling cookies.
   c clicking 'agree.'
5 Online retailers use techniques other than cookies to try to monitor your browsing. They also use …
   a web beacons.
   b alternate browsers.
   c business profiles.

DISCUSSION

SYNTHESIZING

9 Work with a partner. Use ideas from Listening 1 and Listening 2 to answer the following questions.

1 Do you think you will change your browsing behaviour after reading about behavioural targeting? Why / Why not?
2 What are some other positive aspects of electronic tracking technology? Could it be applied outside retail? How?

SPEAKING

CRITICAL THINKING

At the end of this unit, you are going to do the speaking task below.

> Present data that you have collected from a survey and the conclusions that you have drawn from it.

SKILLS

Eliciting information via surveys

In some forms of research, surveys can be a helpful tool. In contrast to interviews, which focus on individual responses, survey research often focuses on trends across a whole group of respondents.

Surveys are particularly good for eliciting information of two types:
opinions/beliefs: *Should tech companies be obliged to help the police identify criminals?*
behaviour: *What do you do to protect your information online?*

When you develop a survey, you need to have a specific question or issue as the goal and build your survey items around it. Items should be neutral in tone so that respondents can answer honestly and comfortably.

Analyzing data

When analyzing a survey, you should focus on the key research questions first. Your data will be raw numbers, percentages and anecdotal data. The more people you ask, the more sure you can be about the results of your survey.

You should compare different groups of people that you asked, e.g. have older and younger people got different views? Men and women? People who are confident with technology and people who aren't? Filtering your data into different subgroups can reveal different trends.

You can also compare your data set to other surveys, e.g. surveys of a similar subject for your country.

1 Work in small groups. Consider the two issues that are explored in this unit: **internet use and protecting personal information** (review Listening 1) and **privacy and crime** (review Listening 2). What opinions or behaviour do you want to investigate? Brainstorm a list of topics. (e.g. *how people ensure their online security*.)

REMEMBER

_____ _____

_____ _____

_____ _____

_____ _____

APPLY

 EVALUATE

2 Consider the topics you wrote in Exercise 1. Are they about behaviour (B) or opinions (O)? Label them.

3 Work in small groups. Discuss which of these questions would work well in a survey. Explain your choices.

1 How many internet-enabled devices do you use at least once per day?
2 Do you ever disable cookies when you surf the internet?
3 How do you protect your information on the internet?
4 Do you think tech companies should help the police?
5 How often do you click 'I agree' when a website asks permission to send you something?
6 'The police should have to get permission from a judge before obtaining an individual's private information.' Do you agree, disagree or have no opinion?

 CREATE

4 Work with your group. Complete the tasks to create your survey.

1 Choose an issue from Exercise 1 as the topic of your survey. _____
2 Write five questions that you feel will give you the information you need to address the issue.

Q1: _____
Q2: _____
Q3: _____
Q4: _____
Q5: _____

 EVALUATE

5 Exchange surveys with another group. Complete the other group's survey in order to give feedback on the points below.

- **clarity of questions:** Are they easy to understand?
- **neutrality of tone:** Will your respondents be comfortable answering the questions?

6 Think about the results you will get from your survey. Answer the questions.

1 Who are the respondents to your survey? What is their age, gender, country of origin, socio-economic status (e.g. are they middle class, rich, etc.), and level of education?
2 How much do you think these factors will affect their responses?
3 How much do you think you can generalize from your survey responses to a larger population?

PREPARATION FOR SPEAKING

PRONUNCIATION FOR SPEAKING

> ### Question intonation
>
> Intonation rises at the end of *yes/no* questions and it falls at the end of *wh-*(information) questions. Using the correct intonation helps listeners understand the type of question you are asking.
>
> ↗
> Should companies have to hand over information about their customers?
>
> ↘
> What do you think?

1 🔊 3.5 Listen to the questions and decide whether each one ends with rising intonation or a falling intonation. Choose the correct arrow (a or b).

1 a ↗   b ↘   3 a ↗   b ↘   5 a ↗   b ↘
2 a ↗   b ↘   4 a ↗   b ↘

2 Conduct your survey. Gather answers from at least 20 respondents either by distributing the survey in written form or by conducting the survey in person and recording the responses. You may ask friends and acquaintances or people you do not know.

3 Make a table like the one below for each of your survey questions. Count up the responses and express them as percentages (for example, 8 out of 20 = 40%). Analyze the data you have collected. Use the Explanation box in Critical thinking to help you.

Question 1: _____	
category	percentage of respondents
strongly agree	

PRESENTING SURVEY DATA

Tables, charts and graphs are useful ways to present survey data. Presenting data visually can help your audience understand your ideas and results more easily.

Phrases like these are commonly used when describing visual data:
This [type of graph] compares ...
This [type of graph] shows ...
As you can see from this [type of chart], ...
From this, it can be seen that ...
X demonstrates that ...
The majority of respondents said ...
The distribution of responses here is even/uneven ...

4 Work in small groups. Look at the pie chart. Practise describing the data to your group. Use some of the phrases in the Explanation box.

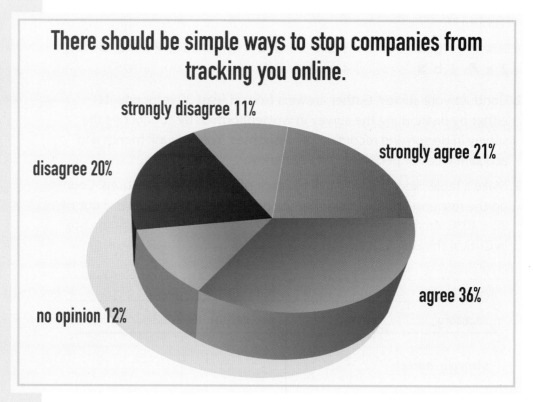

There should be simple ways to stop companies from tracking you online.

strongly disagree 11%

disagree 20%

strongly agree 21%

agree 36%

no opinion 12%

PRESENTING CONCLUSIONS FROM RESEARCH

Here are some phrases that are commonly used when presenting conclusions that have been drawn from survey data or other forms of research:

Survey results indicate that …

It is clear that …

This stands in contrast to …

It follows that …

It can be concluded that …

We can conclude that …

Taking all the results into account, …

Remember to use cautious language in generalizations whenever you don't have a clear result. In addition, remember that your conclusions are based on a small group of respondents so any generalization based on your results should be modest.

5 What can you conclude based on the pie chart? Practise presenting your conclusions to others in your group. Use phrases from the Explanation box.

SPEAKING TASK

Present data that you have collected from a survey and the conclusions that you have drawn from it.

PREPARE

1 Work with your group. Look back at the issue you chose as the topic of your survey (Critical thinking, Exercise 4 on page 74) and the tables of analysis of your survey questions (Preparation for Speaking, Exercise 3). Does the data you gathered in your survey adequately address the issue you chose? If not, what questions should be asked in a further survey?

2 What kind of graph or graphs would work best to display your results: a pie chart (for data that adds up to 100%), a bar graph (with a bar for each kind of response), or some other type? Create your graph(s). Do you want to present all the graphs, or just one or two that present the most important results?

3 With your survey group, review your data analysis from Preparation for speaking, Exercise 3 on page 75. What are the limitations of your survey results? How general can you be in your conclusions? How will you express those limitations in your presentations (e.g. *This was a survey of 20 middle-class female university students in the UAE.*)?

4 Prepare talking points, but do not write out what you will say. Make sure you include the following:

- a description of your survey and data collection process, including a description of the population you surveyed and the number of people who participated
- an explanation of your results, including any graphics you wish to use
- the conclusions you have drawn from the data
- limitations on your conclusion

5 If you are doing a group presentation, assign roles. Who will ...

- introduce your presentation?
- provide background to your survey?
- present your graphs?
- present your conclusions?

Think about how to make transitions from one speaker to another.

6 Refer to the Task checklist as you prepare your presentation.

TASK CHECKLIST	✔
Describe your survey process.	
Use an effective visual.	
Explain your results.	
Use appropriate expressions to refer to your results.	
Make smooth transitions between speakers.	
Draw appropriate conclusions based on your results.	

PRACTISE

7 Take turns presenting your graphs and conclusions to another group. Use some of the phrases from the boxes on pages 76–77. Give feedback to other students. Listen carefully to the others and offer feedback. Consider the feedback that they give you and revise your conclusions if needed.

PRESENT

8 Give your presentation.

OBJECTIVES REVIEW

1 Check your learning objectives for this unit. Write *3, 2* or *1* for each objective.

   3 = very well   2 = well   1 = not so well

   I can ...

   watch and understand a video about internet security. _____

   listen for facts and supporting information. _____

   listen for opinions. _____

   elicit information in surveys. _____

   use subject-verb agreement with quantifiers. _____

   explain data from graphics. _____

   present conclusions from research. _____

   present survey data and conclusions. _____

2 Use the *Unlock* Digital Workbook for more practice with this unit's learning objectives.

UNLOCK ONLINE

WORDLIST

clear your cookies (v phr)	law-abiding (adj)	secure network (n phr)
combat crime (v phr)	law enforcement (n)	surf the internet/the web/the net (v phr)
compel (v)	legitimate (adj) ⊙	take steps (v phr)
disable (v)	livelihood (n)	target (v) ⊙
disable cookies (v phr)	move on (phr v)	trace (v) ⊙
enable cookies (v phr)	offline (adj)	trade-off (n)
encryption (n)	organized crime (n phr)	warrant (n) ⊙
identity theft (n)	personalize (v)	
insight (n) ⊙	public safety (n)	
in the interest of (idiom)	retailer (n)	
	search engine (n)	
	search terms (n pl)	

⊙ = high-frequency words in the Cambridge Academic Corpus

LEARNING OBJECTIVES	IN THIS UNIT YOU WILL ...
Watch and listen	watch and understand a video about the tech hub in East Africa.
Listening skills	listen for definitions; understand figurative language; identify figurative language.
Critical thinking	persuade your audience in a business presentation.
Grammar	emphasize and contrast.
Speaking skill	craft a mission statement; craft a pitch.
Speaking task	make a pitch to get funding for a new venture.

UNLOCK YOUR KNOWLEDGE

Work with a partner. Discuss the questions.

1 How have retail businesses changed the way they interact with their customers in the past twenty years?

2 How has what customers expect from businesses changed?

3 Consider some charitable organizations that you know (e.g. the Red Cross, UNICEF). In what ways are they like businesses?

PLUS

WATCH AND LISTEN

PREPARING TO WATCH

ACTIVATING YOUR KNOWLEDGE

1 Answer the questions about smartphone apps. Then work with a partner and compare your answers.

1 Which of these types of apps do you have on your phone? Which do you use most frequently?

social media ☐	instant messaging ☐	news/weather ☐
business ☐	banking ☐	music/radio ☐
fitness ☐	gaming ☐	TV/films ☐
education ☐	shopping ☐	travel/tourism ☐

2 Which apps do the people you know spend the longest using? Why?

3 Which apps are free and which do you have to pay for? What other ways do technology companies make money from apps?

PREDICTING CONTENT USING VISUALS

2 You are going to watch a video about the tech hub growing in East Africa. Before you watch, look at the pictures and discuss the questions with your partner.

1 What part of the world do you think this is? What proportion of people here do you think own a smartphone?

2 Do you think the same apps would be popular here as in your county? Why / Why not?

3 What kind of business do the people work in? Do you think they are successful? Why / Why not?

GLOSSARY

market (n) the business or trade in a particular product

entrepreneur (n) someone who starts their own business, especially when this involves seeing a new opportunity

mentoring (n) the activity of supporting and advising someone with less experience to help them develop in their work

tech hub (n) a centre which supports new technology businesses when they are starting out

concentration (n) a large number or amount of something in the same place

disposable income (n) the money that is left over after you have paid your bills that you can spend as you wish

WHILE WATCHING

UNDERSTANDING
MAIN IDEAS

3 ▶ Watch the video. Write *T* (true), *F* (false) or *DNS* (does not say) next to the statements below. Correct the false statements.

_____ 1 The Ugandan smartphone market is growing quickly.

_____ 2 Ugandan tech companies are developing apps for a global market.

_____ 3 The game Mutatu has become popular all over the world.

_____ 4 Young people in Africa have money to spend on games.

_____ 5 Very few people want to invest in African tech companies.

UNDERSTANDING
DETAIL

4 ▶ Watch again. Complete the sentences with one to three words in each gap.

1 Jasper Nunu developed a successful _____ called *Mutatu*.

2 In Kenya, one in every five people _____ through their phones.

3 The Mutatu app was a finalist in Google's Android _____ for Sub-Saharan Africa.

4 Google provided _____ which led to more than 60,000 downloads of Mutatu.

5 Popular _____ systems are an example of how the tech industry is growing in East Africa.

6 Africa has more _____ than any other part of the world.

7 Investors want to access East Africa's local _____ .

8 As well as being consumers, Africans hope to become _____ of content.

WORKING
OUT MEANING
FROM CONTEXT

5 ▶ Work with a partner. Explain the words and phrases in bold.

With a successful gaming app already [1]**under his belt**, Jasper Nunu has joined [2]**the growing ranks** of East Africa's [3]**whizz kids**, helping to [4]**propel** the region into the tech [5]**spotlight**.

East Africa has experienced a dramatic tech-hub [6]**boom**, [7]**spurred on** by [8]**collaborative workspaces** such as Nairobi's iHub.

Increasingly, investors are looking to [9]**break into** these [10]**lucrative** local markets.

DISCUSSION

6 Work in a small group. Discuss the questions.

1 Why do you think Google run developer competitions in Sub-Saharan Africa?

2 What traditional games are there from your country? Which of them have been or could be made into apps?

3 Do you know where the apps you use were developed? Were any developed in Africa? Were any of the apps you use developed in your country?

4 What are the biggest markets for growth and investment in your country at present? Why are they growing?

LISTENING

LISTENING 1

PREPARING TO LISTEN

1 Read the sentences and choose the best definition for the words in bold.

1 The plans for the new office building are so **elaborate** that very few people can understand them.
   a late and rushed
   b old and out of date
   c detailed

2 We have submitted a proposal and we are hoping the bank will provide a loan for our **venture**.
   a new business
   b trip
   c factory

3 She is **wary** of using her company credit card over the internet and prefers to shop in person.
   a careful in the face of possible danger
   b resisting new ideas and developments
   c frightened

4 I have been dealing with an email **overload**, but I think I have finally cleared out my inbox.
   a too much of something
   b an unsafe situation
   c something that is too heavy

5 The bank charges a small fee for each international **transaction**.
   a an activity that requires legal permission
   b an activity that involves hiring or firing somebody
   c an activity that involves the movement of money

6 Online-only banking has been really **disruptive** to the banking industry.
   a changing the traditional way that an industry operates
   b changing how customers feel about something
   c creating the appearance of change

7 I have too many things to do. I have just **dumped** all of my files on my desk. I'll sort them out later.
   a threw in different directions
   b left behind
   c put something somewhere without caring where

8 The speaker used all the right **buzzwords** for online marketing, but he really didn't say anything useful.
   a words and expressions that cause a lot of disagreement
   b popular words or expressions that are sometimes overused in a field
   c words or expressions that people outside a field often misunderstand

2 You are going to listen to a lecture about disruptive innovation. Before you listen, take the survey below. Compare your responses with a partner.

---

1 Where would you be most likely to buy a book?
   a a bookshop   **b** online   **c** other: _____

2 How are you most likely to book a flight?
   a on an airline's website
   b with a travel agent
   c on an online site such as Expedia, Skyscanner, etc.

3 Where would you be most likely to buy car insurance?
   a at an agent's office
   b on an insurance company's website
   c other: _____

4 When you travel, where would you be most likely to book a room?
   a a hotel website
   b on a review website such as Trip Advisor or Hotels.com
   c on a sub-letting service like Airbnb or similar

5 Which of these sites have you used? Circle all that apply.
   a Amazon   **c** Uber   **e** Etsy
   b eBay   **d** Craigslist **f** Mechanical Turk

---

3 Work with a partner. Discuss the questions.

  1 Do you think you (or somebody like you) would have given the same answers to the survey ten years ago? Why / Why not?

  2 What *innovations* – new ideas or ways of doing business – are responsible for recent changes in how we get products and services?

4 🔊 4.1 Listen to the beginning of the lecture. Circle the questions you think this lecture will answer.

  a What has happened to mainframe computers? ✗

  b What are some other examples of markets that have been disrupted by the internet?

  c How did the internet redefine business transactions?

  d What new business models emerged as a result of the internet?

WHILE LISTENING

5 🔊 4.2 Listen to the lecture. Check your predictions in Exercise 4. Take notes on the answers if and when these topics are addressed. Write an X if the topic is not addressed.

Listening for definitions

Speakers often provide a signpost of definition either before or after giving the definition. Some signposts of definition to listen for include:

X, which is ...   In other words, ...   The word/term for
By X, I mean ...   This means ... ,   this is X.
X, meaning ...   The definition of X is ...   ... is referred to as ...
... , that is, ...   We can define X as ...   X is the term for ...

Speakers do not always use such obvious markers, however. Often a definition is given in a more conversational way, simply by linking the term and a definition with *is* or pausing briefly between the term and its definition.
In the current economy, it is difficult for many start-ups — new, fast-growing businesses — to survive.

LISTENING FOR DETAIL

6 🔊 4.2 Listen again. Match the term (1–7) that is being defined with its definition given in the lecture. (a–g).

1 disruptive innovation __d__
2 universal access __a__
3 aggregators __b__   __f__
4 frictionless capitalism _____
5 curation __c__
6 power sellers __e__
7 concierge __g__

a anyone with a computer and a network connection could access all kinds of information
b businesses, such as Amazon, which bring together every product imaginable
c sifting activity
d when a new technology or business model fundamentally changes a market
e participants who act as intermediaries on the site, buying and selling
f the smooth and easy exchange of goods and labour
g a middleman who will actually do everything for them

POST-LISTENING

MAKING INFERENCES

SKILLS

Understanding figurative language

Figurative language includes words and expressions that do not have their usual or literal meaning. If you know the literal meaning of a word or expression, you can often infer the figurative meaning from the context.

7 Work with a partner. Complete the table for the figurative language in bold in the excerpts. Use a dictionary to help you.

excerpt	literal meaning	figurative meaning
'The internet has become the **engine** of disruptive innovation in dozens of markets, from travel to publishing to insurance.'		something that provides power or energy for a process
'... it's allowed the automation of transactions, reducing what Bill Gates referred to as "**friction**" in the market.'	the force that makes it difficult for one object to slide past another	
'These new "curators" have become experts at **harnessing** the power of the internet.'		
'A final **casualty** of the elimination of the middleman has been luxury.'		

PRONUNCIATION FOR LISTENING

SKILLS

Pausing and thought groups

Speakers pause after important words, such as transition words, and after thought groups.

Thought groups are words that go together to form an idea. They are usually grammatical units, such as clauses (noun + verb), noun phrases (article + noun) or prepositional phrases (preposition + noun).

Speakers connect words within thought groups and signpost the end of a thought group with a slight change in intonation and a pause. This helps listeners to hear where one idea ends and another begins.

8 🔊 4.3 Listen to the example sentence below. Notice the change in intonation and pauses marked at the end of each thought group. Then listen to the sentences and mark the end of each thought group that you hear.

The classic example / is the personal computer / which was pioneered by IBM / a company that had previously dominated the market / for large mainframe computers.

1 With IBM's new smaller model however computers became accessible to an entirely new group of customers.

2 The internet has become the engine of disruptive innovation in dozens of markets from travel to publishing to insurance.

3 Firstly suddenly anyone with a computer and a network connection could access all kinds of information – information that had previously only been available to professionals.

4 Travel sites such as Expedia and Kayak aggregate information on dozens of airlines and car rentals and thousands of hotels allowing customers to compare and make their choices from a single site.

5 With online transactions there is no need for people no need for interaction which could slow things down.

9 Work with a partner. Read the paragraph and mark where you think you should pause. Then practise reading it aloud. Give each other feedback.

> Next I'd like to talk about some successful non-profits. One example is Kiva a non-profit organization based in San Francisco. Its mission is to alleviate poverty by connecting people who need loans to people who donate money to them through Kiva's website. Through Kiva people can lend money to entrepreneurs and students from more than 80 countries around the world.

DISCUSSION

10 Work in small groups. Discuss the questions.

1 The presenter ends by saying, 'And so disruptive innovation has brought us full circle.' What do you think that means?

2 What services mentioned by the presenter (i.e. curation, concierges, power sellers) have you used? What do you think about them?

EMPHASIZING AND CONTRASTING

Make a greater impact when you speak by including extreme contrasts and emphasizing extremes.

even

The word *even* emphasizes that something is unusual or extreme.

The massive amount of information a consumer encounters online may lead to <u>indecision</u>, in some cases, **even** <u>decision-making paralysis</u>.

Here, *decision-making paralysis* is an extreme form of *indecision*.

let alone

The phrase *let alone* emphasizes that something is extremely unlikely by contrasting it with a related unlikely event. It usually occurs in sentences that contain a negative.

It can appear before a verb, noun, adjective or adverb.

Customers no longer have to visit <u>different websites</u>, **let alone** <u>different shops</u>, to get everything they need.

let alone introduces a more extreme option.

not to mention

The phrase *not to mention* usually occurs after a list of at least two qualities, activities or things. It introduces an additional example (often the most important, obvious or extreme in the eyes of the speaker) that supports and emphasizes the point.

The company's owner is <u>talented</u> and <u>intelligent</u>, **not to mention** rich.

1 Complete the sentences with *even*, *let alone* or *not to mention*.

1 She didn't tell her own mother about her plans, _____ her colleagues at work.

2 I didn't learn computer programming until university, but today _____ young kids are building their own websites.

3 The organization accepts donations of any size; _____ a pound can make a difference.

4 It would have saved a lot of time and energy, _____ money, if you had planned this project better from the start.

5 It seems unlikely that the government, _____ an individual, can change the way this is done.

6 I'm so busy these days that I don't have time to go shopping, cook, clean, do laundry, _____ sleep!

PLUS

2 Complete the sentences with your own ideas.

1 Everyone will be affected by the new law: big businesses, small shops, *even* _____ .

2 The employment rate does not give a complete picture. It doesn't include individuals who buy and sell on eBay and those who sell their services on the internet, *not to mention,* _____ .

3 *Alibaba* is so dominant that it is difficult for other businesses to enter the market, *let alone* _____ .

ACADEMIC ALTERNATIVES

VOCABULARY

Academic communication often includes lower-frequency words with the same or similar meaning as everyday vocabulary. Often, however, these academic words have more specific or specialized meanings than their higher-frequency counterparts. This allows speakers and writers to be more precise.

3 Work with a partner. What, if anything, is the difference in meaning between the words in these word pairs? Use a dictionary to help you.

high	low
business (n)	venture (n)
choice (n)	option (n)
come out (phr v)	emerge (v)
large (adj)	considerable (adj)

high	low
main (adj)	primary (adj)
sign (n)	trace (n)
sort through (phr v)	analyze (v)
stop using (v phr)	abandon (v)

4 Complete the sentences with the correct form of an academic word or phrase from Exercise 3.

1 The marketing team will have to _____ all the data to find a better way to reach our customers.

2 A lot of people have _____ books completely and do all their reading on mobile devices.

3 There are no _____ of yesterday's celebration. Everything has been cleaned up.

4 Several innovative ideas _____ during our discussion yesterday.

5 This has been an extremely successful _____ , making a profit in its first year.

6 My _____ reason for using an online service is the lower cost.

7 I think we should look at some other _____ . The prices of the tickets here are too high.

8 The bill for the new company headquarters is a _____ sum, but the complex has five multi-storey buildings.

PLUS

5 Choose four of the academic words from the box in Exercise 3. Write a sentence for each one that is relevant to its meaning.

LISTENING 2

PREPARING TO LISTEN

1 Use the correct forms of the words in the box to complete the sentences below.

UNDERSTANDING KEY VOCABULARY

> **concisely** (adv) expressing information in a way that is short, without using unnecessary words
>
> **donor** (n) someone who gives money or goods to a person or organization that needs them
>
> **enterprise** (n) a business or organization
>
> **oversight** (n) responsibility for a job or activity and for ensuring it is being done correctly
>
> **overview** (n) a short description giving the most important facts about something
>
> **scope** (n) the range of a subject covered by a book, programme, discussion, class, etc.
>
> **status** (n) the official or legal position of a person or organization
>
> **worthy** (adj) deserving respect, admiration or support

1 The director gave us a(n) _____ of the new product line.
2 The company gives money every year to a _____ cause, usually a children's charity.
3 The company will not consider your application until they determine your residency _____ in this country.
4 I'm afraid this matter is not within the _____ of my responsibility. You'll have to take it to the manager.
5 Several of our wealthy _____ are interested in this new project and may be willing to contribute money.
6 He has _____ of the day-to-day running of the fundraising arm of our charity.
7 Your presentation is disorganized and far too long. Rewrite the introduction and state your ideas more _____ .
8 Although his new _____ was innovative, he struggled to get funding for it.

PLUS

2 Work in pairs. You are going to listen to a presentation on US non-profit organizations. Before you listen, look at the table and answer the questions.

A selection of the ranking of 145 countries for acts of generosity, defined as charitable donation, volunteering, and helping strangers, 2015

COUNTRY	RANKING	COUNTRY	RANKING	COUNTRY	RANKING
Myanmar	1	Malaysia	10	Sierra Leone	54
USA	2	Kenya	11	South Korea	64
New Zealand	3	United Arab Emirates	14	Vietnam	79
Canada	4	Guatemala	16	Portugal	82
Australia	5	Thailand	19	Mexico	90
UK	6	Germany	20	Japan	102
Netherlands	7	Kuwait	24	Brazil	105
Sri Lanka	8	Costa Rica	36	Russia	129
Ireland	9	Saudi Arabia	47	Burundi	145

Source: Charities Aid Foundation, 2015

1 Which country is number 1 (the highest ranking)?
2 Which countries have a ranking that surprises you? Why?

3 Work in small groups. Discuss the questions.

1 Do you think that donating money and volunteering time are the best ways to help people in need? What other ways are there to help?
2 Do you think that charitable organizations do a good job of helping people in need? Give an example of an organization that you are familiar with and the work it does.

WHILE LISTENING

4 🔊 4.4 Listen to the talk. Write *T* (true), *F* (false) or *DNS* (does not say) next to the statements below. Then correct the false statements.

_____ 1 The purpose of the presentation is to give the students an introduction to the non-profit world and persuade them to consider it as a career.
_____ 2 The main difference between a for-profit business and a non-profit organization is that a non-profit has no revenue.
_____ 3 Donations to non-profits cannot be used for administrative functions.
_____ 4 Non-profit organizations have no owner.
_____ 5 90% of non-profit revenue comes from fundraising.
_____ 6 Non-profits are not affected by market forces.

5 🔊 4.4 Listen again and take notes about the terms listed below. Then use your notes to write definitions of the terms as they relate to non-profit organizations in the US.

1 non-profit organization: _____

_____

2 mission: _____

_____

3 revenue: _____

_____

4 programme: _____

_____

5 equity: _____

_____

6 board of directors: _____

_____

_____

7 fundraising: _____

_____

6 Use the correct forms of the terms from Exercise 5 to complete the paragraph.

(1)_____ differ from businesses that operate for a profit in that they cannot keep the money they raise or distribute it to owners or shareholders as (2)_____ . Instead, their (3)_____ , most of which is provided through (4)_____ , must be used to pay for the organization's (5)_____ . To ensure that the (6)_____ of the organization is protected, a (7)_____ maintains oversight of all operations.

POST-LISTENING

Identifying figurative language

One type of figurative language is *personification*, which is when speakers attribute human traits to something that is not human.

The flames **danced** in the dark.   The waves **attacked** the shore.

Speakers may also attribute the traits or treatment of animals.

The storm raged like an angry **beast**.   The new economic policy is designed to **tame** inflation.

Speakers may also use idioms and comparisons with other experiences as imagery to make their message more powerful.

These children are **fighting a battle** against cancer.

It may seem **like we've got a mountain to climb**, but we'll raise the money we need.

7 Work with a partner. Underline the figurative language in the sentences from the presentation below. Explain why you think the speaker uses this figurative language.

1 I cannot stress enough that fundraising is the lifeblood of a non-profit.
2 Running a non-profit is a little bit like having a child that is always hungry!
3 They can't do those things on a starvation budget.
4 They are learning from the for-profit sector about how to harness market forces, but for social good.
5 There is no better way to make your mark on the world.

8 Underline the figurative language in the excerpts from the presentation below. Answer the questions about each excerpt.

> So that tells you about some of the nuts and bolts of running a non-profit, …

> Money is what makes the wheels of commerce turn, and the same can be said of non-profits.

1 What type of imagery is used?
2 What does the expression mean?

9 Work with a partner. Think of one or two alternative ways to express each idea figuratively.

1 overcome a problem   *climb a mountain, fight a battle*
2 work extremely hard _____
3 accept eagerly _____
4 make people happy _____
5 experience a difficult time in your life _____

10 Write three sentences about (a) charity. Use your ideas in Exercise 9.

The charity tries to help those who are fighting a battle against cancer.

DISCUSSION

11 Work with a partner. Use ideas from Listening 1 and Listening 2 to answer the following questions.

1 How do you (or would you) choose an organization to donate your time or money to?
2 What kinds of lessons do you think non-profits can learn from for-profit businesses?
3 Do you think an aggregator, a curator or a concierge service could work in the non-profit world? Why / Why not?

SPEAKING

CRITICAL THINKING

At the end of this unit, you are going to do the speaking task below.

> Make a pitch to get a venture started. Your goal is to get funding for your peer-to-peer business or non-profit organization.

SKILLS

Persuading your audience in a business presentation

In a business presentation, you need to convince your audience that your proposal is viable. First, there are practical concerns. Your audience needs to know that you have done your research and anticipated challenges in terms of the market you are entering, and that you have the ability and resources to meet the goals you have set. However, you also need to think about the appeal of your presentation. Will your business plan inspire your donors or investors? Are you offering something new and different?

1 Work in small groups. Read the descriptions. Discuss each venture's potential to succeed and to attract interest from investors or donors.

UNDERSTAND

Group A: ideas for P2P businesses

1 The Full Wardrobe: a service to help women with a lot of clothes generate income by renting out their clothing to others

2 Proud City: a service that connects visitors with city residents who can act as guides, giving visitors a richer city experience

3 Many Hands: a service that connects individuals with certified, reliable, and affordable caregivers for family members

Group B: ideas for non-profits working for social good

1 Rain To Go: a group that works with private companies to develop portable water purifiers and distribute them in poor countries

2 Beauty for Good: an organization that makes organic beauty products from crops grown by collective farms in Africa. Part of the profits are returned to the farmers.

3 Reset: a service that provides language classes and job training for refugees who have been displaced by war, conflicts or natural disaster

 ANALYZE

2 Brainstorm ideas for what you think investors or donors might want to know about a venture before they invested/donated. Take notes in the table below.

Non-profit organization	P2P business
General issues	
• What will your mission be? • • •	• Will you be 'disrupting' a traditional business? Which one? • • •
Practical issues	
• How much will it cost to start? • • • •	• How many employees will you have? • • • •
Appeal	
• How will it help the image of the donors? • • •	• What's cool and new about your product/service? • • •

3 Work with your group. Review your work in Exercises 1 and 2, and rank the three ventures in each group.

EVALUATE

    1 If you were an investor, which start-up would you give your money to? Why?

    1 _____   2 _____   3 _____

    2 If you were a donor, which non-profit would you contribute money to? Why?

    1 _____   2 _____   3 _____

4 Now think about your own venture. Work with your group. Follow the steps to select a venture.

CREATE

    step 1: Decide if you would like to do a presentation on a peer-to-peer business or a non-profit organization.

    step 2: Brainstorm ideas for a new P2P business or non-profit organization.

    step 3: Narrow your list down to three possibilities. Make a table listing the pros and cons of each.

    step 4: Choose one business or organization for your presentation.

5 Focus on the idea you chose in Exercise 4 and decide what exactly you want to accomplish. Discuss questions you developed in Exercise 2 in your group to help you develop your pitch. Take notes.

PREPARATION FOR SPEAKING

MISSION STATEMENTS

SKILLS

Every business or non-profit organization has a mission statement. It usually consists of one or two sentences that communicate three basic pieces of information:
- why your organization exists
- who it serves
- how it serves them

Our mission here is to provide inspiration and administrative support for new non-profits that serve children in need.

At eBay, our mission is to provide a global online marketplace where practically anyone can trade practically anything, enabling economic opportunity around the world.

Team Rubicon unites the skills and experiences of military veterans with first responders to rapidly deploy emergency response teams.

An organization's mission statement is not a promotional or advertising slogan; rather it is the guiding principle for day-to-day operations.

1 Rewrite this mission statement more concisely. Then compare your new mission statement with a partner's.

> Our mission is to empower teen youth from low-income families to aspire to higher education by offering educational assistance services and mentoring schemes in a supportive community environment.

_____

_____

2 Work with your group. Write a mission statement for the business or organization you will talk about in the speaking task, in a maximum of two sentences.

_____

_____

3 Practise saying your mission statement.

- Review your statement several times so that you can say it without sounding as if you are reading it.
- Speak with authority to show that you know what you are talking about and that the topic is important.

> Business people say that you should be able to make a pitch in the time it takes to ride to the top story of a building in an elevator. This means you need to communicate all the most important ideas in just a few minutes:
> - Demonstrate that you have a plan.
> - Show that it is viable and practical.
> - Offer a measurement for success.

4 Answer the questions to develop your ideas for your pitch. Take notes, but do not write out your answers.

1 What is your business plan? How can you describe it very briefly?

_____

2 What will you actually do – what services will you deliver? Describe them concisely. _____

_____

3 How do you know it will work? Have you tested it on a small scale?

_____

4 How will you (and your investors/donors) know when you have been successful? _____

_____

CRAFTING A PITCH

SKILLS

Your pitch must also be persuasive and personal, so you need to talk to your listeners, not read something that you have prepared.

- Consider your audience. Not everyone will love your idea as much as you do. Consider the listeners' perspective. Show how investing or donating is good for them.
- Grab their attention by telling a story. Make sure you keep the story very short.
  I started in this business after a trip to Haiti, following the 2010 earthquake.
- Use figurative language or imagery to help them understand the need or opportunity your venture will address.
  I also want you to hold onto your dreams and don't let go just because this is hard.
- Appeal to their emotions (but be sure your ideas are supported by evidence).
  How would you feel if one of your children was in such a terrible situation?
- Make them feel special.
  Only a very special type of person can establish and manage a successful start-up for social good. And I believe that all of you are among those special people.
- Make them feel nervous.
  You'll be left out if you don't do this.
- Finish with a strong statement in support of your project and yourself.
  My years working in the non-profit world have been the most rewarding of my life. There is no better way to make your mark on the world, so I hope some of you will step up and join me.

5 Answer the questions to help you develop the style of your pitch. Take notes, but do not write out your answers.

1 Who is your audience (investors or donors)? What are their goals?

_____

2 What story could you use to help illustrate the value of your idea?

_____

3 What imagery could you use for your pitch?

_____

4 How can you appeal to their emotions?

_____

5 What could you say as a strong statement of support for your idea and yourself? Why should they invest in or donate to your venture?

_____

PLUS

SPEAKING TASK

> Make a pitch to get a venture started. Your goal is to get funding for your peer-to-peer business or non-profit organization.

PREPARE

1 Review your notes in Critical thinking, Exercise 4 on page 97, and in the Preparation for speaking section. Rewrite your notes so that they are clear and organized, but do not write full sentences.

2 If you will make a group pitch, assign roles.

3 Refer to the Task checklist as you prepare for your presentation.

TASK CHECKLIST	✔
Give a clear, concise mission statement.	
Include a story to illustrate the need for your venture.	
Explain how you would achieve your goals.	
Offer a measure of success.	
Appeal to the listeners' emotions.	
End with a strong statement of support for your venture and yourself.	

PRACTISE

4 Practise your pitch several times in your group until you can give it without reading from your notes. Make sure you make eye contact with your listeners.

PRESENT

5 Make your pitch to another group or to the class. Take notes as you listen to the other pitches. Ask questions at the end of each pitch. Offer feedback to other students and listen to the feedback that they give you.

OBJECTIVES REVIEW

1 Check your learning objectives for this unit. Write *3, 2* or *1* for each objective.

3 = very well   2 = well   1 = not so well

I can ...

watch and understand a video about a tech
start-up which has built a mobile app.   _____

listen for definitions.   _____

understand figurative language.   _____

identify figurative language.   _____

persuade my audience in a business presentation.   _____

emphasize and contrast.   _____

craft a mission statement.   _____

craft a pitch.   _____

make a pitch to get funding for a new venture.   _____

2 Use the *Unlock* Digital Workbook for more practice with this unit's
learning objectives.

WORDLIST		
abandon (v) ⦿	dump (v)	primary (adj) ⦿
analyze (v) ⦿	elaborate (adj) ⦿	scope (n) ⦿
buzzword (n)	emerge (v) ⦿	status (n) ⦿
concisely (adv)	enterprise (n) ⦿	trace (n) ⦿
considerable (adj) ⦿	option (n) ⦿	transaction (n) ⦿
corporation (n) ⦿	overload (n)	venture (n)
disruptive (adj) ⦿	oversight (n)	wary (adj)
donor (n) ⦿	overview (n) ⦿	worthy (adj) ⦿

⦿ = high-frequency words in the Cambridge Academic Corpus

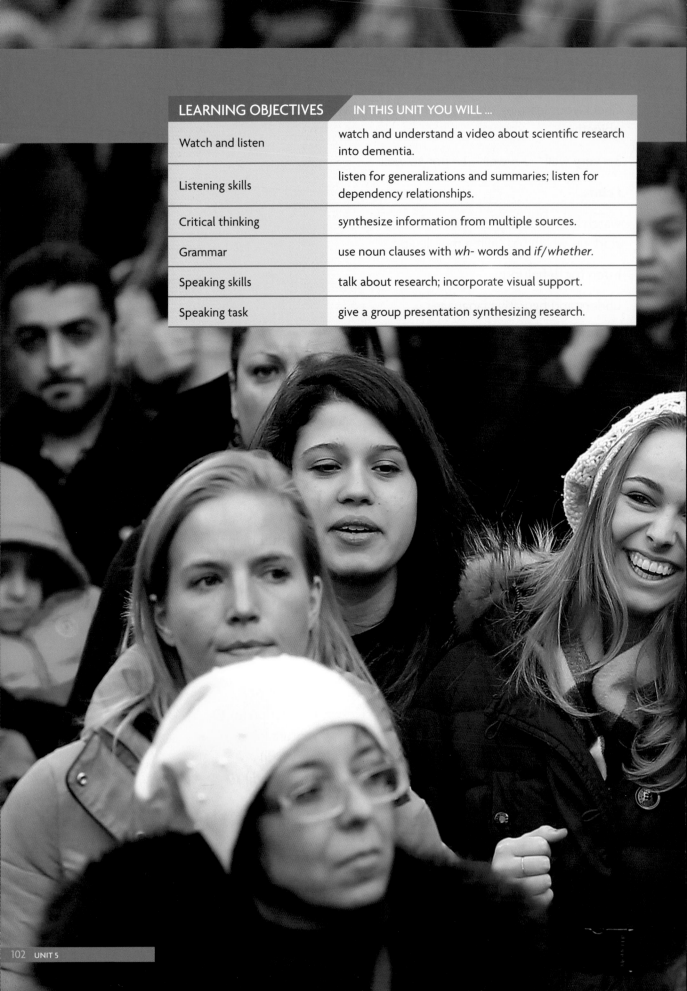

LEARNING OBJECTIVES	IN THIS UNIT YOU WILL ...
Watch and listen	watch and understand a video about scientific research into dementia.
Listening skills	listen for generalizations and summaries; listen for dependency relationships.
Critical thinking	synthesize information from multiple sources.
Grammar	use noun clauses with *wh-* words and *if/whether*.
Speaking skills	talk about research; incorporate visual support.
Speaking task	give a group presentation synthesizing research.

UNL⊘CK YOUR KNOWLEDGE

Work with a partner. Discuss the questions.

1 Do you agree with the sentences below? Why / Why not?
 • I have a good memory for faces.
 • I am a good judge of character.
 • I understand how others feel.
 • I am highly logical.
 • I have an excellent memory for facts.
 • I can quickly make good decisions.

2 Are your strengths things that you have learned or abilities you were born with? Why do you think that?

3 Are there any mental qualities you wish you could improve (either from the list in Exercise 1 or your own ideas)? If so, what are they and why? If not, why not?

PLUS

WATCH AND LISTEN

PREPARING TO WATCH

ACTIVATING YOUR KNOWLEDGE

1 Complete the sentences with your own ideas. Work in a small group and compare your ideas.

1 Dementia is a medical condition which affects _____ .
2 _____ is a common symptom of dementia.
3 People are more likely to suffer from dementia if _____ ,
   or _____ .

PREDICTING CONTENT USING VISUALS

2 You are going to watch a video about scientific research into dementia. Before you watch, look at the pictures and discuss the questions with your partner.

1 What technologies are the scientists using to research dementia?
2 What mental abilities might the researchers be interested in?
3 How might mobile phones be helpful for psychological research?

GLOSSARY

immerse (v) surround the audience, player, etc. so that they feel completely involved

navigate (v) to find the way from one place to another

maze (n) a system of paths or passages that people try to find their way through

spatial awareness (n) the ability to know where your body is in relation to other objects and to understand the relationship within a space between other objects

diagnosis (n) a judgment about what a particular illness or problem is

subtle (adj) small but important; not noticeable or obvious in any way

---

WHILE WATCHING

UNDERSTANDING MAIN IDEAS

3 ▶ Watch the video. Which statement best summarizes the main idea?

a A new game, *Sea Hero Quest*, is being launched to help scientists diagnose dementia in young people via their mobile phones.
b The game *Sea Hero Quest*, which has helped dementia researchers learn about how people navigate, will now be available for virtual reality headsets.
c *Sea Hero Quest* was designed as a mobile phone app, but the game has proved useful in understanding the condition of dementia.

4 ▶ Watch again. Complete the student notes with one to three words in each gap.

Sea Hero Quest

· World's first ¹ _____ for dementia research

· Gameplay = mission at sea   · Collects data on navigation ² _____

Dementia and navigation

In dementia, esp. Alzheimer's, ³ _____ = first ability to be damaged

· Cell level = Brain cells are ⁴ _____

· ⁵ _____ level = impacts real world ability, e.g. find things

  in supermarket

Dementia research

47 million dementia sufferers – expected to ⁶ _____ by 2050

No ⁷ _____ but early diagnosis can help

Sea Hero Quest first launched on ⁸ _____ , data from

3 million people

· Helped scientists understand how ⁹ _____ people navigate

· Discovered ¹⁰ _____ in ability to navigate from 19 years old

---

5 ▶ Watch again. Then answer the questions with a partner.

1 Why do you think early diagnosis techniques for dementia are 'urgently needed'?

2 How do you think Deutsche Telekom helped the scientists with their research?

3 What do you think the scientists hope to discover from the virtual reality version of the game?

DISCUSSION

6 Work in a small group. Discuss the questions.

1 Would you like to take part in the *Sea Hero Quest* study? Why / Why not?

2 In what ways are the *Sea Hero Quest* studies innovative?

3 What different types of technology might be used by psychologists in these activities? How could they use the technology?

   • personality testing
   • counselling clients
   • studying child development

LISTENING

LISTENING 1

PREPARING TO LISTEN

1 You are going to listen to a group of students discussing an assignment on the topic of first impressions. Before you listen, answer the questions then discuss your answers in small groups.

1 How important are these elements when you meet somebody for the first time? Rank them in order from 1 (most important) to 8 (least important). Discuss the reasons for your ranking.

_____ eye contact   _____ attractiveness   _____ voice

_____ clothing   _____ facial expression   _____ handshake

_____ greeting   _____ clean and tidy
                                   appearance

2 Which of the elements above helps you decide if the person is friendly, distant, confident, nervous, etc.?

2 Work in small groups. Discuss the questions.

1 When you meet people, how long does it take you to decide if you like them?

2 How important is physical appearance in forming a first impression of somebody? For example, can you tell if somebody is trustworthy just by looking at the person?

3 What kind of behaviour do you think is most important in making a first impression? What actions are likely to make a positive first impression? A negative one?

4 How strong do you think first impressions are? Do you often change your mind about somebody after you get to know the person better?

3 Read the sentences. Write the words in bold next to their definitions below.

1 I don't have enough information about the situation, so I am not going to **speculate** about why it happened.

2 I attended his job interview and I believe that he is **competent** to manage the project.

3 This type of dog is known for its **dominance** and aggressive behaviour.

4 In the study, **exposure** to cold conditions produced a variety of negative feelings in the test subjects

5 The findings from this study will have many **applications**; for example, it may help businesses find appropriate employees.

6 When he said he was feeling tired, that was my **cue** to leave.

7 I only started to **relate to** the problems they were having when something similar happened to me.

8 Everyone told me that the boss was very serious and rather cold, but I found him very **approachable**.

a _____ (adj) skilled; able to do things well

b _____ (n) experiencing something by being in a particular place or situation

c _____ (v) to guess when there is not enough information to be certain

d _____ (adj) friendly and easy to talk to

e _____ (n) a way in which something can be used

f _____ (n) the quality of liking to take control in a group and being a natural leader

g _____ (phr v) to understand something by connecting it with your own experiences

h _____ (n) a signpost; something that causes a response

WHILE LISTENING

4 🔊 5.1 Listen to the conversation. Circle the topics that the students discuss.

a scientific studies

b newspaper stories

c their class readings

d plans for their presentation

e their professor

Listening for generalizations and summaries

Speakers often help listeners understand their main ideas by providing signposts that they are going to offer a generalization or summarize what they have said. Here are some signposts to listen for:

In general, ... / Generally, ...	We/They can conclude that ...
... a generalization ...	To summarize, ...
Overall, ...	In summary, ...
In short, ...	To sum up, ...
In a nutshell, ... (informal)	The bottom line is ...
To conclude, ... / In conclusion, ...	Basically ...
X leads us to conclude that ...	

**TAKING NOTES
ON MAIN IDEAS
AND DETAIL**

5 🔊 5.1 Listen again. Take notes on the generalizations that you hear after these signposting phrases. Then complete the generalizations.

1 If I had to draw one generalization from all the readings, it would be ... _____

2 Well, in a nutshell ... _____

3 They speculated that, basically, ... _____

4 Overall, it turns out ... _____

5 They conclude that ... _____

6 The bottom line is that ... _____

6 🔊 5.1 Answer the questions below. Then listen to the conversation again to check your answers.

1 Participants in the studies described by the students had to make decisions about people's character based on their faces. What traits were mentioned in the studies? Circle all the traits that were discussed.

a aggressive	**e** thoughtful	**i** sincere
b approachable	**f** dominant	**j** trustworthy
c attractive	**g** likeable	
d competent	**h** nervous	

2 Of these, which four were found to be the most consistent in the studies?

POST-LISTENING

7 Which of the statements are the main ideas (MI) of the studies the students read and which are supporting details (D)?

1 First impressions occur very quickly. _____

2 First impressions are primarily based on physical appearance. _____

3 A specific part of the brain is responsible for first impressions. _____

4 The ability to quickly decide who to trust may have provided an advantage to early humans. _____

5 First impressions are generally accurate. _____

6 One scientist broke down facial expressions into 65 separate features. _____

8 Work with a partner. Look at the computer-generated faces from the last study the students discussed. Which facial features (eyes, eyebrows, nose, smile, etc.) do you think were most important for the subjects' decisions about each of the traits?

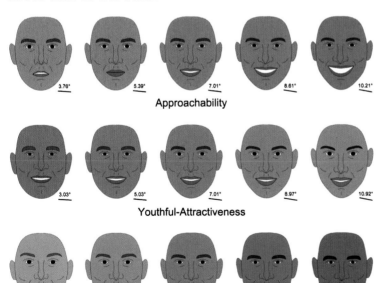

3.76° 5.39° 7.01° 8.61° 10.21°
Approachability

3.03° 5.03° 7.01° 8.97° 10.92°
Youthful-Attractiveness

6.62° 6.81° 7.01° 7.20° 7.40°
Dominance

Emphasis

Emphasis is the extra stress placed on the most important word in a thought group. Usually the last content word in a thought group is emphasized, but sometimes other words, such as transition words or words signposting particular or new information, are emphasized because they are more important.

🔊 5.2 Listen to these examples from Listening 1.

Eva: OK, / so has everybody read / all the material?

Ramzi: Yep. / So how do you think / we should organize it? / There's so much information.

9 🔊 5.3 Listen to the excerpts from the conversation and underline the emphasized word(s) in each thought group.

1 **Eva:** So / what about some of the cues?
   Ramzi: Well, in a nutshell, / it's physical appearance / that's the most important cue / in first impressions …

2 **Ramzi:** Basically / deciding quickly / if you could trust somebody / must have been a really important ability / during early human evolution.
   Eva: It probably still is! / That's really interesting. / I read another study / on a similar topic / but it was a little more specific.

3 **Sara:** Some of the photos / were of really attractive people / and all the participants pretty much agreed / they were fours. / But there were some photos / that only a few people found attractive.

4 **Sara:** Our first response / is to go for somebody who is generally attractive, / what they call / 'a good catch'.

5 **Sara:** But the different preferences / suggest we also make judgments / about who'd be 'a good catch for me'.

DISCUSSION

10 Work with a partner. Discuss the questions.

1 Why do you think some of the judgments of traits in relation to particular facial features were more consistent than others (e.g. trustworthiness)?

2 The authors of one of the studies speculated that there might be an evolutionary advantage to being able to make quick decisions about people. What advantage might it provide today?

PLUS

NOUN CLAUSES WITH *WH-* WORDS AND *IF/WHETHER*

GRAMMAR

We often introduce issues with *wh-* noun clauses. These clauses begin with *what, who, which, when, how, why, whether* or *if* and occur most frequently as the object of a sentence. These clauses present questions within a larger sentence.

Let's talk about **what** we found in our readings and then plan the presentation.
The authors of the study discussed **how** useful this will be in computer-generated graphics in games and films.
Participants had to decide **if** they thought they'd like the person in the picture, on a scale of one to four.

Notice that these noun clauses use the word order in statements, not the word order in questions.
Let's talk about what **we found** in our readings.
Let's talk about what ~~did we find~~ in our readings.

1 Rewrite each pair of sentences as one sentence. Change the question into a noun clause in the new sentence.

1 Who would make a good life partner? This quiz can tell you.

_____

_____.

2 What do people react to in first impressions? It's difficult to say.

_____

_____.

3 Which facial features are particularly significant in first impressions? It's surprising.

_____

_____.

4 Are initial judgments accurate? Researchers wanted to find out.

_____

_____.

5 How fast do people make decisions about traits such as reliability and intelligence? One recent study looked at this.

_____

_____.

2 Write three sentences about first impressions using *wh-* noun clauses.

When I meet people for the first time, I watch how they act in the first few minutes very carefully.

1 _____.

2 _____.

3 _____.

📱PLUS

ACADEMIC WORD FAMILIES

Many nouns that describe personality traits take the endings *-ion, -ness, -ity,* or *-ence / -ance.* Some noun forms require additional spelling changes.

adjective	noun
aggressive	aggression
approachable	approachability
attractive	attractiveness
competent	competence
dominant	dominance
likeable	likeability
thoughtful	thoughtfulness

3 Complete the sentences with the correct form of an academic word in the Explanation box.

1 It was so _____ of you to remember my birthday.
2 Her father was always the _____ member in the family and rarely let anyone else make decisions.
3 The main qualities we are looking for in candidates for this position are past experience and _____ in several technical areas.
4 I saw Serena Williams at a restaurant once. I was nervous about talking to her, but she was surprisingly _____ . She even gave me a signed menu as a souvenir.
5 The physical _____ of a job candidate should never be a factor in hiring decisions.

4 Write two sentences using words from the Explanation box that were not used in Exercise 3.

1 _____
_____
_____ .

2 _____
_____
_____ .

PREPARING TO LISTEN

1 You are going to listen to a lecture on how the brain makes and uses mental maps. Before you listen, work with a partner. Look at the diagram of the brain. Read the description of the parts and then label the diagram.

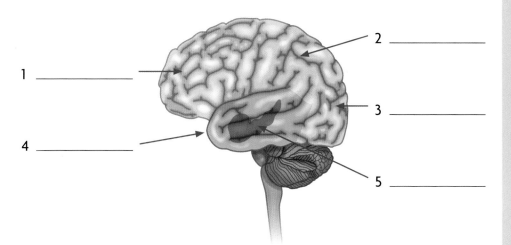

1 _____

2 _____

3 _____

4 _____

5 _____

frontal lobe	**parietal lobe**
• located at the front of the skull	• located at the top/back of the skull
• associated with reasoning, planning, speech, emotions, and problem-solving	• associated with movement, orientation, perception
temporal lobe	**hippocampus**
• located at the bottom of the brain	• located deep inside the temporal lobe
• associated with perception, hearing, memory and speech	• associated with spatial memory and navigation
	occipital lobe
	• located at the back of the skull
	• associated with vision

2 Work with a partner. Only one of these statements about the brain is true. Which one do you think it is?

a Human intelligence is related to brain size.

b Many people use only about 10% of their brains.

c Some people are 'right-brained' and others are 'left-brained'.

d Some people have memories like a camera.

e If you get hit on the head, you could lose your memory. Another knock on the head may bring it back.

f One area of the brain specializes in understanding stories.

g Men's and women's brains are fundamentally different.

3 Read the sentences and choose the best definition for the words in bold.

1 Scientists have been working **intensively** to identify the areas of the brain that control different behaviour.
   a requiring specialized skills
   b involving extreme concentration or effort
   c only on one thing

2 After interviewing dozens of witnesses, the police were able to **reconstruct** what had happened.
   a to create a description of a past event
   b to investigate
   c to understand the reasons for

3 When her health began to **deteriorate**, she decided to move in with her son.
   a to improve
   b to worsen
   c to stabilize

4 I use **landmarks**, such as parks and buildings, to work out where I am.
   a geographical features such as waterfalls and rock formations
   b places or structures that are easy to recognize
   c places in the community where people gather

5 Scientists proved **definitively** that we use 100% of our brains.
   a eventually; after a lot of effort
   b completely; without doubt
   c unexpectedly; when researching something else

6 Pilots once depended on just their eyes to **navigate**, but now they use advanced technology.
   a to find the way from one place to another
   b to read instructions
   c to communicate with others

7 Hunger and lack of sleep can **impair** your ability to think clearly.
   a to change
   b to maintain
   c to damage

8 Our **reliance on** technology has been increasing steadily. I can't manage five minutes without it.
   a the situation in which you always use or need the help of a particular thing
   b the quality of being useful for many different tasks
   c the tools which give you the ability to be creative

4 Work with a partner. Answer the questions.

1 How do you navigate when you are in an unfamiliar place?
2 Is this different from how your parents navigated when you were a child?
3 What do you do when you get lost? How do you find your way?
4 Do you know anybody who has suffered from dementia, that is, a loss of cognitive function as a person grows older? Describe what happened. For example, did the person begin to forget names or other words?

USING YOUR KNOWLEDGE

WHILE LISTENING

5 🔊 5.4 Listen to the lecture. Circle the questions that the lecturer answers in his presentation.

a How do humans navigate?
b How do humans lose memory ability as they age?
c How does memory loss relate to the hippocampus?
d How does navigation experience affect the human brain?
e How do maps impact on human cognition?

LISTENING FOR MAIN IDEAS

6 🔊 5.4 Listen again and take notes. Then use your notes to complete these statements about the main ideas in the lecture. Compare your statements with a partner.

TAKING NOTES ON MAIN IDEAS

1 Scientists have established that the hippocampus _____ _____.

2 Humans use two forms of navigation: _____ and _____ .

3 Research results suggest that the _____ navigation strategy leads to the creation of mental maps.

4 Recent studies suggest that the constant creation of mental maps may result in _____ .

Listening for dependency relationships

Scientific research contains a great deal of language describing dependency relationships. Some relationships are causal – one thing causes another. In other relationships, one element may be a contributing factor to another. Here are some common signposts of dependency relationships.

causal	dependence	partial causality or dependence
X causes	X relies on	plays a role
X is the cause of	X depends on	is a factor
X leads to	X is dependent on	contributes to
X is the result of	reliance on	has an impact/effect on
X is the consequence of	dependence on	influences
because		affects
as a/the result of		promotes
because of		

7 🔊 5.4 Listen again. Listen for the dependency signposts in bold and complete the information.

1 The hippocampus **plays a key role** in _____ .

2 The landmark strategy **relies on** _____ .

3 In the response strategy, your knowledge of the route is **the result of** _____ .

4 In Maguire's first study, MRI images strongly suggest that creating mental maps all the time **had affected** _____ .

5 In her second study, she was able to prove a **causal relationship** between _____ _____ .

SUMMARIZING

8 Work in groups of four. Each group member will give an oral summary of one of the studies described in the presentation. Other members of the group will ask questions.

POST-LISTENING

9 Choose the best answer (a–c) to complete the explanations.

1 The speaker says, 'These are among the first abilities to deteriorate as we age, sometimes ending in dementia. So, you can see why understanding how it (the hippocampus) works is a top priority for researchers today.'

Why is this a top priority?

a because it may tell us how other parts of the brain work

b because dementia affects a growing number of people

c because these abilities are the most important in our daily lives

2 The speaker says, 'So, Maguire did a longitudinal follow-up study.' Why did she choose a longitudinal study?

a because she thought the hippocampi would grow even larger

b because she thought her earlier results might be wrong

c because only a longitudinal study could prove the relation is causal

3 The speaker says, 'Perhaps more important, this group also performed better on a cognitive test that often reveals the first sign of dementia as a person ages.'

Why is this important?

a because behaviour results are considered more meaningful than physical results

b because this result suggests a way to slow dementia

c because it provides a causal link between the use of devices and the onset of dementia

DISCUSSION

10 Work with a partner. Use ideas from Listening 1 and Listening 2 to answer the following questions.

1 Have you ever arrived somewhere 'automatically' without remembering the journey? Describe the experience.

2 Which form of navigation do you use, landmark or response? Do you think there could be an evolutionary advantage to navigating one way or another? How might that work?

SPEAKING

CRITICAL THINKING

At the end of this unit, you are going to do the speaking task below.

▶ Give a group presentation about research on some aspect of human behaviour. Support your presentation with slides.

Synthesizing information from multiple sources

When you present a synthesis of research, you must first analyze individual studies and then find common themes. Ensure that the sources you use are reliable and that the information can be verified.

When you use print sources (books, journal articles), check:
- **author:** Is the author a well-known expert or scholar on this topic? Is his or her work cited in other places?
- **date:** How recent is the publication? In general, it is better to cite more recent sources.
- **publisher:** Is this a university press or a large press with a good reputation?
- **content:** Are the views and facts widely shared, or is this work controversial? If it is controversial, it is important to verify the information in other sources.

When you use a web-based source, check:
- **the extension (i.e. the abbreviation after the full stop):** Educational and government organizations (.ac .edu . gov, etc.) are usually good sources of reliable information. Commercial sites (.co or .com) may be less reliable.
- **purpose:** What is the purpose of the website? Who is the intended audience? Is it trying to convince you of some political point of view? If so, it may be propaganda. Is it trying to sell you something? If so, it may be a type of advertisement. Be very careful about the information on these sites (some have the extension .org). It may be biased.
- **authority:** Who is the author? Look for links like 'Who we are' or 'About us' to find out more about the organization or people behind the site.
- **date:** Most websites don't have obvious dates, but there may be an indication on the bottom of the home page about when the information was updated. Check to see if the links still work. Broken links often indicate that the page is old and no one is taking responsibility for it.

1 Work in groups of four. Read the information about some human behaviour studies (A–C) below. Decide which topic your group would like to present or choose and research an alternative topic (D).

☐ **A** **Perceptual blindness**

Perceptual blindness refers to the failure to see or notice a stimulus that is in plain sight. However, this lack of attention has nothing to do with vision problems. A number of studies have tested this idea, especially when the stimulus is unexpected.

References:
Invisible gorilla experiment
Clown on a unicycle experiment

☐ **B** **The judgment of others**

The halo effect describes the fact that people frequently extend their judgments of others in one area (e.g. physical attractiveness) to another area (e.g. intelligence). Experiments have documented this effect in many different contexts.

References:
The halo effect
Beauty is talent

☐ **C** **Conformity**

Conformity experiments test the degree to which people report their true feelings or beliefs when others around them state opposing feelings and beliefs.

References:
Asch experiments
Sherif: Group norms and conformity

☐ **D** _____

_____
_____
_____
_____
_____
_____

2 Go online and read more about the scientific studies referenced for your topic. Complete the table with notes to answer the questions.

ANALYZE

	study 1	study 2
goal: What was the research question?		
participants: How were they chosen?		
study description: What were the participants asked to do?		
results: What did the study show?		
conclusions: What did the researcher(s) conclude from the results?		

EVALUATE

3 Work in pairs. For each study, verify the reliability of your resources.

1 What website(s) did you consult?

_____

2 What is the purpose of the website?

_____

3 Who is/are the author(s) of the study?

_____

4 When was the study conducted? Are other scholars still citing the findings?

_____

5 Do you believe the website offers reliable information? Why / Why not?

_____

ANALYZE

4 Work with your group. Discuss the questions.

1 In what ways are the studies you read the same? In what ways are they different?

2 Does each study confirm, expand on, or conflict with the findings of the other(s)?

EVALUATE

5 Use the information in the table from Exercise 2 to synthesize the studies. Write notes for your presentation. Use the notes in the boxes as a model for your notes.

1 Why were these research studies conducted? What important questions do they address or answer?

> Scientists wanted to understand how the hippocampus works and the effect of the creation of mental maps on different areas of the brain.

2 What are the areas of overlap, similarity, or contrast?

> Both of Maguire's studies explored how navigation strategies impact the brain. Maguire's first study found a relationship between spatial navigation and larger hippocampi, but not which was the cause and which was the effect. By controlling for the size of participants' hippocampi in the second study, she was able to support the claim that spatial navigation leads to a larger hippocampus.

3 Is it possible to conclude anything from the two sets of results?

> There is a causal connection between the creation of mental maps and the size of the hippocampus.

PREPARATION FOR SPEAKING

TALKING ABOUT RESEARCH

Research presentations generally follow the same format as research papers. Prepare talking points which follow this structure rather than reading out your research paper in full.

- introduction
- research questions
- methods and participants
- results
- conclusions

1 Follow this outline to prepare your talking points.

1 Explain the question(s) that the studies were investigating.
2 Explain why the question is important in a broader context.
3 Make a statement that brings together the two studies.
4 Explain briefly and concisely what happened in each study.
5 Give a brief description of the results of the two studies.
6 Compare the results of the two studies.
7 Draw a conclusion or speculate about future possibilities.

PLUS

INCORPORATING VISUAL SUPPORT

Most formal presentations include slides to support what the speaker is saying.

✔ use just one type of background on all slides.	✘ use too many colours or complicated graphics.
✔ include only the most important information.	✘ have too much information on each slide.
✔ include photographs or other supporting visuals.	✘ have more than one image on one slide unless two need to be compared.
✔ state the source of your information.	

2 Create the slides that will accompany your talking points from Exercise 1. Create a list of talking points for each slide. Ensure the words on the slides are brief and you have more to say on each point than is included on the slide. Note any photographs or other visuals you plan to use, using the information in the box to choose your photographs.

SPEAKING TASK

> Give a group presentation about research on some aspect of human behaviour. Support your presentation with slides.

PREPARE

1 Assign roles for your presentation. Who will …

- introduce the presentation and the central question of the research?
- report on the first study?
- report on the second study?
- bring the results of the two studies together and offer a conclusion?
- make transitions from one speaker to another?

2 Review your talking points and slides.

3 Refer to the Task checklist as you prepare for your presentation.

TASK CHECKLIST	✔
Synthesize the important points of two studies.	
Discuss points of similarity and contrast.	
Follow the formal format for the presentation of a research study.	
Support your talking points with well-crafted slides.	
Add emphasis to the focus words in sentences.	

PRACTISE

4 Practise presenting your parts of the presentation in your group. Consider the advice in the box below. Give other students feedback and consider the feedback they give you. Make any necessary changes to your plan and slides.

- Be enthusiastic.
- Do not speak too quickly. Take the time to say each word clearly.
- Do not read your presentation. Refer to your talking points and notes.
- Anticipate questions. How will you deal with them?
- Observe time limits. Practise your presentation to check length.

PRESENT

5 Give your presentation.

OBJECTIVES REVIEW

1 Check your learning objectives for this unit. Write *3*, *2* or *1* for each objective.

3 = very well   2 = well   1 = not so well

I can ...

watch and understand a video about scientific research into dementia. _____

listen for generalizations and summaries. _____

listen for dependency relationships. _____

synthesize information from multiple sources. _____

use noun clauses with *wh-* words and *if/whether*. _____

talk about research. _____

incorporate visual support. _____

give a group presentation synthesizing research. _____

2 Use the *Unlock* Digital Workbook for more practice with this unit's learning objectives.

UNLOCK
ONLINE

WORDLIST

aggression (n) ⊙	cue (n) ⊙	likeability (n)
aggressive (adj) ⊙	definitively (adv)	likeable (adj)
application (n) ⊙	deteriorate (v)	navigate (v)
approachability (n)	dominance (n) ⊙	reconstruct (v)
approachable (adj)	dominant (adj) ⊙	relate to (phr v)
attractive (adj) ⊙	exposure (n) ⊙	reliance on (n)
attractiveness (n)	impair (v)	speculate (v)
competence (n) ⊙	intensively (adv)	thoughtful (adj)
competent (adj) ⊙	landmark (n)	thoughtfulness (n)

⊙ = high-frequency words in the Cambridge Academic Corpus

LEARNING OBJECTIVES	IN THIS UNIT YOU WILL ...
Watch and listen	watch and understand a video about a job fair.
Listening skill	make inferences.
Critical thinking	understand job descriptions.
Grammar	use degree expressions with *so ... that / such a ... that*.
Speaking skill	prepare for a job interview.
Speaking task	participate in a mock job interview.

UNLOCK YOUR KNOWLEDGE

Work with a partner. Discuss the questions.

1 What is your ideal job? Is it the same as the career you are preparing for?

2 Other than completing your studies, how are you preparing for your future career? If you are already working, how are you planning the next step in your career?

3 Do you think there are more career options for young people today than there were in the past?

PLUS

PREPARING TO WATCH

ACTIVATING YOUR KNOWLEDGE

1 Work with a partner and complete the table about employment with your own ideas. Compare your ideas with another pair.

Problems unemployed people face	Obstacles to getting a job
• _____	• _____
• _____	• _____
• _____	• _____

Ways you can get a job lead	Qualities recruiters look for
• _____	• _____
• _____	• _____
• _____	• _____

PREDICTING CONTENT USING VISUALS

2 You are going to watch a video about jobs for young people in America. Before you watch, look at the pictures and discuss the questions.

1 What kind of area is this? What do you think job opportunities are like for young people in this area?

2 What kind of event is happening?

3 Who do you think has organized the event?

4 Who do you think is attending the event?

GLOSSARY

promising (adj) Something that is promising shows signs that it is going to be successful or enjoyable.

resort (n) the action that you take deal with a difficult situation

irregardless (adv) despite; without being affected by something

zip code (n) in the US, a series of numbers that forms part of an address and refers to the area of the city that somebody lives in

WHILE WATCHING

UNDERSTANDING MAIN IDEAS

3 ▶ Watch the video. Number the main ideas in the order you hear them.

_____ Business and political leaders attended the event.

_____ A large proportion of young people in Chicago are out of work.

_____ Everett wants to work so he can go to university.

_____ Representatives from a number of large businesses met with thousands of young people.

_____ Young people make bad life decisions only when they have no other choice.

_____ If young people work, they are more like to get a university degree.

_____ The 100,000 Opportunities job fair will benefit many young people.

UNDERSTANDING DETAIL

4 ▶ Watch again. Take notes while you watch and then summarize why the words and expressions are mentioned in the video.

1 violent crime _____

2 opportunity youth _____

3 persistence and dependability _____

4 colour, station in life, zip code _____

5 a good personality, outspoken, helpful _____

6 a perfect fit _____

MAKING INFERENCES

5 Work with a partner. Discuss the questions.

1 What do you think was on offer to young people at the event, besides job leads?

2 What do you think the main aim of the event was?

3 What social problems are likely to be caused by youth unemployment in Chicago?

4 In what different ways does being employed help young people in the US to go to university?

5 Why do you think that the employers were interested in Everett?

DISCUSSION

6 Work in a small group. Discuss the questions.

1 What benefits could there be for large companies in working with so-called 'opportunity youth'?

2 What other kinds of job fairs are there? Who organizes them? Why?

3 Have you ever been to a job fair? If so, what was it like? If not, would you like to attend one? Why / Why not?

4 Is higher education equally accessible to everyone in your country? What different ways are there to finance university studies?

LISTENING

LISTENING 1

PREPARING TO LISTEN

1 You are going to listen to a presentation by a careers advisor about different ways to enter the world of work after university. Before you listen, work in small groups. Would you rather work for a large business or work for yourself? What are the pros and cons of each? Compare your table with other groups' tables.

	pros	cons
work for a large business	Good salary	work-life balance
be your own boss	work-life balance	

2 Work with a partner. Look at the pie chart and discuss the questions.

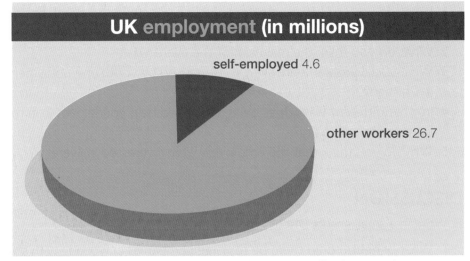

Source: Office for National Statistics, 2016

1 What does the chart show?
2 What kinds of jobs do you think the self-employed workers have?
3 Do you think most of the self-employed people are *entrepreneurs*, that is, people who start an often risky business based on a new idea?
4 What kind of work do you think has the largest proportion of self-employed workers?

3 Read the sentences. Write the words in bold (1–8) next to their definitions below (a–h).

1 These are two **distinct** ideas and should not be confused.
2 At the end of the **probationary period**, you will be eligible to join the pension scheme and your salary will automatically increase by 2.5%.
3 I hope Jin is available to help. I don't want to **be landed with** doing all the work for this party.
4 The company has placed a **cap** on salary increases until the economic crisis eases.
5 When we **started out** in this business, we had just one small office and two employees.
6 If you are thinking of starting your own company, it's important to have a clear **vision** for how it can compete with established companies.
7 I would like to start my own business, but it is pretty **daunting**. I hear that the failure rate is more than 50%.
8 If you feel you have been a victim of harassment or **discrimination**, you should report it to our office at once.

a ___2___ (n phr) the time during which a new employee is monitored to ensure they are suitable for their role and can easily be removed if unsuitable
b ___7___ (adj) making you feel less confident; frightening
c ___8___ (n) unfair treatment, especially based on sex, ethnic origin, age or religion
d ___4___ (n) a limit on the amount of money that can be charged or spent
e ___6___ (n) idea for how something could develop in the future
f ___1___ (adj) clearly separate and different
g ___5___ (phr v) to begin the part of your life when you work (in a job or particular industry)
h ___3___ (phr v) to be forced to take responsibility for something or somebody unpleasant

WHILE LISTENING

4 🔊 6.1 Listen to the presentation and take notes. Then use your notes to answer these questions.

1 What is the purpose of the presentation?

_____

2 Who is the audience for the presentation?

_____

3 What are the three options that the careers advisor discusses?

_____
_____
_____

5 🔊 6.1 Listen again. Take notes in the table.

	pros	cons
work for a company	job security	prohibition period
work as a consultant / independent contractor / freelance worker		
establish your own start-up company		

POST-LISTENING

6 Work with a partner. Compare your tables from Exercise 5. Then compare your ideas in Exercise 5 with your ideas in Exercise 1 on page 128. Which pros or cons were new to you?

Exercise 1 on page 128

Making inferences

Sometimes speakers do not directly say everything they mean. Sometimes they say just enough to allow listeners to understand what they mean. They do this because it is often quicker and more efficient. It is also often more elegant and less boring than saying everything directly. Listen to what speakers say directly to infer meaning that they may leave out. You can also use your own knowledge of the topic to infer speakers' intended meanings.

For example, in the opening sentences, the speaker says:
We wanted to target this session at all of you in computer science and related degree programmes because, frankly, you'll probably have a lot more options when you finish your degree than other graduates.

She does not say that this information would not be useful for other graduates.

7 🔊 6.2 Listen to the excerpts from the presentation (1–6). Use logic and your own knowledge to infer the speaker's meaning (a, b or c).

1 a So, you don't really need to worry about anything.
   b So, you could lose your job during this period.
   c So, you shouldn't choose a big company for your first job.
2 a Undergraduates are unlikely to choose this option.
   b Start-up companies are the best career option for those with advanced degrees.
   c This option has the most problems.
3 a You will not experience these problems.
   b If you do experience these problems, you have protection.
   c You may experience these problems anyway.

4 a This is a problem.
  b This is an advantage.
  c This is legally required.
5 a The speaker thinks the answer is obvious – the second.
  b The speaker wants to know what the students in the audience think.
  c The speaker is testing the students' knowledge of the job market.
6 a Be sure that you and your friend agree about everything before
    you begin.
  b It is probably a bad idea to go into business with friends.
  c Do not let your start-up destroy your friendship.

PRONUNCIATION FOR LISTENING

Reduction of auxiliary verbs

Reductions are unstressed words that are spoken quickly and linked to surrounding words. The vowel is often pronounced as the /ə/ sound.

Common reductions include auxiliary verbs such as *do, have, can, could, should, will* and *would*. Other reduced forms include *going to*, which sounds like 'gonna', and *want to*, which sounds like 'wanna'.

You **can** immediately start using the skills and knowledge you've gained in your studies.

Reduced words are not always essential to understanding the meaning of a sentence, but it is important to pay attention to them to understand the finer points of meaning, especially with modal verbs.

8 🔊 6.3 Listen to the sentences. Write the missing words in full.

1 Keep in mind that some of the legal issues and government regulations that we're _____ discuss may not apply to you.
2 You _____ also consider the option of using those skills without joining a company.
3 This is what I meant earlier when I said our topic _____ be the UK market.
4 I don't _____ scare you, but, as in the case of consultants, you're your own boss.
5 You _____ engage in some self-reflection.
6 You _____ take credit for all aspects of that success, and that _____ be incredibly rewarding.
7 I _____ emphasize how stressful starting a new company _____ be.

9 Work with a partner. Practise saying the sentences in Exercise 8. Use reductions of auxiliary verbs.

DISCUSSION

10 Work in small groups. Complete the tasks.

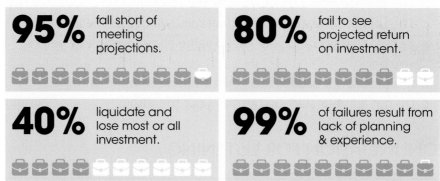

Failure rates of start-ups

95% fall short of meeting projections.

80% fail to see projected return on investment.

40% liquidate and lose most or all investment.

99% of failures result from lack of planning & experience.

Data from various sources including Harvard Business School, University of Tennessee Research, StatisticBrain.com, and others.

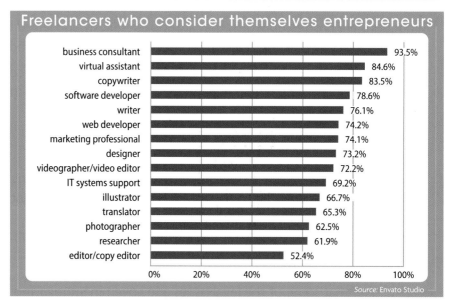

Freelancers who consider themselves entrepreneurs

business consultant	93.5%
virtual assistant	84.6%
copywriter	83.5%
software developer	78.6%
writer	76.1%
web developer	74.2%
marketing professional	74.1%
designer	73.2%
videographer/video editor	72.2%
IT systems support	69.2%
illustrator	66.7%
translator	65.3%
photographer	62.5%
researcher	61.9%
editor/copy editor	52.4%

0%   20%   40%   60%   80%   100%

Source: Envato Studio

1 Look at the information in *Failure rates of start-ups*. Why do you think so many of these businesses fail? Explain each of the four business situations using the example of a new restaurant.

2 Why do you think that entrepreneurs continue to open new businesses when the chance of failure is so high?

3 Look at the second graph. What does it show? What is the relationship between these two sets of data?

4 How might a freelance photographer be an entrepreneur? What activities do you consider make somebody an entrepreneur?

11 Work in small groups. Discuss the questions. Explain your answers.

1 What career advice would you give a recent undergraduate in computer science?

2 What career advice would you give somebody graduating with an advanced degree in computer science?

⦿ LANGUAGE DEVELOPMENT

DEGREE EXPRESSIONS WITH *SO ... THAT; SUCH A ... THAT*

GRAMMAR

To show the consequences of extreme conditions or behaviour, you can use *so ... that* with nouns and verbs (with the quantifier *much* or *many*; *few* or *little*), and adjectives or adverbs. The extreme condition or behaviour is expressed with *so,* and the consequence follows *that.*
You shouldn't **prepare so much** (<u>that</u>) your answers sound rehearsed or mechanical.

EXTREME CONDITION   CONSEQUENCE

The responsibility and uncertainty are **so daunting** (<u>that</u>) they don't even consider it.
The entrepreneur was **so successful** (<u>that</u>) he became a billionaire by age 30.

With nouns, use *such / such a ... that.*
This is **such an important point** (<u>that</u>) I'll repeat it.

1 Rewrite the two sentences in each item to create a single sentence using a degree expression *so ... that* or *such / such a ... that.*

1 Most businesses can make a profit. The current market is very strong.
_____

2 She cannot get to work most days. She has very little energy.
_____

3 Everyone asks her for business advice. Her company has been very successful.
_____

4 We can't find anywhere to put it. We bought a lot of equipment.
_____

5 Nobody can hear the sound. The volume is very low.
_____

6 I made a quick decision. I didn't have much time.
_____

PLUS

2 Write four sentences about a new start-up company, two with *so ... that* and two with *such (a) ... that.*

1 _____

2 _____

3 _____

4 _____

EMPHATIC EXPRESSIONS OF BELIEF AND CERTAINTY

These are common expressions to show emphasis, especially in spoken English:

there is no question   believe me

make no mistake   it is beyond question

that/it goes without saying   without a doubt

These expressions usually precede the statement that the speaker wishes to emphasize; however, they may stand alone after the speaker has already made an argument.

Make no mistake, not every computer science graduate is going to become a millionaire.

Technology skills are highly valued in today's labour market. **That goes without saying.**

3 Work with a partner. Write three strong statements about the job market using emphatic expressions.

1 _____
   _____

2 _____
   _____

3 _____
   _____

PLUS

LISTENING 2

PREPARING TO LISTEN

UNDERSTANDING KEY VOCABULARY

1 Read the sentences and choose the best definition for the words in bold.

1 My **dreaded** presentation is going to be in front of the company director. I'll be a nervous wreck!
   a unwelcome because of being frightening
   b difficult because of being confusing
   c scary because of being mysterious

2 We're getting too emotional about this. We need to take a more **analytical** approach to the problem.
   a creative and expressive
   b critical and negative
   c careful and organized

3 The teacher requires a specific **format** for the list of references at the end of the paper.
   a font
   b level of detail
   c organization
4 After she explained the lab experiment twice, our teacher **reiterated** the importance of going slowly, for safety reasons.
   a insisted on
   b repeated
   c listed
5 One of the director's most important **accomplishments** has been increasing the number of women working for the company.
   a something done successfully
   b something that has been promised but not done
   c something identified as a goal for a project
6 The speaker **rambled** on for half an hour and never got to the point.
   a spoke in a complicated way
   b spoke in a boring and confused way
   c spoke in a loud and angry manner
7 The new park is the result of a **collaboration**. The city, the county and private businesses all helped to build it.
   a donation
   b a long time and a lot of work
   c cooperative effort
8 The teacher didn't believe his story about missing the test because of a car accident. It all sounded too **rehearsed** and insincere.
   a practised and unnatural
   b emotional and dramatic
   c suspicious and intriguing

PLUS

2 You are going to listen to a workshop about job interview skills. Before you listen, work in small groups. Discuss the questions.

USING YOUR KNOWLEDGE

   1 Have you had a job interview? If so, what was it like? If not, what do you imagine it would be like?
   2 How would you prepare for an interview?
   3 How can you make a good first impression at a job interview?

3 Write five questions that you think are likely to be asked at a job interview.

1 _What is ur weakness?_
2 _Why did you choose this job?_
3 _What is ur expected salary?_
4 _What are ur experiences?_
5 _Why should we hire you?_

WHILE LISTENING

4 🔊 6.4 Listen to the workshop and take notes. Then circle any of your questions in Exercise 3 that were mentioned.

5 Answer the questions.

1 What is the main theme of the presentation?

_____

2 What is the careers advisor's most important advice?

_____

6 🔊 6.4 Review your notes and answer the questions. Listen again to check your answers or find missing information.

1 What are three of the things the careers advisor suggests you should do to prepare for a job interview?

_____
_____
_____

2 What topics should you expect questions about?

_____   _____
_____   _____

3 How should you respond to a question about weaknesses?

_____

4 What kind of advice does the careers advisor give about answering questions in general?

_____
_____
_____

5 What should you do after the interview?

_____

POST-LISTENING

7 🔊 6.5 Listen to the excerpts from the workshop. What information can you infer from each of the speaker's statements? Choose the best answer (a–c).

1. a There is no need to do research on anybody in Human Resources.
   b You should find out as much as you can about anybody you are being interviewed by.
   c Interviewers from Human Resources are more likely to ask difficult questions.
2. a Do not memorize your answers.
   b Just write out a few answers.
   c Rehearse your answers.
3. a You should have each step of your career planned.
   b Your interviewer will want to hear that you expect to stay with the company for five or ten years.
   c You need to think about your whole career, not just this position.
4. a They will think that you are lying.
   b You may think it is an original idea, but it's not.
   c It's OK not to say anything at all.
5. a The person interviewing won't have a lot of time.
   b Most interviewers prefer quiet candidates.
   c Inexperienced job candidates sometimes talk too much.

DISCUSSION

8 Work with a partner. Use ideas from Listening 1 and Listening 2 to answer the following questions.

1. Do you think the careers advisor in Listening 2 offered good advice? Why / Why not?
2. Would you add anything further to the advice offered by the careers advisor?
3. Would you prepare differently for an interview with a big company versus a small start-up? If so, how? If not, why not?

SPEAKING

CRITICAL THINKING

At the end of this unit, you are going to do the speaking task below.

▶ Participate in a mock job interview as an interviewer and/or as a job candidate.

SKILLS

Understanding job descriptions

A job description on a job search site usually starts with an introduction that gives information about the company, followed by two main sections:

Duties/Responsibilities: information about the available position
Skills required: information about the skills, experience and traits that a successful candidate would need

The key words and descriptions within the job description are important when you are deciding whether a job is suitable for you, when submitting your application for a job and within a job interview. These words and descriptions can tell you what the job is and what the employer is looking for. Using key words from the job description in a job interview can help persuade an employer that you are a good candidate for the job.

 REMEMBER

 ANALYZE

1 Work in small groups on the first step toward a job interview – the evaluation of job descriptions. What kinds of information would you expect the different sections of a job description to include? Brainstorm ideas.

2 Look at the job advertisements and answer the questions. Compare your answers with your group.

1 What elements are common to both job advertisements?

_____

_____

2 What kind of language is used to describe duties and responsibilities (e.g. verbs, nouns)? What language is used to describe the skills required?

_____

_____

3 What personal attributes of candidates are **not** specified in the job advertisements?

_____

_____

GRADUATE RESEARCH ASSISTANT

RESPONSIBILITIES:

This research assistant will join a multidisciplinary research team that analyzes consumer decision-making behaviour.

DUTIES:

- Assisting with preparation of manuscripts, presentations, grants and reports (e.g. references, literature reviews, tables)
- Coordinating research team meetings
- Updating program website

- Working on research activities with faculty, data analysts and other graduate students from diverse disciplines
- Other tasks, as requested

SKILLS AND QUALIFICATIONS:

- Graduate student in a masters or doctoral program
- Good interpersonal skills and ability to work productively as part of a team
- Excellent oral and written communication skills

- Dependable, organized and detail-oriented
- Strong ethical conduct
- Prior research and data analysis experience preferred

MARKETING ASSISTANT

JOB DESCRIPTION:

Assisting the director in developing and carrying out marketing and advertising campaigns, tracking sales data and preparing reports.

RESPONSIBILITIES:

- Assists with marketing and advertising campaigns by assembling and analyzing sales forecasts; preparing marketing and advertising strategies.
- Collects and summarizes sales data for sales reports.
- Supports sales staff by providing sales data, market trends, forecasts and new product information.
- Researches competitive products by identifying and evaluating product characteristics, pricing and advertising.

SKILLS REQUIRED:

- Superior communication skills
- Ability to think creatively and innovatively
- Budget management skills

- Analytical skills to identify trends, opportunities and challenges
- Ability to work on a team and independently

EDUCATION AND EXPERIENCE:

Minimum qualification: BA in Business Administration or related field; One year of work experience.

3 Which of the two jobs would you be a better candidate for? Look at the key words used in that job description. Complete the first column of the table. Tick (✔) the attributes and experience that you have.

attributes/experience in the job description	example

4 For each attribute/experience in the job description that you ticked in Exercise 3, think of a concrete example from your education or work history. Complete the second column of the table.

5 Work with a partner. Look at your partner's table from Exercise 3 and 4. Do you think your partner is a good candidate for the job? Why / Why not?

6 Which attributes/experiences listed in the job description does your partner not have? Do they have experiences from another area of life they could make relevant? Brainstorm ideas with your partner and add them to the table.

BODY LANGUAGE

SKILLS

Body language is an important aspect of communication. It refers to how we position and move our bodies, as well as facial expressions and how and where our eyes focus. Having positive body language is important in a job interview.

Do ...
- ✔ sit or stand with your back straight and your shoulders back, to show confidence.
- ✔ shake hands firmly, to show confidence and maturity.
- ✔ lean forward slightly, to show interest and enthusiasm.
- ✔ make eye contact, to indicate you are engaged. It also conveys openness and honesty.
- ✔ smile! It suggests that you feel at ease and are happy to be there.

Do not ...
- ✘ cross your arms, as this signposts resistance or defensiveness.
- ✘ hold your arms behind your back, as this indicates nervousness.
- ✘ fidget or touch your face, as this conveys nervousness and anxiety.

1 Work with a partner. Look at the photographs. Does each photograph show positive or negative body language? Explain your answers.

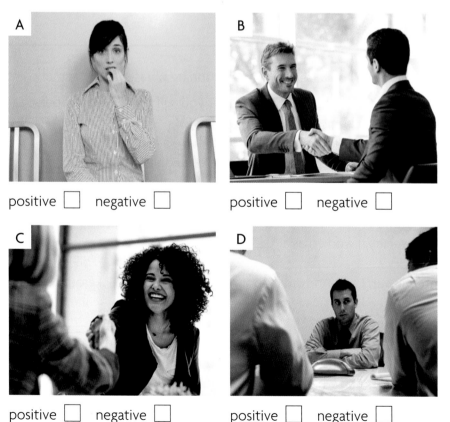

A

positive ☐ negative ☐

B

positive ☐ negative ☐

C

positive ☐ negative ☐

D

positive ☐ negative ☐

PRESENTING YOURSELF IN A JOB INTERVIEW

SKILLS

When you prepare for a job interview, try to use the language that was used in the job description. Think about how you can present yourself as a good fit for this position in terms of:

- your skills and personal attributes
  I'm very good at ... (e.g. time management, coding)
  I'm skilled at ...
  I work well ... (e.g. under pressure, in a team)
  I consider myself a ... (e.g. a people person)

- your background (education and experience)
  I have ... years of experience in/as ... (e.g. in marketing, as a manager)
  I studied ... at ...
  I have learned to ... (e.g. deal with difficult situations)

- your goals
  I hope to develop my skills/further my career in ...
  I hope to accomplish ...
  I want to focus on ...

- appropriateness for the position
  I'm a good fit for this position because ...
  ... make me a good fit/match for this position.
  Your company is exactly ...
  I'd really love to work at ... because ...
  The company culture is ...

2 Complete the conversation with appropriate phrases.

Interviewer: So tell us a little bit about yourself. What kinds of personal assets do you bring to the job?

Interviewee: Well, I've always hoped to have a career in sales.
(1)_____ with all kinds of people and
I (2)_____ at persuading people.

Interviewer: Have you had any sales experience?

Interviewee: Yes, I have (3)_____ in sales. While I was at university, I worked as a (4)_____ at
(5)_____ .

Interviewer: I see. And what about your educational background? I see your degree is in management.

Interviewee: Yes, I have (6)_____ from (7)_____ .
I wanted to get a more general business degree, but all my work experience is in sales and that is where I hope to continue in my career.

Interviewer: And what attracts you about this job and our company in particular?

Interviewee: I think both my educational and professional experience (8)_____ . I have been working in a similar environment for several years.

Interviewer: And can you tell us a little bit about what you hope to accomplish professionally in the next couple of years?

Interviewee: I hope (9)_____ in consumer behaviour research and data analysis. Personal interaction is a crucial part of sales, but it is also important to understand the quantitative aspects of the field.

3 Work with a partner and take turns. Using some of the phrases you have learned, prepare a short presentation about yourself including the points below. Give feedback to your partner.

   1 What kind of a worker are you? Describe your best personal attributes in a work setting?

   2 Describe your educational background.

   3 Describe your past work experience.

SPEAKING TASK

▶ Participate in a mock job interview as an interviewer and/or as a job candidate.

PREPARE

1 You are going to interview another student for one of the jobs you read about in Critical thinking. You are going to be interviewed for one of the jobs from Critical thinking. Complete the tasks for both interviewers and interviewees.

Interviewer

1 Imagine you are interviewing candidates for the position in the advertisement. What questions would you definitely ask? Use your notes from Critical thinking to help you identify the key attributes and experience.

   a _____

   b _____

   c _____

   d _____

   e _____

   Add more questions, including any common interview questions mentioned in Listening 2.

2 Think about how you will begin the interview: introductions, etc.

3 Think about how you will end the interview.

Interviewee

4 Read the advertisement and prepare the talking points you want to make sure you mention in your interview. Use your notes from Critical thinking to help you identify the key attributes and experience. Be prepared to speak for 2–3 minutes about yourself and your background.

5 Write down questions you think you will be asked.

6 Prepare responses to possible questions. (You can take notes, but remember that you will not be able to look at them during the interview.)

- How would you answer the accomplishments question mentioned in Listening 2?
- How would you answer the weakness question mentioned in Listening 2?

7 Prepare three questions to ask the interviewer.

a _____

b _____

c _____

2 Review the Task checklist as you prepare for your interview.

TASK CHECKLIST	✔
Read the job advertisement carefully to plan and/or anticipate questions.	
Make a good impression with your initial greeting and body language.	
Ask and answer questions appropriately.	
Maintain positive body language throughout the interview.	

PRACTISE

3 Work with a partner. Decide which interview you will conduct first. Review your notes for this interview from Exercise 1. Organize your space so that you are sitting opposite each other, if possible, with a desk between you.

4 Review the information on body language in Exercise 1. Practise your initial greeting with your partner. Give each other feedback.

- How was your handshake?
- Did you make eye contact?
- Does your posture indicate interest and enthusiasm?

DISCUSS

5 Conduct your first interview.

6 Change roles and review your notes in Exercise 1. Conduct your second interview.

OBJECTIVES REVIEW

1 Check your learning objectives for this unit. Write *3, 2* or *1* for each objective.

3 = very well   2 = well   1 = not so well

I can ...

watch and understand a video about a job fair.   _____

make inferences.   _____

understand job descriptions.   _____

use degree expressions with *so ... that*.   _____

use degree expressions with *such a ... that*.   _____

prepare for a job interview.   _____

participate in a mock job interview.   _____

2 Use the *Unlock* Digital Workbook for more practice with this unit's learning objectives.

WORDLIST		
accomplishment (n)	discrimination (n) ⊙	ramble (phr)
analytical (adj) ⊙	distinct (adj) ⊙	rehearsed (adj)
be landed with (phr v)	dreaded (adj)	reiterate (v)
cap (n)	format (n) ⊙	start out (phr v)
collaboration (n) ⊙	probationary period	vision (n) ⊙
daunting (adj)	(n phr)	

⊙ = high-frequency words in the Cambridge Academic Corpus

LEARNING OBJECTIVES	IN THIS UNIT YOU WILL ...
Watch and listen	watch and understand a video about the impact of a chemical leak on the water supply.
Listening skills	make unstructured notes as you listen; identify persuasive appeals.
Critical thinking	understand motivation.
Grammar	establish cohesion with *so* and *such*.
Speaking skills	use inclusive language.
Speaking task	participate in a community meeting about a local health controversy.

HEALTH SCIENCES

UNIT 7

UNLCK YOUR KNOWLEDGE

Work with a partner. Discuss the questions.

1 Look at the picture. How does this image relate to the topic of health?

2 What environmental factors can cause health problems? Give examples.

3 How are health conditions which are caused by environmental factors different from other health issues or conditions?

WATCH AND LISTEN

PREPARING TO WATCH

1 Work with a partner. Discuss the questions.

1 Where does your local drinking water come from?
2 In what kinds of communities are people most likely to be concerned about the safety of their food and drinking water?
3 How can food or water become contaminated?
4 What should governments do to protect the food and water their citizens consume?

2 You are going to watch a video about an environmental problem in West Virgina in the US. Before you watch, look at the pictures from the video. Answer the questions.

1 What do you think the problem is?
2 How do you think this problem began?
3 Where do you think the drinking water in this area comes from?

GLOSSARY

---

contaminate (v) to make something dirty, polluted or poisoned

pose (v) to cause a problem

MCHM (n) a chemical used to clean coal

coal country (US n, informal) a part of the country that produces a large amount of coal

reignite (v) to cause something such as a disagreement or worry that was disappearing to suddenly grow stronger

trump (v) surpass (something) by saying or doing something better

senator (US, n) a politician who has been elected to be one of a group of senior lawmakers

governor (US, n) a person in charge of a particular political unit or area

plant (n) a factory in which a particular product is made or power is produced

WHILE WATCHING

3 ▶ Watch the video. Write *T* (true) or *F* (false) next to the statements below. Then correct the false statements.

_____ 1 A week after the chemical leak, the state of West Virginia tried to convince people that the water was safe to drink.

_____

_____ 2 The effects of the chemical MCHM are known.

_____

_____ 3 The former governor does not support legislation that requires regular inspections of chemical facilities.

_____

_____ 4 Matilda is concerned about allowing her children to drink the water.

_____

4 ▶ Watch again. Complete the summary.

There was a chemical ⁽¹⁾_____ in West Virginia. It ⁽²⁾_____ the water supply that supports 300,000 residents. State officials tried to convince the residents that the water was ⁽³⁾_____ to drink; however, residents like Matilda Murray were uncertain of the water's safety. Many feel that the state is putting the interests of ⁽⁴⁾_____ above their citizens' health. The former governor ⁽⁵⁾_____ legislation that would require regular ⁽⁶⁾_____ of chemical storage facilities, preventing tragedies like this from happening again.

5 Circle the statements that can be inferred from the video. Explain your answers to a partner.

1 People became sick after drinking the contaminated water.
2 The business responsible for the leak had to pay the costs of the environmental clean-up.
3 Matilda Murray supports the new legislation.
4 Regular inspections had not occurred prior to the chemical leak.
5 If the law does not pass, similar accidents are likely to occur in other states.

DISCUSSION

6 Work with a partner. Discuss the questions.

1 Do you think that the business interests of the coal companies outweigh the environmental concerns in West Virginia? Why / Why not?
2 What could Matilda Murray and other residents do to voice their concerns?
3 Are you familiar with cases similar to this one? Describe the situations.
4 What other environmental disasters have posed serious risks to human health?

LISTENING

PREPARING TO LISTEN

USING YOUR
KNOWLEDGE

1 You are going to listen to a talk about asthma. Before you listen, work with a partner to answer the questions. Use a dictionary to help you with any unfamiliar words or expressions.

1 Do you or anybody you know have *allergies* to something in the environment, such as dust, pets and certain kinds of plants? Describe the symptoms.

2 Do you or anybody you know have *asthma*? Describe the symptoms.

PREDICTING
CONTENT
USING VISUALS

2 Asthma symptoms are responses by the *immune system* to triggers in the environment. Which of these photos show asthma triggers?

a

b

c

d

e

f

g

h

3 Read the definitions. Use the correct forms of the words in bold to complete the sentences below.

> **allergy** (n) an abnormal physical reaction, such as a rash or breathing problems, when exposed to a particular substance, for example animal hair or pollen
>
> **correlation** (n) a connection between two or more things
>
> **disparity** (n) a lack of equality
>
> **guidelines** (n) formal advice (usually written) about how to do something
>
> **hygiene** (n) cleanliness; keeping yourself and your environment clean
>
> **incidence** (n) the rate at which something happens
>
> **obesity** (n) the state of being extremely fat in a way that is dangerous for health
>
> **severity** (n) seriousness, how bad something is

1 The UK government has attempted to tackle _____ by raising taxes on sugary drinks.
2 The government has issued its _____ for meals served in primary schools.
3 No one predicted the _____ of the outbreak of the disease, in which thousands of people died.
4 There is a growing _____ between the life expectancies of the rich and the poor in this country.
5 The _____ of asthma is lower in the Middle East than in the US and UK, but it is increasing in the Gulf States.
6 I had to stop eating bread because I've got a wheat _____ .
7 There is a significant _____ between educational achievement and health, but this does not mean that one is the cause of the other.
8 Poor _____ is a contributing factor to the spread of disease.

WHILE LISTENING

Taking unstructured notes as you listen

Taking notes in ordered lists, outlines and tables can be effective, but it is not always possible to know in advance how a lecture or presentation will be organized. Even if speakers provide an outline or summary, they may not follow it exactly or may include other information when they speak.

For the listener taking notes, sometimes a looser organization is necessary and even preferable. Going back to these unstructured notes later allows you to see connections and relationships that you might not have recognized otherwise. Once you understand these connections, you can organize your notes into tables or ideas maps.

4 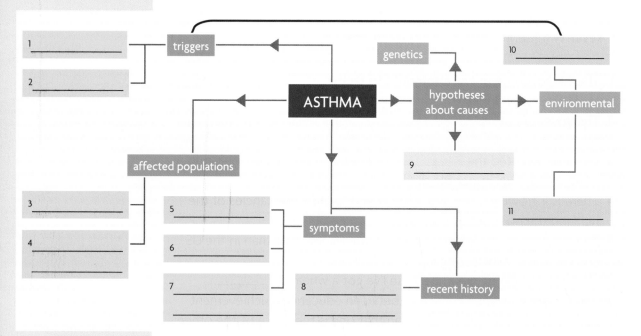 7.1 Listen and make unstructured notes. Do not try to organize your notes yet. Leave space so you can add details later.

5 7.1 Review your notes. Underline the parts that you think may be main ideas. Circle any parts that you are not sure of and want to listen to again. Then listen to the presentation again and add to your notes.

6 Work with a partner. Using your notes from Exercise 5, write a summary of one of the two hypotheses about the environmental causes of asthma. Give each other feedback.

POST-LISTENING

7 Use your notes from Exercise 5 to complete the ideas map.

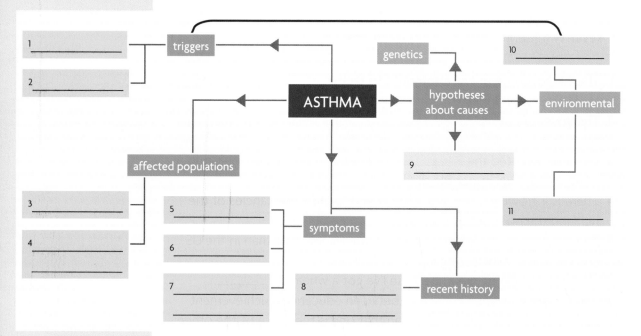

8 With a partner, discuss what the blue line at the top of the ideas map in Exercise 7 means. What kind of connection does it describe? Mark other connections like this on the ideas map.

9 7.2 Use your notes to create a separate ideas map like the one below about the two main competing *environmental* hypotheses (on the right side of the ideas map in Exercise 7). Add boxes for supporting details, examples and counter-examples for each hypothesis. Then listen to that part of the presentation again to check your ideas.

ENVIRONMENTAL
HYPOTHESES

PRONUNCIATION FOR LISTENING

Contrastive stress

Contrastive stress is the extra stress or emphasis that is placed on words to show contrast or difference. Listening for contrastive stress can help you understand when a speaker is comparing or contrasting ideas.

Indoor pollution includes dust, mould, tobacco smoke, pet hair and various chemicals used for cleaning. _Outdoor_ pollution includes particulate matter and ground-level ozone.

10 🔊 7.3 Listen to the sentences and write the contrasting information.

1 situation for some asthmatics: _____

_____

situation for other asthmatics: _____

_____

2 more common: _____

less common: _____

3 don't know: _____

do have: _____

11 🔊 7.4 Listen to the sentences and make a note of what is being contrasted and the contrasting information in each sentence.

1 _____

_____

2 _____

_____

3 _____

_____

DISCUSSION

12 Work in small groups. Discuss the questions.

1 After having heard all the evidence, what do you think is the most likely explanation for the recent increase in the incidence of asthma?

2 Do you know anybody who suffers from asthma? What are his or her triggers?

ESTABLISHING COHESION WITH *SO* AND *SUCH*

GRAMMAR

Cohesion refers to the use of grammatical structures and words to tie a text together, especially across sentences. There are many ways to establish cohesion. One way is to use the words *so* and *such* to link new information with ideas that came earlier in a text or conversation.

So

So is often used to avoid repeating a phrase. It is used with *be* or a modal or auxiliary verb, often *do*.

The city thought the water was safe and **so did I**.

(I also thought the water was safe.)

The city has improved its air quality, and by **doing so**, it may have helped to reduce asthma rates.

(By improving its air quality, the city may have helped to reduce asthma rates.)

Such

Such can also be used to refer to previous information. It usually has the meaning 'like the one(s) just mentioned'.

Cities are required to test lead levels regularly. **Such measures** are critical to public health.

(Measures like the one just mentioned are critical.)

Every city is required to have a plan to test water for acidity. And that's where the council was at fault. They had no **such plan**.

(The council had no plan like the one just mentioned.)

---

1 Rewrite the ideas using *so* or *such* for cohesion.

1 Asthma rates have risen dramatically. Rates of other allergies have risen dramatically.

2 Early remedies for asthma included warm milk and cool baths. Unfortunately, treatments like warm milk and cool baths do little to relieve the symptoms.

3 My aunt recently quit smoking. The major change in behaviour of quitting smoking may have reduced her chances of getting asthma, cancer and other diseases.

4 Vigorous exercise contributes to asthma attacks. Ironically, a sedentary lifestyle also contributes to asthma attacks.

5 Some cities require monthly reports on water and air pollution. Unfortunately, my city does not have any requirement for monthly reports on water and air pollution.

2 Write three new sentences with *so* or *such* to show cohesion.

PLUS

ADJECTIVES OF STRONG DISAPPROVAL

The English language is rich in synonyms, especially when it comes to emotions.

Adjectives expressing how a person feels

Many of these adjectives are the past participle forms of verbs. They often appear as passives with a *by* phrase.

aghast   appalled   dismayed   horrified   outraged   shocked

I was **outraged** by their lack of concern.

Adjectives describing a situation or activity

These adjectives have similar meanings to the adjectives above.

appalling   atrocious   deplorable   dreadful   outrageous   shocking

It was an **appalling** lack of judgment.

Use a dictionary to help you understand some of the subtle differences between them.

3 Choose the correct adjective to complete each sentence.

1 We were *shocked / shocking* at the amount of taxpayers' money spent on entertainment by politicians.

2 The food was bad and the service was *aghast / atrocious*. I'll never go to that restaurant again!

3 The inspectors were *appalled / appalling* at the filthy kitchen.

4 It was *outraged / outrageous* that the situation had been going on for so long.

5 The doctors were *dismayed / dreadful* that the medicine had suddenly stopped working.

6 After being in the hot sun all day, she had a *dreadful / horrified* headache.

7 When the full story was made public, I was *aghast / deplorable*. How could such a thing happen in our little town?

 PLUS

4 Write three statements that express strong disapproval of something that you have read or heard about recently in the news. Read them with a partner. Did you both use the correct adjectives and the correct forms?

1 _____

_____

2 _____

_____

3 _____

_____

PREPARING TO LISTEN

1 You are going to listen to a moderated community meeting about water quality. Work with a partner. Answer the questions.

1 What do the photographs show?
2 What do you know about the safety of your drinking water? Who ensures its safety?
3 What health problems can unsafe drinking water cause?

2 Read the sentences and choose the best definition for the words in bold.

1 Exposure to some drugs can **compromise** your immune system and lead to chronic illness.
   a harm   **b** decrease   **c** elevate

2 Doctors found a high **concentration** of dangerous chemicals in the patient's blood.
   a damage   **b** amount   **c** increase

3 It was clear from the student's poor performance on the test that he had made **minimal** effort to prepare for it.
   a very small
   b no
   c initial, in the beginning

4 Lead has some useful **properties** – it doesn't rust and has a low melting point – but it can also be poisonous.
   a functions   **b** qualities   **c** ingredients

5 Toxic chemicals from the nearby gold mine have **contaminated** the town's drinking water.
   a poisoned   **b** filtered   **c** improved

6 The police **intervened** to protect the wider public.
   a asked for assistance
   b shouted or spoke in a loud voice
   c entered a situation to stop it from getting worse

3 🔊 7.5 Listen to the moderator's introduction. Circle the people you expect to hear speak.

a a doctor in Swansbeck
b the mayor of Swansbeck
c an environmentalist
d a public relations person from local government
e one or more residents of Swansbeck
f a teacher from one of Swansbeck's schools

WHILE LISTENING

4 🔊 7.6 Listen to the community meeting. Check your predictions in Exercise 3. Then complete the cause-and-effect chain (a–d) below with the items in the box.

LISTENING FOR
MAIN IDEAS

> behavioural and cognitive problems   damaged pipes
> contaminated water   lead poisoning

Swansbeck changed water source

↓

water supply more acidic

↓

a ___ → b ___ → c ___ → d ___

5 🔊 7.6 Listen again. What evidence is presented during the panel discussion for each of the items in the cause-and-effect chain in Exercise 4?

LISTENING FOR
DETAIL

a _____

_____

b _____

_____

c _____

_____

d _____

_____

Identifying persuasive appeals

When speakers are trying to persuade listeners, they may use different kinds of appeals to make their case. They consider the people in their audience and think about what is important to them.

Appeal for trust

Speakers may try to show that they are trustworthy. They – or somebody else – may cite their credentials (e.g. their education or their job history); they may talk about their experience and expertise or give other reasons why the audience should trust their judgment and accept their point of view.

I have been a government inspector for 25 years ...

Appeal to emotion

Emotions are powerful motivators. Speakers may try to shock, frighten or worry their listeners. They may try to make them feel guilty, happy, angry or sad. They may flatter their audience. They may illustrate their point with stories in order to evoke emotions. Or they may use strong words and expressions to demonstrate how important the issue is.

*It's **completely unacceptable** that ...*

*We cannot allow such **shocking conditions** to continue.*

Appeal to logic

To prove that what the speaker is saying is logical and reasonable, speakers may cite statistics, research and established facts. They may use assertive language to convince their listeners.

*You **must see** that ...*

*It's **obvious** that ...*

6 🔊 7.6 Listen again, this time for appeals. Take notes in the table below. Use the script on pages 259–260 to help you.

TAKING NOTES ON DETAIL

- What appeals are used?
- What type of appeals are they?
- Who made each appeal (scientist, private citizen, etc.)?

appeal for trust	
appeal to emotion	
appeal to logic	

POST-LISTENING

7 Review your notes in Exercise 6. Then work with a partner. Discuss the questions.

1 Which kinds of appeals were typical for the different speakers?
2 Why do you think they chose that type of appeal?
3 Were any strong emotional words used? What were they? Why do you think the speaker used them?
4 Which types of appeals do you think were most effective?

DISCUSSION

SYNTHESIZING

8 Work in a small group. Use ideas from Listening 1 and Listening 2 to answer the following questions.

1 Do you think there is a link between diet and asthma? Why? What changes could someone make to their diet to improve their asthma?
2 Should businesses be responsible for the impact they have on people's heath? Why / Why not?
3 Do you think a situation like this could happen in your city? Why / Why not?
4 What would you do if this happened where you live? Explain your answer.

SPEAKING

CRITICAL THINKING

At the end of this unit, you are going to do the speaking task below.

> Participate in a meeting in which you discuss whether a fast-food restaurant should open at a local commercial complex. You will each take on the role of somebody involved with and/or affected by this decision.

SKILLS

Understanding motivation

Controversial issues can often provoke emotional responses because the stakes are high. If you want to understand a person's point of view, it is useful to understand their motivation – what they want and what makes them behave as they do. Understanding the motivation of all parties in a situation can help you anticipate and challenge others' points of view. It may also help you to persuade others to adopt your position.

 ANALYZE

1 Study the facts and figures and read the article about a country on page 161. Then work with a small group and answer the questions.

1 How favourable is the market for fast-food restaurants? What approximate level of growth between 2003 and 2018 is shown in Figure 1?
2 What kinds of economic and societal changes may have occurred during this period?
3 How might the increase in fast-food consumption have affected the population's diet? Their health?
4 What do the diseases in Figure 2 have in common?
5 Did the rate of obesity for adults rise or fall between 2003 and 2018? For children? What might the difference between the two figures mean for the future health of the population?

 UNDERSTAND

2 🔊 7.7 Listen to part of a radio programme from the country in Exercise 1. Take notes on the reason(s) each caller took part in the radio programme. Compare your notes with a partner.

Figure 1: Growth of Fast Food

	2003	2018
number of fast food restaurants	378	658
number of fast food meals per week	0–1	2–5

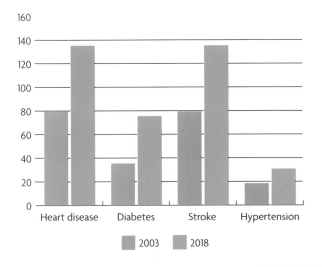

Figure 2: Death rate (per 100,000 people)

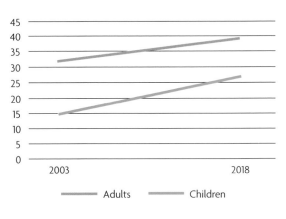

Figure 3: Percentage of the population considered obese

CHRONIC DISEASES ON THE RISE

There was a time when we were worried about diseases like tuberculosis, cholera and polio. Happily, those days are in the past. However, chronic diseases like heart disease, stroke, diabetes and kidney disease, which were once mostly Western problems, have replaced them as the most serious threats to public health. These are so-called 'lifestyle' diseases because they have emerged as we have adopted many aspects of Western lifestyle.

Two specific changes in lifestyle go a long way towards explaining our current health crisis. A generation ago, most people in the country were engaged in physical labour, either in their jobs or in their homes. Today, we spend our days at desks in offices and we hire others to perform physical tasks. We rarely walk; instead, we drive everywhere. As a result, we get very little exercise. But this issue is overshadowed by a bigger problem – diet. Traditionally, we had a very healthy diet: primarily grains, fruits and vegetables. Furthermore, the quantity of food we ate was restricted; quite simply, people did not always have extra food. But our diets, like our jobs, have changed with increasing prosperity. We eat much more fat, salt and sugar than in the past, and a lot of it comes in the form of fast food. Fast food is fine as a treat once

in a while, but that is not what is happening. In a recent survey in Mexico, almost 50 percent of the respondents said they ate fast food between one and three times a week. In Kuwait, fast-food restaurants are so busy they have established call centres to handle the volume of orders. The manager of one call centre said that about 15 percent of his customers order four times a week or more. Across the Middle East and North Africa, McDonald's makes six million dollars in sales every day, with plans to increase that by 60 percent by 2020.

What happens with these changes? More than 30 percent of the population is obese, a condition that can lead to an alarming number of chronic health problems. Increasingly, the leading causes of death are heart disease, stroke and diabetes. The list of countries with the 20 highest rates of diabetes in the world includes Kuwait, Saudi Arabia, Qatar, Bahrain, UAE, Malaysia, Egypt, Mexico and Oman. One recent study projected that half the population of Saudi Arabia will have diabetes by 2030. It is already the number one killer in Mexico. And the picture for coronary heart diseases is just as depressing. Many people are wondering if our prosperity is killing us.

3 Work with a partner. Using information from the radio programme, the text and the graphs, complete the table for how each group would be affected by a fast-food restaurant opening at a local commercial complex.

	What concerns might they have?	What do they want the outcome to be?
manager/owner of the complex		
business owners near the location		
owner of FryKing		
children		
high-school students		
local parents		

 EVALUATE

4 Your classroom will become the meeting room at a local commercial complex. Work as a class. Assign roles for your meeting. Make sure there are roughly equal numbers of people 'for' and 'against' the FryKing.

- the complex manager
- a parent of a student at the tutoring centre
- an owner of a business that might benefit from FryKing's presence
- an owner whose business might be hurt by FryKing's presence
- the owner of the tutoring centre
- a student who goes to the tutoring centre
- a parent who brings her child to the play area in the complex
- a local doctor

5 Work individually. Based on Exercise 3, construct a position statement for the person you are representing.

Against:
- Your position statement should say who you are and how you, your family or your business would be affected. Consider using adjectives of strong emotion. Include information about health considerations.

_____

_____

_____

_____

For:
- Your position statement should say who you are and how you, your family or your business would be affected. Use your imagination to provide details about the person you are representing. Consider using adjectives of strong emotion.

_____

_____

_____

_____

Complex manager:
- Consider how you will respond to both sides. Think about how you could resolve their differences by offering a compromise.

_____

_____

_____

_____

6 Prepare your talking points for the meeting.

- Rewrite your position statement in note form so you do not have to read it.
- Consider the motivation of other participants. Which of them do you think might challenge or object to your position? How would you reply to them?
- Consider what kinds of appeals will be the most effective forms of persuasion. Will you appeal for trust, to emotion or to logic?
- Take notes on what you want to happen and how you will respond to opposing suggestions and compromises.

_____

_____

_____

_____

_____

_____

_____

PREPARATION FOR SPEAKING

INCLUSIVE LANGUAGE

When speakers want to persuade others, they often try to include listeners in the perspective they are taking. They may use the pronouns *we, us, our* and *everyone.* Using inclusive language can make people more willing to listen to your argument.

If **we** want to prevent this from happening in the future, we need to know what happened.

Perhaps he can answer **our** questions.

Fast food is killing **our** young people.

Now **everybody** eats burgers and fried fish. **Everyone** I know is on medication.

They may suggest that they are just like their listeners.

Like all of you, I want to know why ...

They may address their listeners directly.

So, what do **you** think? What kind of life do they have to look forward to?

1 Rewrite the sentences below with more inclusive language.

  1 This factory is a threat to public health and should close down.

  _____

  2 Why hasn't there been any public discussion of these important issues?

  _____

  3 The food at fast-food restaurants is not part of a healthy diet, so people should stop going to them so often.

  _____

  4 I don't think it is a good idea to have these kinds of businesses near children's schools.

  _____

  5 The testing procedures are flawed and the laboratory has done nothing to improve them.

  _____

2 Review the statement that you prepared in Critical thinking, Exercise 5 on page 163. Write one more sentence that contains inclusive language and add it to your statement.

  _____

PRONUNCIATION FOR SPEAKING

Emphasis for emotional appeal

Speakers often emphasize words that carry strong emotions or words that they hope will resonate with their audience and generate sympathy for the argument that they are attempting to make.

It is **utterly** **unreasonable** to expect local residents to bathe in bottled water.

You **must understand** that the council is doing **everything within its power** to resolve the situation.

3 🔊 7.8 Listen to the excerpts from Listening 2. Write the missing words you hear. Why do you think these words are emphasized?

1 Lead is _____ toxic – to the nervous system, to the reproductive system, but most of all, it affects _____ development.
2 And the most _____ part is that the damage is _____ .
3 My kids got _____ rashes and _____ stomach pains.
4 The council is _____ sorry for the problems this has caused your family.
5 You need to understand that _____ level of lead in the blood is considered safe.
6 What I found was _____ , I would say, even _____ .

4 With your partner, take turns reading the sentences aloud. Emphasize the words that show emotion. Did you both emphasize the same words?

1 This situation is unacceptable.
2 I've never seen such appalling conditions.
3 We simply cannot stand by and watch this happen any longer.
4 It's obvious that the council has done nothing to address these problems.
5 Every resident of this community has been affected.
6 I want you to know that the council is taking this problem very seriously.

SPEAKING TASK

> Participate in a meeting in which you discuss whether a fast-food restaurant should open at a local commercial complex. You will each take on the role of somebody involved with and/or affected by this decision.

PREPARE

1 Review your talking points from Critical thinking Exercise 6 on page 163 and the challenges that you anticipate.

2 Refer to the Task checklist as you prepare for your discussion.

TASK CHECKLIST	✔
Make a statement which clearly expressed your position.	
Use adjectives of strong emotion where appropriate.	
Use contrastive stress where appropriate.	
Anticipate the motivation and objections of other parties.	
Use inclusive language to gain support for your points.	
Make or respond to demands as appropriate for your role.	

PRACTISE

3 Practise delivering your position statements in small groups. Give the other students feedback. Consider the feedback your group gives you. Make any necessary changes to your notes.

4 Consider the advice in the box below.

> - Identify yourself. Say your name and what role you have in the situation.
> - Do not speak too quickly. Speak clearly and with emotion.
> - Refer to your talking points and notes, but keep your head up and speak directly to the audience or to the members of the panel.
> - Listen to what others say and respond when appropriate.

DISCUSS

5 Hold your meeting. Your teacher will be the moderator. He or she will begin by stating the purpose of the meeting and calling on people to introduce themselves, make contributions and ask questions.

OBJECTIVES REVIEW

1 Check your learning objectives for this unit. Write *3, 2* or *1* for each objective.

3 = very well   2 = well   1 = not so well

I can …

watch and understand a video about the impact
of a chemical leak on the water supply.   ———

make unstructured notes as I listen.   ———

identify persuasive appeals.   ———

understand motivation.   ———

establish cohesion with *so* and *such*.   ———

use inclusive language.   ———

participate in a community meeting about a local
health controversy.   ———

2 Use the *Unlock* Digital Workbook for more practice with this unit's learning objectives.

UNLOCK ONLINE

WORDLIST		
aghast (adj)	deplorable (adj)	minimal (adj) ⊙
allergy (n)	dismayed (adj)	obesity (n)
appalled (adj)	disparity (n) ⊙	outraged (adj)
appalling (adj)	dreadful (adj)	outrageous (adj)
atrocious (adj)	guidelines (n) ⊙	property (n) ⊙
compromise (v) ⊙	horrified (adj)	severity (n) ⊙
concentration (n) ⊙	hygiene (n) ⊙	shocked (adj)
contaminate (v) ⊙	incidence (n) ⊙	shocking (adj)
correlation (n) ⊙	intervene (v)	

⊙ = high-frequency words in the Cambridge Academic Corpus

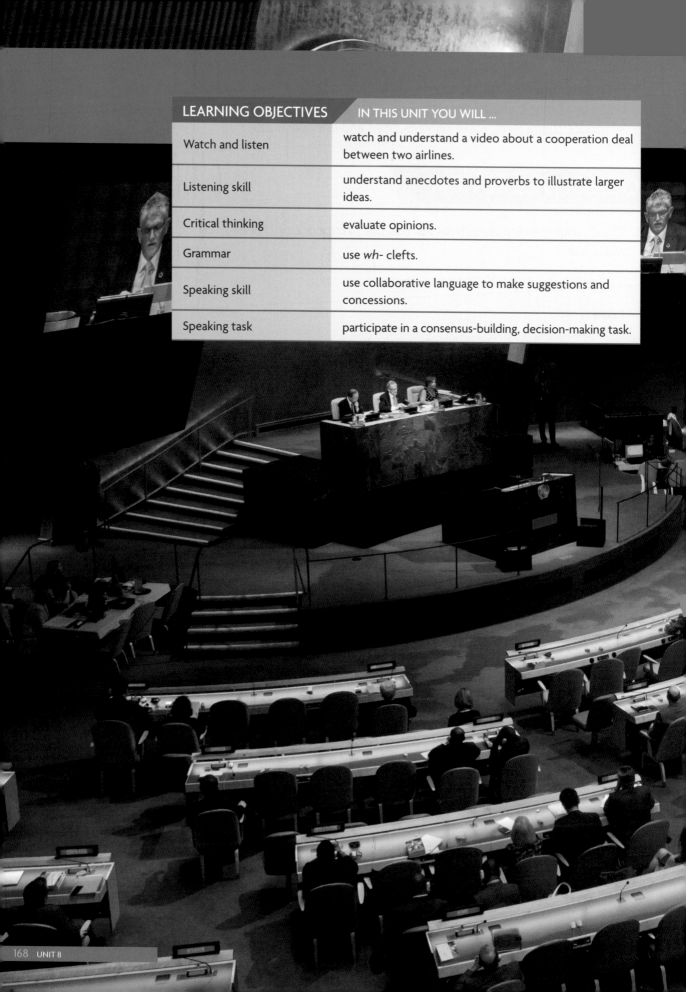

LEARNING OBJECTIVES	IN THIS UNIT YOU WILL ...
Watch and listen	watch and understand a video about a cooperation deal between two airlines.
Listening skill	understand anecdotes and proverbs to illustrate larger ideas.
Critical thinking	evaluate opinions.
Grammar	use *wh*- clefts.
Speaking skill	use collaborative language to make suggestions and concessions.
Speaking task	participate in a consensus-building, decision-making task.

UNL⊘CK YOUR KNOWLEDGE

Work with a partner. Discuss the questions.

1 Describe a personal experience you had in making an important decision as a group. How long did it take? What kind of experience was it: productive, pleasant, frustrating?

2 How do formal groups, such as government bodies and businesses, make decisions?

3 How do you think collaboration can be a part of decision-making? Give an example.

PLUS

WATCH AND LISTEN

PREPARING TO WATCH

ACTIVATING YOUR KNOWLEDGE

1 Work with a partner. Discuss the questions about each pair of companies.

Why would these companies collaborate with each other? What might be the benefits? What could go wrong?

1 A multinational chain of hotels and a multinational airline
2 A Korean fashion design house and a European department store chain
3 A multinational tech company and a tech start-up
4 A French car manufacturer and a Japanese car manufacturer

PREDICTING CONTENT USING VISUALS

2 You are going to watch a video about a business collaboration. Before you watch, look at the pictures and discuss the questions with your partner.

1 What companies can you see in the pictures? What different aspects of their businesses can you see?
2 Do you know which country each company is based in? How might this be important in their collaboration?
3 What other benefits could there be for these two airlines in collaborating with one another?

GLOSSARY

aviation (n) the activity of flying aircraft, or of designing, producing, and keeping them in good condition

subsidiary (n) a company that is controlled by another

freight (n) transporting goods by ship, aircraft, train, or truck

procurement (n) BUSINESS the process by which an organization buys the products or services it needs from other organizations

---

WHILE WATCHING

UNDERSTANDING MAIN IDEAS

3 ▶ Watch the video. Write *E* (Etihad), *L* (Lufthansa) or *B* (both).

1 _____ want to find other ways to work together in the future.
2 _____ have agreed to pay $100,000,000 for catering services.
3 _____ own one of the largest aircraft maintenance companies.
4 _____ will share their international flight routes.

4 ▶ Watch again. Complete the student notes with one to three words or a number in each gap.

Etihad and Lufthansa deal

CEOs signed:

- (1)_____ worth $100 million for the provision of (2)_____ catering services
- Agreement for maintenance and (3)_____

Deal is first part of (4)_____ for growth in the (5)_____ aviation market:

- Lufthansa's Sky Chefs = Etihad's (6)_____ caterer outside Abu Dhabi –
  (7)_____ cities worldwide for (8)_____ years
- Etihad to gain (9)_____ of Lufthansa Technik
- Lufthansa Technik to find (10)_____ with Etihad Airways Engineering

Poss. future partnerships: (11)_____ operations, procurement and (12)_____ services.

---

5 Choose a meaning (a–e) for each word or phrase in bold (1–5).

1 They will be **dishing up** the goods in sixteen cities ...   _____

2 ... Etihad Airways Engineering, who **provide a portfolio of** similar services.   _____

3 As the new partners **reached for the skies** together ...   _____

4 ... new so-called '**feeder** markets' throughout the Indian Subcontinent.   _____

5 ... the important business **hubs** of Frankfurt and Rio de Janeiro ...   _____

a a centre of an activity
b to do something ambitious
c to offer a range of
d to provide
e something that provides a large supply

DISCUSSION

6 Work in a small group. Discuss the questions.

1 How long do you think it took Etihad and Lufthansa to negotiate a deal? What do you think would have been the main points of discussion? What difficulties might there have been?

2 What other examples of international collaboration can you think of outside of the business world?

3 How do you think decisions are made in the following types of international collaboration?
  - a university exchange programme
  - a trade agreement
  - a friendly sports match

LISTENING

PREPARING TO LISTEN

1 You are going to listen to a training session on group dynamics. Before you listen, work with a partner. Discuss the questions.

1 What can an individual do to make sure a group in which they are a member works well and that it accomplishes its tasks? What kind of behaviour makes group work more effective?

2 What can an individual do to disrupt the work of a group and prevent it from accomplishing its tasks? What kind of behaviour impairs group work?

3 Have you ever had an experience in which one member of a group behaved inappropriately and prevented the group from working well together? If so, describe what happened.

4 If you have had, or know about, a negative experience like this, what did you, or anybody else in the group, try to do to respond to this individual?

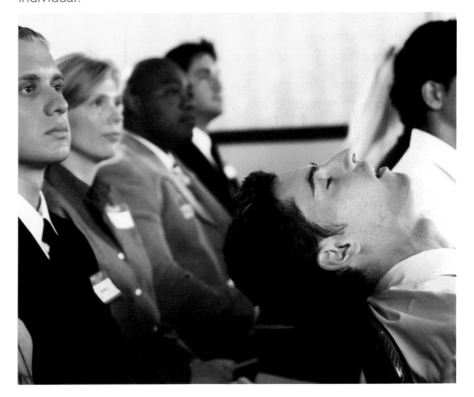

2 Take the quiz about work styles. Then work in small groups and compare your scores. What is your style, according to your score? How accurate do you think your score is?

WHAT IS YOUR WORK STYLE?

Do you work well in collaborative settings? Write *T* (true) or *F* (false) for each statement to find out your style.

1 I tend to give in to group pressure easily. ___

2 I produce my best results when I work on my own. ___

3 My work would be so much easier if I didn't have to depend on others to do it. ___

4 Other people will almost always let you down. ___

5 I don't care about my job that much; I just do what they tell me to do. ___

6 If too many people are working on the same thing, it usually doesn't turn out very well. ___

7 I usually know what's best and get impatient when I have to listen to a lot of other opinions. ___

8 Some of the people I work with really annoy me. ___

9 When somebody talks, I think about how to respond while they're speaking. ___

10 You have to protect your own interests because nobody else will. ___

11 When you disagree with somebody, the best course of action is to stay silent. ___

12 Meetings are usually a waste of time. ___

13 Creativity is something that applies to individuals not groups. ___

14 I always seem to end up doing the most work on a group project. ___

15 I do my best to avoid conflict. ___

16 I hate(d) working on group projects in school. ___

17 When somebody challenges my ideas, I just stay quiet. ___

18 If I want the job done right, I do it myself. ___

19 We spend too much time discussing and not enough time doing. ___

20 I'd rather just go with what the rest of the group wants than fight for my idea. ___

Now calculate your score. Give yourself five (5) points for each F.

YOUR SCORE

95–100: You are a collaboration superstar. You generally trust others and enjoy working in collaborative situations.

80–90: You are a team player. You will probably function well in a group. But some of your beliefs and attitudes could interfere with your ability to get the most out of collaboration.

65–75: You are a doubter. You don't always see the value in collaborative work. Perhaps you've had a bad experience in the past.

60 and below: You are a loner. You find collaborative work difficult, and you don't see the value in it. You prefer tasks that allow you to work independently and be rewarded for your own work. When you have to work in groups, you respond negatively.

3 Read the words and their definitions. Use the correct forms of the words in bold to complete the sentences below.

> **bully** (v, n) to intentionally frighten someone who is smaller or weaker, or someone who acts in this way
> **constructive** (adj) helpful, positive
> **counteract** (v) to reduce the negative effect of something
> **defuse** (v) to make a situation calmer or less dangerous
> **dynamics** (n pl) forces that produce change in a system or group
> **perception** (n) a belief or opinion based on observation
> **prevail** (v) to eventually become the controlling force
> **resentment** (n) anger at being forced to accept something

1 It's important to understand a group's _____ before you add or remove team members.
2 Public _____ of the community centre has changed since it was built. It is a lot more popular now.
3 _____ feedback from the community is an important part of the decision-making process.
4 He made a joke to try to _____ the tension in the room.
5 I know that this is a difficult time, but we hope that good sense will _____ in the end.
6 His rude behaviour has created a great deal of _____ among his colleagues.
7 Every school seems to have a _____ , who frightens the smaller and younger children.
8 He drank three cups of coffee to _____ the effects of two sleepless nights.

WHILE LISTENING

4 🔊 8.1 Listen to the presentation and summarize the main idea in one or two sentences. Compare your summary statement with a partner.

_____

_____

_____

_____

5 🔊 8.1 Listen again. To support her claim, the speaker reports on a research study. Take notes on how she explains the study and its results. Use your notes to complete the table below.

Participants: _____

Methods (How was the study organized and carried out?):

_____

Results: _____

_____

Conclusion: _____

_____

POST-LISTENING

Using anecdotes and proverbs to illustrate larger ideas

Speakers will sometimes use stories, anecdotes or proverbs as shortcuts to express their ideas. These shortcuts can illustrate broader ideas or principles. For example the proverb 'When in Rome, do as the Romans do.' means act the same way as the people around you. A speaker may use a short version of the proverb, for example, just 'When in Rome.' The listener can then infer the rest of the meaning if they know the proverb.

6 🔊 8.2 Read the tasks and then listen to the excerpt from the presentation. Complete the tasks.

1 Consider the proverb, 'One bad apple can spoil the barrel'. Explain the literal meaning and then explain how it applies to the content of the presentation. _____

_____

_____

2 The presenter names three types of 'bad apples' and gives examples of their behaviour. Complete the table with information from the presentation.

	type of bad apple	examples of behaviour
a		exhibits lack of interest in task
b	naysayer	
c		

7 Work in small groups. Discuss the meaning of each of the proverbs. What larger principles or ideas do they illustrate?

1 You can lead a horse to water, but you can't make it drink.
2 There is no smoke without fire.
3 There is no such thing as a free lunch.
4 Too many cooks spoil the broth.
5 The grass is always greener on the other side of the fence.

PRONUNCIATION FOR LISTENING

Connected speech: linking words with vowels

When people speak fluently, they often insert an extra linking sound between words without noticing. When one word ends in a vowel sound and the following word begins with a vowel sound, speakers may insert another sound in-between them. Common linking sounds are /j/ and /w/.

They may not actively ⌣/j/⌣ oppose the ⌣/j/⌣ actions and ideas of other members of the group.
What will you do ⌣/w/⌣ if your group has a 'bad apple'?
Research suggests that it only takes one member of a group to ⌣/w/⌣ act badly.

When *the* precedes a word that begins with a vowel sound, it is pronounced /ðiː/ and the /j/ sound links the two words.

The ⌣/j/⌣ other members of the group often resent the bad apple.

8 🔊 8.3 Listen to the sentences. Circle the pairs of words with /j/ or /w/ links between them. Compare answers with a partner.

1 They'll insist on doing things their way and only their way.
2 Of course, individual members of a group may also have their own goals, which may or may not be consistent with the group goal.
3 The other members began to adopt the same negative behaviour.
4 'This will never work,' or 'This is so stupid', other members also became critical or began to express similarly negative views.
5 And perhaps just as importantly, everybody had a negative response to the entire experience.

DISCUSSION

9 Work with a partner. Discuss the questions.

1 What is the best way to deal with each type of bad apple?
2 Why do you think negative behaviour and attitudes spread so easily? Do you think positive behaviour spreads as easily? Why / Why not?

WH- CLEFTS

GRAMMAR

Wh- clefts are constructions that allow speakers to focus the listener's attention on one part of a sentence – the part that contains new or unknown information.

A *wh-* cleft consists of a clause that begins with a *wh-* word (often *what*), followed by a form of the verb *be*.

The researchers found that the behaviour of one bad apple can spread to the whole group.

What these researchers found was that the behaviour of one bad apple can spread to the whole group.

        CLEFT   NEW INFORMATION

Wh- clefts are also used to express a speaker's perspective on new information or to clarify new information:

I guess **what I'm saying is** that not everybody is going to have that kind of time.
What surprised me was that the results were so consistent.
What I didn't agree with were the study's conclusions.

1 Rewrite the sentences using *what* clefts.

  1 The report revealed that bad apples destroy group dynamics.
     What the report revealed was that bad apples destroy group dynamics.
  2 The participants said their group didn't have a good leader.
  3 The researchers saw an increase in negative behaviour.
  4 The study showed that one member can have a disproportionate effect.
  5 We found that people are easily influenced by others to behave badly, which really surprised me.

2 Rewrite the sentences as clarifications using *what* clefts. Use the words in brackets in the clefts.

  1 This was a poorly designed study. (I'm telling you)
     What I'm telling you is that this was a poorly designed study.
  2 Nobody was aware of the effect his behaviour had on them. (you mean)
  3 The results were the same for children, teens and adults. (you're saying)
  4 Studies like this are hard to replicate because every group of people is different. (I mean)

PLUS

3 Now complete three sentences containing *wh-* clefts expressing your opinions about environmental issues.

1 What worries me is _____ .
2 What we need to do is _____ .
3 Where we've made some progress is _____ .

DEPENDENT PREPOSITIONS

VOCABULARY

Many familiar verbs and verb phrases collocate with particular prepositions.

verbs with *on*	verbs with *in*	verbs with *with*
depend on	*believe in*	*interfere with*
concentrate on	*engage in*	*agree/disagree with*
rely on	*participate in*	*argue with*
insist on	*result in*	*engage with*
plan on	*succeed in*	*provide (somebody) with*
agree/disagree on		*present (somebody) with*
		compare (somebody/something) with

4 Complete the sentences with a verb from the Explanation box and its dependent preposition. Make sure the verbs are in the correct form. Some items may have more than one correct answer.

1 The psychologist recruited more than 50 students to _____ _____ the study as research subjects.
2 They've asked us to _____ them _____ all kinds of information that will take a considerable time to pull together.
3 There are many different directions we could go with this in the future, but I think we really need to _____ _____ the fundamental issues for now.
4 Some less reputable researchers have been known to _____ _____ the data to exaggerate the significance of their findings.
5 Although I believed it was unnecessary, the lead researcher _____ _____ repeating the study, just to make sure that the initial findings were correct.
6 When we _____ the data for the control group _____ that of the experimental group we got a shock.

PLUS

5 Write three sentences about working in groups using the verbs and their dependent prepositions in the Explanation box.

1 _____
2 _____
3 _____

LISTENING 2

PREPARING TO LISTEN

1 You are going to listen to a talk comparing two systems for decision-making. Before you listen, read the definition and answer the questions with a partner.

USING YOUR
KNOWLEDGE

> Majority rule is a principle that states that a majority, usually constituted by 50% plus one of an organized group, have both the right and the power to make decisions that apply to and govern the entire group.

1 What institutions operate by majority rule?
2 Have you ever participated in a group that operates by majority rule? Describe the group and why it operates this way.
3 Do you think majority rule is a fair system? Is it an effective one?
4 Are there any downsides to majority rule?

2 With your partner, read the quote and answer the questions.

> 'I do not believe in the doctrine of the greatest good for the greatest number. It means … that in order to achieve the supposed good of fifty-one percent, the interest of forty-nine may be, or rather should be, sacrificed. It is a heartless doctrine and has done harm to humanity.'
>
> Mahatma Gandhi (1909)

1 What did Gandhi mean? Why is the doctrine 'heartless'?
2 What kind of harm was he referring to? Can you think of any decisions or laws that were supported by a majority in the past but now might be considered unjust? Why has opinion changed?
3 What are the alternatives? Should the majority always prevail?

3 Read the sentences. Write the words in bold next to their definitions below.

1 We won't know the **outcome** of these decisions for at least a year.
2 Many of us still have very serious **reservations** about this plan.
3 A lot of different people have a **stake** in this project, so it will not be easy to please all of them.
4 We need to **resolve** this dispute or we'll never make a decision.
5 This proposal is a **hybrid** of several earlier proposals.
6 After discussing the matter for several hours, we reached a **consensus** on how to move forward.
7 The important advances he has made in the field will be his **legacy** to society.
8 The people in this community feel a real sense of **ownership** of the new park. They worked hard to make it a success, and they look after it.

a _____ (n) result
b _____ (n) a generally accepted opinion or decision
c _____ (n) something you do that becomes part of history and remains after you are gone
d _____ (n) attitude of accepting responsibility for something
e _____ (v) to solve or end a problem or difficulty
f _____ (n) something that is a combination of two or more things
g _____ (n) a personal interest or investment
h _____ (n pl) doubts

WHILE LISTENING

4 🔊 8.4 Listen to the discussion. Use the table to take notes on what the students say about the two approaches to decision-making.

voting	consensus building

5 Work with a partner. Use your notes to review the discussion. Complete the tasks.

1 Describe the issue that the class was trying to resolve.
2 Report the outcome of the first decision-making process: voting.
3 Briefly report the outcome of the second decision-making process: consensus-building.

6 🔊 8.4 Listen again. Focus on the processes in the two different approaches. Think about these questions as you listen and add details to your notes in Exercise 4.

LISTENING FOR DETAIL

- In what ways are they similar? In what ways are they different?
- Who participated? Can you describe their participation?
- How did the participants feel about the two processes at the end?

7 Work with a partner. Using your notes, give an oral summary of one process to your partner. Listen as your partner gives an oral summary of the other process. Did you both include the most important details?

SUMMARIZING

POST-LISTENING

8 Work in small groups. Discuss the questions.

MAKING INFERENCES

1 Why do you think the students responded differently to the two processes?

2 Why do you think the teacher wanted his students to participate in this activity? What was his goal?

9 Work in groups of three. Complete the tasks.

1 In Japan, most large businesses make decisions by consensus. What do you think the advantages and disadvantages of this are in the global business environment?

2 Does your country have a jury system? Are jury systems all the same internationally? Go online to find out more. Then discuss the question below.

- Do you think a jury should operate using the first approach the class used or the second?

DISCUSSION

10 Work in a small group. Use ideas from Listening 1 and Listening 2 to answer the following questions.

SYNTHESIZING

1 How do you think a bad apple would affect the consensus-building process?

2 Do you think it is easier to deal with a bad apple in a group that uses consensus-building or majority-rule to make decisions?

3 How could group dynamics affect the decision-making process of a jury or other group that has to make a judgment (for example the best film or piece of art in an exhibition)? Do you think these groups decide by consensus? Explain your answer.

4 Which form of decision-making would you prefer to use in groups or organizations where you are a member? Give reasons for your answer.

SPEAKING

CRITICAL THINKING

At the end of this unit, you are going to do the Speaking task below.

> Participate in a consensus-building decision-making task. Your goal is to choose one of three options for future food-service operations at your university.

Evaluating options

Important business decisions require a careful analysis of the pros (benefits) and cons (costs) of every option. A formal method for doing this is called a *cost-benefit analysis*.

The benefits of biking to work, for example, might include a saving in transport expenses and some good exercise; costs might include longer commute times and the discomfort of riding in bad weather.

In considering options, also consider the 'winners and losers'. Which people will get the greatest benefit from each of the options? Who will suffer the greatest costs?

 **REMEMBER**

1 Work in small groups. Discuss the questions.

  1 What are the dining options on your campus or near your college/university?

  2 Do you ever eat at fast-food restaurants? If so, what do you like about them? If not, why not?

  3 Describe your experiences of eating in 'institutional' dining facilities (those found in hospitals, schools, etc.).

2 Listen as a university administrator describes each of the possible dining options at the campus Student Centre. Take notes as you listen.

1  8.5 DINESCO (a commercial food services provider)

_____

_____

_____

2 🔊 8.6 Sharzad (a fast-food restaurant)

_____

_____

_____

3 🔊 8.7 Unihub (a café run by students studying Hospitality and Catering)

_____

_____

_____

3 Work with a partner on a cost-benefit analysis of the three options. Who would be the winners and who would be the losers in each option? Compare your notes in Exercise 2 and complete the table.

	DINESCO	Sharzad	Unihub
costs			
benefits			
winners			
losers			

4 Imagine that you go to this university. Which option would be best for you? For the community? Are the two answers the same? Decide on your position. Write a position statement in which you say which option you support and why.

_____

_____

STEPS FOR CONSENSUS BUILDING

The consensus-building process is one type of formal, structured process for making decisions. It has a sequence of formal steps. Depending on the goal of the project, some steps might be given more attention than others.

step 1: Describe the situation in objective terms. Generate key questions that must be answered in the process. State the needs and concerns of all participants.

step 2: Generate ideas. Accept everything at this point in the process. Avoid criticizing others' ideas.

step 3: Discuss the costs and benefits of each idea. Discuss consequences of each option for all the stakeholders.

step 4: Summarize what has been discussed so far. Look for points of agreement and try to synthesize them to create a preliminary proposal.

step 5: Check for concerns and reservations members of the group may have.

step 6: Amend your proposal(s) to accommodate concerns or objections.

step 7: Summarize the proposal that is on the table. Test for agreement among the group members. (See Testing for agreement, below.)

step 8: If there are no blocks, finalize your agreement, dealing with reservations and concessions if possible. If there are blocks, return to step 3 and repeat the consensus-building process.

1 Work with a partner or in small groups. Review each of the steps for consensus-building. Discuss any questions you have.

Testing for agreement

During the testing for agreement stage, participants have a range of options:

- **block:** 'I have a basic disagreement with the proposal and I cannot support it in its current form. I propose that we reconsider a crucial aspect of the proposal …'
- **stand aside:** 'I don't support this proposal for these reasons … However, I understand why others do, so I will stand aside and let the process continue.'
- **reservation:** 'I have some doubts about this project. I am willing to let it go forward, but I would like us to consider one small change.'
- **agreement:** 'I fully support the proposal.'

2 🔊 8.5 The students in Listening 2 followed the consensus-building process outlined in the Explanation box. Listen to the discussion again and identify some of the steps in their description.

COLLABORATIVE LANGUAGE: SUGGESTION AND CONCESSION

SKILLS

When building consensus around a decision, the original proposal is often changed or amended to satisfy all parties. Participants should offer suggestions for changes in a respectful, non-aggressive way.

How about / What about … ?
Let's try / think about / consider …
Why don't we try / think about / consider … ?
What do you suggest/propose?

Participants also need to be open to changes in their own positions for the good of the group or project. They can do this graciously by acknowledging objections, conceding points or offering conditions that would make the idea acceptable.

I understand that this proposal includes things that you don't like, but would you be willing to support it anyway?
I would be willing to support this proposal if we add something for vegetarians.

Collaborative language often refers to shared goals, values and interests. It may also include the use of *we, us, our* and *let's*.

Let's think about this in a different way …
None of us wants to stand in the way of progress, do we?

3 Work with a partner. Read Scenario 1 and the list of responses (a–g) from a consensus-building process.

1 Decide if each response is:
- block
- reservation
- stand aside
- agreement

2 Circle the responses that use collaborative language.

Scenario 1

Your group is trying to decide where to place a facility for former prisoners who were convicted of non-violent crimes. The former prisoners will live in the facility for six months under supervision before they are released. At the testing-for-agreement stage, the proposal is to place the facility at the edge of town in an old school that has not been used for six years.

---

a I don't like this, but I recognize that it is a difficult decision for all of us in the community. Since everyone else seems to agree, I will not oppose it.
stand aside

b This proposal makes no sense at all and I cannot support it.
_____

c I still think this is a dangerous proposal. Perhaps if we could consider some additional security measures, it would be more acceptable to the whole group.
_____

d I think this is the best possible solution to a difficult problem. How can we make it more acceptable for the rest of you?
_____

e This is a solid and sensible plan and I say we should move forward.
_____

f How about we consider an alternative site – one a little farther from the centre of population? This site is just too close to our homes for me to feel comfortable supporting it.
_____

g I don't like this proposal at all, but I will abstain (= not vote).
_____

4 Work with a new partner. Read Scenario 2. Write a response of each type to the proposal. Use collaborative language.

> **Scenario 2**
> Currently, your school has a very harsh policy regarding plagiarism. Any student found guilty of plagiarism is expelled from the school. Administrators want to adopt a new policy that gives students a chance to learn and change. The first offence would result in a failing grade for that assignment, plus the student would have to attend a seminar on how to avoid plagiarism. The second offence would result in a failing grade in the class. The third offence would result in expulsion from the school.

1 block: _____

_____

2 stand aside: _____

_____

3 reservation: _____

_____

4 agreement: _____

_____

5 Work in small groups. Discuss the scenarios in Exercises 3 and 4. Which position would you actually take for each scenario? Why?

SPEAKING TASK

> Participate in a consensus-building decision-making task. Your goal is to choose one of three options for future food-service operations at your university.

PREPARE

1 Review the table in Critical thinking, Exercise 3 on page 183, about the costs and benefits of each proposal and the winners and losers for each proposal.

2 Review the position you chose in Critical thinking, Exercise 4:

- What are the main arguments for the proposal that you support?
- What concessions would you be willing to make?
- What arguments do you think others will make for the other two proposals?
- What will you say in response to them?
- What could make the other two proposals more attractive to you?

3 Refer to the Task checklist as you prepare for your discussion.

TASK CHECKLIST	✔
Start with a position statement.	
Offer a cost-benefit analysis of the proposal that you support.	
Use collaborative language as you discussed the ideas of other students.	
Anticipate and respond to competing proposals.	
Participate appropriately in the consensus-building process.	

PRACTISE

4 With a partner, practise presenting the reasons that favour your proposal, responses to the arguments that you anticipate from others, and suggestions or concessions that you would be willing to make. Make sure you include collaborative language. Give each other feedback.

DISCUSS

5 Follow the steps for consensus-building (Preparation for speaking, page 184) to carry out the speaking task. The facilitator (your teacher) will begin the discussion by describing the general situation.

6 When you have finished the task and made your decision, discuss the questions below as a group.

- Was the process successful? Explain your answer.
- Why do you think it was (un)successful?
- What do you think of the consensus-building process? Would you use it again? Why / Why not?

OBJECTIVES REVIEW

1 Check your learning objectives for this unit. Write *3*, *2* or *1* for each objective.

3 = very well   2 = well   1 = not so well

I can ...

watch and understand a video about a cooperation deal between two airlines.   _____

understand anecdotes and proverbs used to illustrate larger ideas.   _____

evaluate opinions.   _____

use *wh-* clefts.   _____

use collaborative language to make suggestions and concessions.   _____

participate in a consensus-building decision-making task.   _____

2 Use the *Unlock* Digital Workbook for more practice with this unit's learning objectives.

WORDLIST		
bully (v, n)	hybrid (n) ⊙	resentment (n)
consensus (n) ⊙	legacy (n) ⊙	reservations (n pl)
constructive (adj) ⊙	outcome (n) ⊙	resolve (v) ⊙
counteract (v)	ownership (n) ⊙	stake (n) ⊙
defuse (v)	perception (n) ⊙	
dynamics (n pl) ⊙	prevail (v)	

⊙ = high-frequency words in the Cambridge Academic Corpus

LEARNING OBJECTIVES	IN THIS UNIT YOU WILL ...
Watch and listen	watch and understand a video about an anthropomimetic robot.
Listening skill	listen for examples; supporting speculation.
Critical Thinking	provide supporting detail.
Grammar	use hypothetical future.
Speaking skills	leave and return to the topic; ask for clarification and confirmation.
Speaking task	take part in an informal discussion.

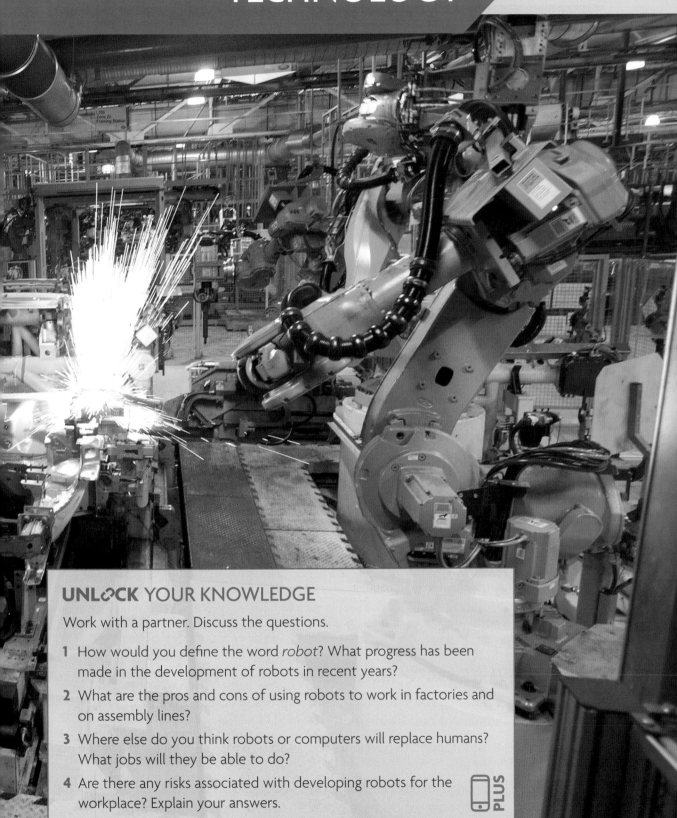

TECHNOLOGY

UNL*O*CK YOUR KNOWLEDGE

Work with a partner. Discuss the questions.

1 How would you define the word *robot*? What progress has been made in the development of robots in recent years?

2 What are the pros and cons of using robots to work in factories and on assembly lines?

3 Where else do you think robots or computers will replace humans? What jobs will they be able to do?

4 Are there any risks associated with developing robots for the workplace? Explain your answers.

PLUS

WATCH AND LISTEN

  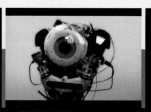 

PREPARING TO WATCH

ACTIVATING YOUR
KNOWLEDGE

1 Work with a partner. Discuss the questions.

1 What is the meaning of *artificial intelligence* (AI)?
2 What human tasks do robots excel at?
3 What human abilities are difficult to replicate in robots?

PREDICTING
CONTENT
USING VISUALS

2 You are going to watch a video about an unusual robot. Before you watch, look at the photos and discuss the questions with a partner.

1 Is the robot shown in the pictures different from other robots that you have seen? If yes, how is it different? If no, where have you seen similar robots?
2 The robot in the pictures is an *anthropomimetic* robot, which means that it mimics the human body. In what ways is it human-like?
3 The robot in the picture has no skin or flesh. What does this suggest about the specific aspects of human ability the scientists are trying to replicate in this robot?

GLOSSARY

mimic (v) in science, to copy or imitate another living thing or the way that they behave

anthropomimetic (adj) in robotics, human-like in senses, behaviour, movement and interaction

condition (v) to train or influence a person or an animal so that they do a particular thing without thinking about it

draughts (n) a game for two people, each with twelve circular pieces that they move on a board with black and white squares

---

WHILE WATCHING

UNDERSTANDING
MAIN IDEAS

3 ▶ Watch the video and check your predictions in Exercise 2. Which statement best expresses the main idea of the video?

a Anthropomimetic robots will be able to replace humans in a variety of jobs.
b In order to replicate human intelligence, robots need a human-like body.
c Until now, robots have not been able to mimic human movements.

4 ▶ Watch the video again. Answer the questions.

1 What is the importance of a body in creating AI?

_____

2 What parts of the robot's body resemble the human body?

_____

3 How does creating human-like robot help scientists understand human intelligence?

_____

4 In what ways were the first robots different from the human-like robots?

_____

5 What type of tasks were difficult for the first robots to perform? Why?

_____

_____

UNDERSTANDING DETAIL

5 Read the sentences from the video (1–5). Choose the best synonym (a–c) for each word or phrase in bold.

1 Our physical form actually **helps shape** the way we think.
   a influences   b understands   c controls
2 This is an **extraordinary** piece of engineering.
   a typical   b amazing   c strange
3 How does it help in actually getting **insight into** intelligence?
   a increases in   b understanding of c sympathy for
4 Human intelligence simply cannot be **divorced** from the human body.
   a linked   b imitated   c separated

WORKING OUT MEANING FROM CONTEXT

6 Work with a partner. Discuss the questions.

1 The presenter says that: 'the hunt for AI has ended up on an alternative path'. What does he mean by *an alternative path*?
2 Based on what you saw in the video, how close do you think scientists are to creating human-like intelligence?

MAKING INFERENCES

DISCUSSION

7 Work with a partner. Discuss the questions.

1 What different reasons can you think of for scientists wanting to create human-like machines?
2 Do you agree with the scientist when he says that 'human intelligence simply cannot be divorced from the human body'?
3 What do you think would happen in wider society if scientists actually managed to create a human-like machine?

LISTENING

PREPARING TO LISTEN

UNDERSTANDING
KEY VOCABULARY

1 Read the definitions. Use the correct form of the words in bold to complete the sentences below.

> **confronted with** (phr v) to be in a difficult situation or to be shown something which may cause difficulties
>
> **constitute** (v) to make up a proportion of something
>
> **disposable income** (n phr) the money that is left over after you have paid your bills that you can spend as you wish
>
> **peer** (n) a person who is the same age or has the same social position as other people in a group
>
> **rational** (adj) based on facts and not affected by emotions or imagination
>
> **related to** (phr v) connected
>
> **reluctant** (adj) not willing to do something and therefore slow to do it
>
> **verify** (v) to prove something is true, or to do something to discover if it is true

1 We tried to _____ that the report was accurate, but there wasn't enough data available.
2 Many school head teachers were _____ to buy the new interactive whiteboards because of their high price.
3 Men _____ 80% of the buyers of this product.
4 It doesn't seem _____ to be afraid of the internet – it cannot hurt anybody!
5 Many people are influenced by the opinions and behaviour of their _____ .
6 Most older people have concerns _____ to the impact of technology on younger people.
7 We are continually _____ a wider and wider array of attempts to steal our data.
8 Young professionals without children often have _____ to spend on fashion and leisure.

PREDICTING
CONTENT
USING VISUALS

2 You are going to listen to a lecture about how people in society respond to new technology. Before you listen, work with a partner. Look at the graph on page 195 and answer the questions.

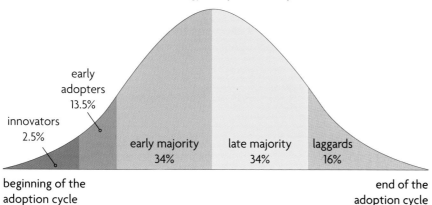

The technology adoption life cycle

1 What does the graph show?
2 Which group of people are the first to adopt a new technology? Which are the last?
3 Which group of people might agree with these statements?
   'I only change when there's no other choice.'
   'I'll try anything once!'
   'I'll only try something new once it's fully established.'
4 What do you think some of the characteristics of *laggards* are?

WHILE LISTENING

3 ◀ 9.1 Listen to the lecture and take notes on the main ideas. Use a table to organize your ideas. Leave a column for examples and details.

LISTENING FOR MAIN IDEAS

4 Review your notes from Exercise 3 and circle the five main ideas (a–h) that you heard. There are three ideas which are not mentioned in the lecture. Make any necessary changes to your notes.

a The introduction of new technology can cause negative feelings in some people.
b The invention of weaving machines helped craftsmen improve their products.
c Fear of technology is not always irrational; sometimes people are right to be afraid.
d Historically, governments have often played a crucial role in spreading new technology.
e People tend to believe bad things they hear about new inventions without checking them.
f Laggards refuse to use technology because of negative experiences with technology in their pasts.
g Innovators and early adopters are crucial to the acceptance of new technology by society.
h Peers have a significant influence over an individual's decision to use, or not use, new technology.

Listening for examples

Speakers may use a variety of linking expressions to introduce examples, such as:

For instance, ...
Let's look at an example ...
To illustrate the point ...
The examples demonstrate that ...
It is an example of ...

However, speakers do not always introduce examples so explicitly. Listening for adverbials of time and place can also help you to identify examples.

At the turn of the century, ...
In the North, ...

Note that examples may sometimes be given before the main idea is explicitly stated.

5 🔊 9.1 Listen to the lecture again and complete your notes. Add examples and details to the table you created in Exercise 3. Then compare your notes with a partner and make any necessary changes.

6 Use your notes from Exercises 3–5 to answer the questions.

1 What does the example of *computer phobia* illustrate?

2 What happened to the craftsmen in the late eighteenth and early nineteenth centuries?

3 How did the government react to the workers' protests?

4 What kind of fear is exemplified by the example of these craftsmen?

5 What did some people in the 1820s think of travelling by train?

6 What does the train example illustrate?

7 What technology was believed to cause cancer in the late 1990s?

8 What differentiates normal feelings from irrational feelings according to the speaker?

9 What do innovators and early adopters have in common?

10 When is the tipping point in the adoption of technology?

POST-LISTENING

7 Answer the questions. Use your notes or script 9.1 on pages 264–265 to help you. Then compare your answers with a partner.

1 The lecturer expresses some bias when describing the groups of people mentioned in her lecture. Which group of people is she biased against? Which groups of people is she biased towards?

_____

_____

2 Which words, expressions and statements used by the speaker show bias?

_____

_____

3 The lecturer implies that all *laggards* are technophobes. Do you agree with her opinion?

_____

_____

PRONUNCIATION FOR LISTENING

SKILLS

Connected speech: elision

In spoken English, some sounds are often omitted (elided) for ease of pronunciation.

Awareness of these lost sounds can make it easier to distinguish the words that are being said when listening.

Elision often occurs in words with:
- unstressed vowels (schwa).
  during the nineteenth cent~u~ry   many people believed
- consonants /t/ and /d/ when they appear in clusters (groups of two or more). Note that if the consonant begins a stressed syllable it cannot be elided.
  by skilled craf~t~smen   to ignore scientific fac~t~s

Elision also occurs with consonant clusters across word boundaries:
- when a word ends with /t/ or /d/ and the following word begins with a consonant.
  firs~t~ wave of resentment   tha~t~ time
- when a word ends with a consonant and the following word begins with an unstressed /h/.
  But this ~h~as not always been the case.   as you might ~have~ guessed

8 🔊 9.2 Listen to the excerpts. Underline the sounds which are omitted.

1 An irrational fear which is often unfounded and based on hearsay.
2 Many people refused to get on the train.
3 Scientists have refuted these claims.
4 Any new technology will be accompanied with a great deal of anxiety.

9 🔊 9.3 Listen and complete the sentences with one word in each gap.

1 The Industrial Revolution sparked the first wave of _____ _____ new technology.
2 Many specialized _____ were _____ during the nineteenth century.
3 These speculations had no scientific _____ .
4 Similar accusations _____ been levelled at modern technologies.
5 They're usually the _____ _____ adopt new technology.
6 Not all people are _____ _____ _____ new technology.
7 They're more likely to make an _____ _____ .

DISCUSSION

10 Work with a partner. Discuss the questions.

1 Look at the graph on page 195 again. Which group of adopters do you think you belong to? Why?
2 What advice would you give to workers who lose their jobs due to mechanization?

⊙ LANGUAGE DEVELOPMENT

NEGATIVE PREFIXES

Using adjectives with negative prefixes: *ir-*, *im-*, *un-*, *il-*, and *in-* demonstrates a wider vocabulary range than if you form negatives with *not* + adjective. Adjectives with negative prefixes make your speech more concise and effective. Their use creates a positive impression on listeners in more formal contexts such as presentation and interviews.

These examples demonstrate feelings that are **not rational**, in that they are based not on research, but on rumours. (less concise)

These examples demonstrate **irrational** feelings in that they're not based on research, but on rumours. (more concise)

Skilled workers were replaced by labourers who were **not skilled** and only had to know how to operate the machines. (less concise)

Skilled workers were replaced by **unskilled** labourers who only had to know how to operate the machines. (more concise)

1 Work with a partner. Discuss the meaning of each adjective in the table below. Check your answers in a dictionary.

il-	illegal, illegible, illiterate, illogical
im-	immobile, immoral, imperfect, impersonal, implausible
ir-	irrational, irreplaceable, irreversible, irrevocable
in-	inconsiderate, indispensable, inefficient, insignificant, insufficient
un-	unavoidable, undesirable, unproductive, unscrupulous, unsustainable

2 Replace the words in bold in the sentences with an adjective with the same meaning from the table in Exercise 1 (in the correct position). More than one answer may be possible.

1 Some people claim that replacing skilled jobs with mechanized production was **morally wrong**.
2 I find the idea that there is a link between mobile technology and cancer **hard to believe**.
3 The meeting was **not very useful**; we did not make any decisions or reach any meaningful conclusion.
4 Human creativity is not **something than can be substituted**.
5 Developing artificial intelligence (AI) may reduce people's motivation to work; that would **not** be **a welcome outcome**.
6 Innovators and early adopters are **very important** in the diffusion cycle of new technology.
7 Most technology-related phobias are **not based on logical reasoning**.
8 The rise of music streaming services has caused damage to the CD industry **that cannot be reversed**.
9 I don't like talking to automated customer support; it is **missing the human touch**.
10 The speed with which digital technology is taking over our lives is **not something which should be allowed to continue**.

PLUS

3 Write four sentences about technology using adjectives from the table in Exercise 1. Then compare your sentences with a partner.

1 _____
   _____
2 _____
   _____
3 _____
   _____
4 _____
   _____

HYPOTHETICAL FUTURE

Use hypothetical future forms to describe a possible future scenario, for example, to describe the consequences of future developments in technology and science.

To talk about the hypothetical future use *would, could* (for possibility, not ability), or *might* in the main clause.

Use past tenses in any dependent clauses.

The use of driverless cars **might not be** sustainable whilst there **were** millions of human drivers looking for jobs.

Once human-like robots **were granted** human rights, there **would be** no way to turn back the clock.

It **would be** difficult to live in a world where there **were** no prospects for gainful employment.

Whatever we **did**, it **would be** impossible to stop once we **had reached** the tipping point of AI adoption.

Without expert knowledge of how the robots **worked**, we **would not be able to** shut them down.

One day it **might be** possible that highly intelligent robots **could take over** skilled jobs.

4 Rewrite the statements to make them refer to a hypothetical future.

1 People whose jobs are given to robots struggle to find a place in society.

_____

_____

2 Even if they look human, they cannot think like us.

_____

_____

3 Once robots take over the AI industry, they will create super-intelligent robots.

_____

_____

4 While robots keep evolving, human cognitive skills gradually diminish.

_____

_____

5 It is difficult for young people to find part-time jobs because they have been filled by robots.

_____

_____

6 How people spend the free time created by the widespread use of AI will be determined by how much disposable income they have.

_____

_____

5 Imagine a future world where all motor vehicles were driven by AI. Write three sentences. Then compare your sentences with a partner.

1 _____
_____

2 _____
_____

3 _____
_____

4 _____
_____

5 _____
_____

PREPARING TO LISTEN

UNDERSTANDING KEY VOCABULARY

1 Read the sentences. Write the words in bold next to their definitions below.

1 It would be great to have a machine to perform **mundane** tasks, such as cleaning up the kitchen, opening mail, and paying bills.

2 Many more jobs would be **at stake** if robots with human capabilities became cheaper to produce.

3 The aim is to develop a robot with basic **dexterity**; one that can button a shirt or tie shoelaces.

4 The impact of technology on the labour market has been both deep and **pervasive**.

5 I can't explain how I knew that this would work out well – I suppose it was **intuition**.

6 He shows a lot of **compassion** for animals; he volunteers at the local animal shelter and he is a vegetarian.

7 The lecturer asked the student to **elaborate** on the point she had made.

8 The programme can **mimic** the cognitive processes of the human mind, but it cannot think for itself.

a _____ (v) to explain or give more detail about something that you have said

b _____ (phr) in a situation where something valuable may be lost

c _____ (n) the ability to perform an action or actions skilfully with your hands

d _____ (adj) very ordinary and therefore not interesting

e _____ (adj) present and noticeable everywhere

f _____ (n) the ability to understand or know something immediately, based on your feelings rather than facts

g _____ (v) in science, to copy or imitate another living thing or the way that they are or behave

h _____ (n) a strong feeling of sympathy for someone or something suffering and a wish to help them

PLUS

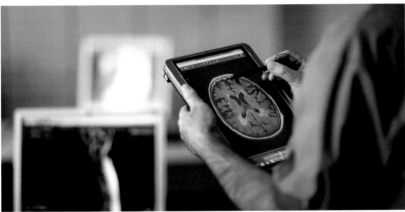

2 You are going to listen to a university seminar about computers and robots replacing human jobs. Work with a partner. Look at the photographs above and answer the questions.

PREDICTING
CONTENT
USING VISUALS

1 As a restaurant owner, what would the benefits of using a robot waiter be? What do you think some of the limitations of robot waiters might be?

2 How would you feel about hospital staff using AI to analyze your symptoms and diagnose your conditions?

3 Make a list of jobs that can be performed by computers or robots today.

_____

_____

_____

3 🔊 9.4 Listen to the introduction to the seminar. Answer the questions.

1 What jobs does the speaker mention that are done by robots and computers?

_____

_____

_____

2 Are any of these similar to your answers to question 4 in Exercise 2?

WHILE LISTENING

4 🔊 9.5 Listen to the seminar. Match the speakers (1–3) to the topics they talk about (a–f).

1 Faiz _____ _____   2 Enrique _____ _____   3 Ayşe _____ _____

a an example of a job that is likely to be replaced by droids
b the distinction between graduate jobs and other skilled jobs
c the limitations on robots in most factories
d zero net job loss from the impact of AI
e jobs that are unlikely to be replaced by droids
f an explanation of AI

5 🔊 9.5 Listen to the seminar again and make detailed notes.

6 Use your notes in Exercise 5 to answer the questions. Then compare your answers with a partner.

1 What type of factory jobs have been replaced by robots?
_____

2 What is the difference between robots and AI?
_____

3 What is an intelligent robot? Why aren't they widely used?
_____

4 What kinds of professional jobs are being replaced by droids now, or are likely to be replaced in the future?
_____

5 What kinds of jobs are least likely to be replaced? What sorts of skills or qualities do these jobs require?
_____

POST-LISTENING

Supporting speculation

In a discussion or presentation, speakers may speculate about what might happen in the future. When you listen, it is important to distinguish between occasions when speakers are just guessing and when they are supporting their speculation with currently known facts, expert opinions, and examples. You can be more confident about relying on speakers' speculations when they are supported.

We'll start our studies and then the jobs will disappear! (speculation)
They (robots) can crawl and run, and pick up injured soldiers. (support)
So, it's possible that in the future, all robots might have the same level of dexterity as humans. (speculation)

7 🔊 9.6 Listen to some speculations from the discussion. Take notes on the support that each speaker provides for their speculation.

1 In the future, AI will threaten jobs which require thinking skills.

_____

2 These machines are … and frankly not in very wide use. And I don't imagine that will change any time soon.

_____

3 There won't be any jobs for any of us! I mean maybe there'll be some jobs, but not enough for all of us.

_____

4 I don't think things will really be so different than in the past.

_____

5 Although jobs in any industry may be vulnerable to advances in technology, skilled manual work is less vulnerable than the analytic jobs we …

_____

6 Jobs that involve creativity and compassion, like teaching, medicine, or nursing, will be pretty safe. I think.

_____

8 Work in small groups. Compare notes on the speculations in Exercise 7. What kind of support did each speaker provide (facts, expert opinions, examples)?

DISCUSSION

9 Work with a partner. Use ideas from Listening 1 and Listening 2 to answer the following questions.

SYNTHESIZING

1 Should we try to protect human jobs from further automation? If so, why? What could be done? If not, why not?

2 Do you think that our acceptance of AI has to go through a process similar to the innovation adoption life cycle? If so, which jobs will take the longest to get through the cycle? If not, why not?

3 Fully automated shops and fast-food restaurants, that is, without humans, are already appearing. Do you think you are likely to be an early adopter of this type of commerce, or would you resist adopting it? Give reasons for your answer.

SPEAKING

CRITICAL THINKING

At the end of this unit, you are going to do the speaking task below.

> Have a group discussion about the future of specific professions. Consider the likelihood that these jobs will be replaced by an AI program by 2040.

ANALYZE

1 Read the opinions about developing AI. Do you agree (✔) or disagree (✘)? Why? Compare your ideas with a partner.

1 Even if droids could make medical evaluations and diagnoses, they should not act as doctors. _____

2 Robots might evolve so much that there would be no need for human engineers to maintain them. They would create their own super-intelligent robots and take over the world. _____

3 We should not be afraid of robots; they are very useful. _____

4 Developing droids and robots that can do human tasks is unwise; if we continue, there will be no jobs left for us in the future. _____

5 If robots had emotions like humans, they'd need laws to protect them. _____

6 Robots can never completely replace humans. _____

7 People will not accept the use of droids and robots in some jobs. _____

SKILLS

Providing supporting detail

When speakers present ideas or facts without supporting details, listeners may not be convinced that they are true or plausible. To make sure that your arguments come across clearly, always develop your ideas by adding supporting details, that is, details that are clearly connected to your argument and make it stronger. These may include examples, facts, statistics, research results, or statements by experts.

APPLY

2 The ideas in Exercise 1 are opinions; they are not well-developed or supported. Work with a partner and add supporting details to each idea.

3 Decide on a profession you would like to investigate and talk about. You may select one from the list below, or come up with one of your own. Do some research on the skills that the job requires (e.g. creativity, dexterity, etc.), the future outlook for the job, and whether the job, or some aspects of the job, are likely to be replaced by AI. If so, when is this replacement likely to happen? In the near or distant future?

- home plumber
- dentist
- graphic designer
- civil engineer
- chef

- pharmacist
- bank clerk
- nurse
- artist
- firefighter

- software developer
- lorry driver
- HR manager
- journalist
- salesperson in a shop

4 Add notes about why you think this job is (un)likely to be replaced by AI. Write a supporting detail for each of the points you will present to support your claim.

5 Work in small groups with other students. Evaluate each other's points and suggest additional details if necessary.

PREPARATION FOR SPEAKING

LEAVING AND RETURNING TO THE TOPIC

When you give a presentation, you will occasionally have to go off-topic, perhaps because someone asks a question, you sense your audience is not following, or perhaps you suddenly remember something you need to explain. It is important to mark these digressions (the times when you leave the topic). In other words, you need to inform your audience that you are leaving the main topic temporarily and to inform them again, when you return to it.

Digressing	Returning to the point
First let me take / let's take a moment	Anyway,
Oh, before I forget,	Returning to my point,
That reminds me,	Getting back to my point, / the topic,
Changing the topic for a moment,	Let's return to
Incidentally,	That brings us back to
Before I/we get to / discuss ... I just want to clarify something	As I said earlier,

1 🔊 **9.7** Listen to the sentences. Complete the gaps with the missing phrases.

1 OK, _____ before we start our discussion. Perhaps you've seen news stories about robots working in hotels, restaurants or hospitals. _____

2 For example, driverless taxis use AI but they are not robots. So, now _____ , with a focus on the broader issue of AI. _____

3 _____ , I just want to make sure I understand. So, you're not asking about robots in factories? _____

4 OK, _____ . Faiz has given us a good explanation of AI. Now, what about robots? _____

5 The impact of AI – minus the robotics, in contrast, has been far more pervasive. _____ Ayşe, what did you think of the predictions in the article? _____

6 Perhaps that's a bit dramatic, but I'm glad you mentioned that, because _____ . Are the jobs that require a university education most at risk? Ayşe? _____

📱 PLUS

2 Decide if each item in Exercise 1 is an example of digression or returning to the topic. Write *D* (digression) or *R* (returning) next to each sentence. Compare you notes with a partner.

ASKING FOR CLARIFICATION AND CONFIRMATION

SKILLS

During an informal discussion, you may want to ask speakers to explain or clarify their point.

Asking for clarification
What do you mean by saying that '**the impact of AI has been more pervasive**'?
What do you mean by saying that (repeat their words)?
Could you be more specific/explicit?
I want to make sure I understand …
I'm not sure I understand what you're getting at. Could you elaborate?

Confirming the meaning of others
To confirm you understood their idea correctly, paraphrase what they said.
Are you saying that **it is impossible to build a robot with emotions**? (paraphrase)
Are you saying that (paraphrase)?
Do you mean that (paraphrase)?

Clarifying or modifying your own meaning
What I mean is that **this is not going to happen anytime soon**. (clarification)
What I'm trying to say is (clarification)
What I mean to say is (clarification)
I mean, in other words, (clarification)

3 Work in pairs. Practise using these phrases to clarify your ideas and to ask for clarification. Student A will explain the concept and Student B will ask for clarification, then student A will clarify what he or she means. Take turns being Student A and Student B.

1 diffusion theory   3 financial liquidity   5 robots
2 laggard   4 AI

PLUS

PRONUNCIATION FOR SPEAKING

SKILLS

Assimilation in connected speech

Assimilation occurs when the sound at the end of a word changes so as to make it easier to pronounce the next word. In the following examples, the underlined consonants change their sound.

🔊 9.8 Listen.

Would you say that it's important?   They want you to believe that.
Do you mean that?   Don't you agree?

Notice the pronunciation of the letter *n* in *mean* before the letter *b*.

What do you mean by saying ... ? (/n/ changes to /m/)

4 🔊 9.9 Listen to these sentences. Underline all the consonants that change their sound. Work with a partner. Practise reading the questions.

Use assimilation where appropriate.

1 Could you be more specific?
2 What do you mean by saying that?
3 Don't you think that robots will soon be in every workplace?
4 Would you elaborate, please?
5 Wouldn't you see a robot doctor, if you needed medical attention?

SPEAKING TASK

▶ Have a group discussion about the future of specific professions. Consider the likelihood that these jobs will be replaced by an AI program by 2040.

PREPARE

1 Work in groups of four. Take turns telling your classmates about the profession you have chosen. Focus on the key skills in the profession and whether it would be possible for a droid to accomplish each of the skills. Ask the speaker for clarification if anything is unclear.

2 As a group, decide if you agree with each classmate's assessment of the profession's future. Make sure your arguments are well supported. Consider possible counter-arguments.

3 Refer to the Task checklist as you prepare for your discussion.

TASK CHECKLIST	✔
Present persuasive arguments for your point of view.	
Successfully refute counterarguments.	
Use negative adjectives with prefixes where possible.	
Use hypothetical future.	
Use signposts if you digressed from the topic and then returned to it.	
Ask for clarification and confirmation.	
Decide how to categorize each profession and explain your decision in terms of required skills.	

PRACTISE

4 Work in your groups. Practise presenting your arguments and refuting any counterarguments.

DISCUSS

5 Have a class discussion with the following goals:

   a Decide which skills determine the likelihood that a profession will be replaced by a droid.

   b Place each of the professions into one of three categories: Very likely / somewhat likely / unlikely to be replaced by 2040.

OBJECTIVES REVIEW

1 Check your learning objectives for this unit. Write *3, 2* or *1* for each objective.

3 = very well   2 = well   1 = not so well

I can ...

watch and understand a video about an anthropomimetic robot.   _____

listen for examples.   _____

identify supported speculation.   _____

provide supporting detail.   _____

use hypothetical future.   _____

leave and return to the topic.   _____

ask for clarification and confirmation.   _____

take part in an informal discussion.   _____

2 Use the *Unlock* Digital Workbook for more practice with this unit's learning objectives.

UNLOCK ONLINE

WORDLIST		
at stake (phr)	imperfect (adj) ⊙	mimic (v)
compassion (n)	impersonal (adj)	mundane (adj)
confronted with (phr v)	implausible (adj)	peer (n) ⊙
constitute (v) ⊙	inconsiderate (adj)	pervasive (adj) ⊙
dexterity (n)	indispensable (adj)	rational (adj) ⊙
disposable income (n)	inefficient (adj)	related (adj)
elaborate (v) ⊙	insignificant (adj) ⊙	reluctant (adj) ⊙
illegal (adj) ⊙	insufficient (adj) ⊙	unavoidable (adj)
illegible (adj)	intuition (n) ⊙	undesirable (adj)
illiterate (adj)	irrational (adj) ⊙	unproductive (adj)
illogical (adj)	irreplaceable (adj)	unscrupulous (adj)
immobile (adj)	irreversible (adj)	unsustainable (adj)
immoral (adj)	irrevocable (adj)	verify (v) ⊙

⊙ = high-frequency words in the Cambridge Academic Corpus

LEARNING OBJECTIVES	IN THIS UNIT YOU WILL ...
Watch and listen	watch and understand a video about language diversity.
Listening skill	note down follow-up questions while listening.
Critical thinking	ask appropriate and productive questions.
Grammar	use complex gerunds and infinitives.
Speaking skill	interrupt and handle questions.
Speaking task	conduct an in-depth semi-structured interview.

UNL⌖CK YOUR KNOWLEDGE

Work with a partner. Discuss the questions below.

1 What languages do you think are the most different from your first language? What are the differences?

2 In what ways does language reflect culture? Can we have culture without a language?

3 How has your first language changed in the last fifty years? Are there any words or expressions that your grandparents use that younger generations no longer use?

4 What are some reasons that languages change over time?

PLUS

WATCH AND LISTEN

PREPARING TO WATCH

ACTIVATING YOUR
KNOWLEDGE

1 Work with a partner. Discuss the questions.

1 In what ways are languages around the world similar? And in what ways are they different from each other?

2 Do people in your country speak one language, or are there different dialects? If so, what are the dialects? How are they different from the official language?

3 Is your language similar to any other languages that you know of? In what ways?

PREDICTING
CONTENT
USING VISUALS

2 You are going to watch a video about the history of languages. Before you watch, look at the photos and discuss the questions with a partner.

1 What words can you read on the diagrams? What do they have in common?

2 What do you think the diagrams show?

USING YOUR
KNOWLEDGE TO
PREDICT CONTENT

3 Work with a partner. Use your knowledge to answer the questions.

1 Sanskrit is a(n) _____ language.
   a dying   **b** ancient   **c** modern

2 English is a _____ language.
   a Romance   **b** Slavic   **c** Germanic

GLOSSARY

philologist (n) an academic who studies literary texts and written records

psycholinguist (n) an academic who studies the psychological aspects of language acquisition and use

Grimm (n) Jacob and Wilhelm Grimm were nineteenth-century German academics and philologists.

Germanic language (n) a language that belongs to, or is related to, the group of languages that includes German, English, and Swedish

Indo-European (adj) describing languages related to the group of European and Asian languages that are spoken in most of Europe and in parts of Asia which include English, French, Greek, Russian and Hindi

Proto-Indo-European (PIE) (n) the ancient language that linguists think Indo-European languages developed from, but there are no written records

WHILE WATCHING

4 ▶ Watch the video and check your predictions in Exercises 2 and 3.

5 ▶ Read the questions. Watch again and take notes. Then discuss the answers with a partner.

UNDERSTANDING MAIN IDEAS

1 What does Grimm's Law imply?

_____

2 Which language is the root of other Asian and European languages?

_____

3 According to the professor, what is the importance of language?

_____

6 ▶ Watch again. Complete each gap with a word from the video.

UNDERSTANDING DETAIL

Linguists noticed that there were similarities between many words in different languages despite $^{(1)}$_____ distances between their countries of origin. They believe these differences are not usually $^{(2)}$_____ . Grimm's Law shows that there are consonants that are related. For example, $^{(3)}$_____ in Latin, Greek, corresponds to $^{(4)}$_____ in Germanic languages. Linguists believe that these similarities derive from a Proto-Indo-European language which was used thousands of years ago. As time passed and people $^{(5)}$_____ across Europe and Asia, this language spread and evolved into many separate $^{(6)}$_____ which formed the basis of a large number of modern languages. Proto-Indo-European may not have been the first language that humans spoke, but it is the earliest one that we have found $^{(7)}$_____ for. Even though various European and Asian languages seem unrelated, they have a common $^{(8)}$_____ .

7 Work with a partner. Discuss the questions.

MAKING INFERENCES

1 What kind of evidence do you think we have of PIE? How do you think we know that there were earlier languages?

2 The professor says: 'Whatever we know, whatever we have done over the centuries, [it's] just based on language – on languages and language.' Can you explain what he means by this?

DISCUSSION

8 Work with a partner. Discuss the questions.

1 Do you agree that language is what distinguishes humans from other species? Why? / Why not?

2 What non-verbal forms of communication exist among humans? Are these similar or different around the world?

3 What do you think is the difference between a language and a dialect? What examples can you think of from your own region?

LISTENING

LISTENING 1

PREPARING TO LISTEN

1 Read the sentences. Write the words in bold next to their definitions below.

1 The translation was **incomprehensible**. I could not make any sense of it.
2 The **complexities** of Chinese dialects make them difficult for machines to translate.
3 In my French class, the teacher make us use French all the time. The use of English is **frowned upon**.
4 His argument was **vague**, so I asked for clarification.
5 This company has some **radically** new ideas about computer translation.
6 Even twenty years ago, the idea of automatic translation did not seem even **remotely** likely.
7 It's not always easy to **determine** which word in your language is the best equivalent to an English word.
8 Researchers have used **statistical** methods to trace the origins of the languages we use today.

a _____ (n pl) the features that make something difficult to understand or explain
b _____ (v) to discover the facts or truth about something
c _____ (adj) not clearly expressed, described, etc.
d _____ (adj) related to numbers and trends
e _____ (phr v) to disapprove of something
f _____ (adv) in a very slight way
g _____ (adj) impossible to understand
h _____ (adv) in a thorough way; completely

2 The excerpt from a travel blog on page 217 has been translated into two different languages using machine translation. It was then translated back into English. Read the English original and the two translations and answer the questions. Then work in small groups and compare your answers.

1 What do you think of the accuracy of the translations? Which sentences has the machine done the best job of translating?
2 Which individual translation mistake is the most misleading, in your opinion?
3 Which language seems more problematic for the translation machine? Why do you think that is?

English original

Things are on the up[1]. There's a lot of renovation going on, especially in Moscow. High-end cars like Porsches and Mercs accelerating with boy-racer[2] menace down city streets. English is spoken in most settings – it's not difficult to get by if you can speak English. People are friendly, helpful, smiley and care about you and each other. Being able to read the Cyrillic alphabet is a big bonus, especially when on foot around the city, with street signs and Metro stops. Carrying a table with Cyrillic/Roman letter equivalents helps, or being lucky enough to have a fluent travelling companion with you, as I do.

Machine translation from Russian

Things are on the rise[3]. There's a lot of renovation going on, especially in Moscow. High-quality cars like Porsches and Mercs **accelerating the boy-racer face down[4] city streets.** English is spoken in most **installations – it is not hard to get,** if you can speak in English. People are friendly, helpful, smiley and take care of you and with each other. Being able to read Cyrillic big bonus, especially when on foot around the city, with street signs and subway stops. **Carrying out** a table with Cyrillic/Roman letters **helps equivalents**, or be lucky enough to have a **free companion** with you, as I do.

Machine translation from Simplified Chinese

Things are up[5]. There are a lot of renovations, especially in Moscow. High-end cars such as Porsche and **Meyers accelerate the threat of boy racing with city streets**. English **can be used** in most environments – and if you can speak English, **it is not difficult to understand**. People are friendly, helpful, smiling and caring about you and each other. Being able to read the Cyrillic alphabet is **a great reward**, especially when **near the city, there are signs** and subway stations. Carrying the **Slavic**/Roman alphabet **forms helps**, or **fortunately is having a fluent companion with you, like me**.

[1]**on the up** (UK, idiom) currently improving in condition, for example, becoming more successful or wealthy

[2]**boy racer** (UK, n, informal) a young man who drives fast and aggressively in high-powered cars around the public roads for fun

[3]**on the rise** (phrase) currently increasing in amount, for example, unemployment, crime

[4]**face down** (phr v / adv) to defeat someone or something that is opposing you by being brave and strong / with the face or front turned towards the ground

[5]**something is up** (phr v) there is a problem or something unusual is happening

WHILE LISTENING

3 🔊 10.1 Listen to a university seminar about machine translation. Circle five challenges of machine translation discussed during the seminar.

a multiple meanings of vocabulary items
b translating between languages with different alphabets
c the need to understand the context to select the correct word equivalent
d the need to create an extremely large database
e translating from languages where nouns have gender
f the need to understand cultural and historical references
g dealing with different sentence structures across languages
h translating figurative language

4 🔊 10.1 Listen to the seminar again and answer the questions. Then compare your answers with a partner.

1 What examples are given of English words and expressions that have multiple meanings?

_____

2 What two types of meaning are mentioned by the student?

_____

3 What problems occurred when the student translated directions into Russian?

_____

4 How long have scientists been working on machine translation?

_____

5 What did the IBM scientists say about the challenge of machine translation?

_____

6 How does rule-based machine translation work?

_____

7 What is the 'statistical approach' in machine translation?

_____

8 How does the student use Google Translate?

_____

9 What examples are given of grammar differences that make machine translation difficult?

_____

10 What aspects of Chinese dialects cause problems when programming machine translators?

_____

Noting down follow-up questions

When you listen to a lecture or a seminar, you may not want to interrupt the speaker to ask questions. As you take notes, underline parts you don't fully understand, or write a question mark in the margin. It is also a good idea to quickly write down questions in the margin, so you don't forget. Listen to see if the speaker has answered your questions by the end of his or her turn. If you still need answers at the end of the speaker's turn, ask your questions then. Some speakers may prefer that you ask questions at the end of the lecture or seminar.

5 🔊 10.1 Listen to the seminar again and take notes. As you do, underline or make a note about anything you don't fully understand. After the lecture, review your notes and write three follow-up questions for the lecturer. Then work in small groups and discuss the questions.

TAKING NOTES ON DETAIL

1 _____

2 _____

3 _____

POST-LISTENING

6 🔊 10.2 Listen to two anecdotes told by the students during the seminar. Answer the questions.

MAKING INFERENCES

1 What's the main difference between these two students' use of translation programmes? Which is closest to your own use?

2 The student mentioned that his university does not approve of using machine translation. What do you think the university's reasons for that might be?

3 Why do you think the lecturer encourages the students to tell anecdotes?

7 Think of a personal anecdote related to machine translation. Work in small groups and tell your anecdotes. Do you have any similar experiences?

DISCUSSION

8 Work with a partner. Discuss the questions.

1 Do you use automatic translators? Are they effective? What aspects of your first language pose the greatest problems for them?

2 In what situations is accurate translation very important? What problems result from relying on machine translation? Are any of them potentially quite serious?

PHRASAL VERBS ABOUT COMMUNICATION

VOCABULARY

Phrasal verbs are a crucial part of English vocabulary. Their meanings can be transparent or idiomatic. One phrasal verb can have multiple meanings, depending on the context or the grammar. Because their meaning may be completely different from the meaning of the root verb, you should learn phrasal verbs as separate vocabulary items.

1 Read the definitions. Use the correct forms of the phrasal verbs in bold to complete the sentences. Write one word in each gap.

> **come across (as something)** to behave in a way that people believe that you have certain characteristics
> **come out with something** to say something unexpectedly or suddenly
> **get at something** to express something in a way that people find difficult to understand
> **get something across** to communicate an idea or a message successfully
> **pick up on something** to notice or understand something that is communicated directly or indirectly
> **talk somebody into / out of something** to persuade somebody to do / not to do something
> **talk somebody through something** to explain an idea, a plan, etc. to somebody

1 He didn't _____ _____ _____ their hints to change the subject and continued for some time.

2 You _____ _____ _____ some strange remarks sometimes. They can be hurtful to some people.

3 Using diagrams and graphics is a great way to _____ complicated information _____ to your audience.

4 Can you _____ me _____ your thesis proposal? What are your research questions and what methods will you use in this study?

5 He can _____ _____ as superficial, but telling jokes is his way of coping with the stress of speaking in a foreign language in front of an audience.

6 I tried to _____ him _____ taking Japanese classes with me, but he wasn't interested.

7 I really don't understand what you are _____ _____ . Can you explain it again please?

PLUS

2 Complete the sentences with your own ideas. Then compare your sentences with a partner.

1 I can usually pick up on _____ .
2 It is easy to talk me out of _____ .
3 I can come across as _____ .
4 When I want to get something across in a presentation,
  I _____ .

COMPLEX GERUNDS AND INFINITIVES

Gerunds phrases are clauses with verb + *ing* forms which are used as nouns in a sentence. The whole clause acts as a noun, not only the verb + *ing* form.

Asking students to work out the language rules on their own may not be feasible with complete beginners or small children.

Not being taught explicit information about rules may be frustrating for some students.

Having both **studied and taught** English gives you a lot of insight, I think.

Infinitives can be with or without *to* and have many uses. They can also form clauses that act as nouns. They appear most frequently as objects:

They didn't have time **to teach** me when I was little.

Some learners just want **to be given** the rules at the outset.

They are more likely **to have achieved** a high level of proficiency.

Gerunds and infinitives can be positive or negative, active or passive. We use the perfect forms to make it clear that the activity is complete and took place in the past. Infinitives also have continuous forms.

	active	passive
simple gerund	**Writing** letters is unusual these days.	Not **being accepted** into university was a great disappointment to me.
perfect gerund	I regret not **having read** more in English when I was a teenager.	**Having been interviewed** before was useful experience.
simple infinitive with *to*	I don't need a translation device **to understand** what they're saying.	Translation devices are not **to be used** during the exam.
perfect infinitive with *to*	You need **to have started** learning the language before you attend classes.	I would hate not **to have been chosen** for the team.
continuous infinitive with *to*	The translation machine seems **to be working** perfectly.	The translation app seems **to be being used** by students for their assignments.

3 Rewrite the two sentences in each item to create a single sentence. Replace the words in bold with a complex gerund formed from the first sentence. More than one answer is possible.

1 We didn't do any speaking activities. **It** had an obvious impact on our fluency. _____

_____

2 We didn't study any grammar. Despite **that**, we were remarkably competent communicators. _____

_____

3 I was not exposed to native speakers at school. **It** didn't really affect me. _____

_____

4 He travelled to different countries. **It** taught him the usefulness of online translation devices. _____

_____

4 Complete the sentences with a correct infinitive form of the verb in brackets. More than one answer may be possible.

1 We would have preferred _____ (not spend) so much time reading.

2 It is exciting _____ (live) in the UK while I am studying for my English exam.

3 Students would have liked _____ (give) more grammar practice.

4 I expected you _____ (finish) this essay by now.

5 Only paper dictionaries are _____ (use) during the language exams.

PREPARING TO LISTEN

1 Read the definitions. Use the correct form of the words in bold to complete the sentences below.

> **aptitude** (n) a natural ability or skill
>
> **coherent** (adj) well-structured and logical, and therefore easy to understand
>
> **discrepancy** (n) a difference between two things that should be the same
>
> **excel** (v) to be extremely good at something
>
> **explicit** (adj) clear and exact
>
> **frustrating** (adj) making you feel annoyed or less confident because you can not achieve something
>
> **grasp** (n) understanding of a subject or issue
>
> **lacking in** (adj) not having a quality

1 It can be very _____ if you can't speak a language after years of studying it.

2 There was a vast _____ between the exam results in these two classes.

3 This essay is not very _____ ; you need to link the ideas between the paragraphs.

4 My sister has always _____ in languages; she is fluent in four.

5 I have a good _____ of English grammar, but my listening skills are not so great.

6 A review found that the programme was _____ specific goals. It was not clear what students would learn.

7 The lecturer gave us _____ instructions on how to submit this assignment.

8 Some children show great _____ for languages from an early age.

2 You are going to listen to an interview with a student teacher of English as a Foreign Language. Before you listen, work with a partner and discuss the questions.

1 In your opinion, what makes a good language teacher?

2 What makes a successful language learner?

3 What are some advantages and disadvantages of learning English with a teacher who is a native speaker?

WHILE LISTENING

3 🔊 10.3 Listen to the interview. Complete the topics and subcategories column of the interview schedule below. Then compare your notes with a partner.

Interview schedule

Student teacher: Maya

topics and subcategories	notes / follow-up questions
1 _____	
a When did you start learning English? _____	
b Were your first teachers native speakers or non-native speakers? _native speakers_____	
c What did you think of your English teachers/lessons at school? _____ _____	Why not qualified?
d What was your experience of high school English lessons? _____ _____	
e Do you think that there is a difference between native speaker and non-native speaker teachers? _____ _____	
2 Beliefs about teaching English: **a** What kind of language teaching methods do you prefer? Why? _____ _____	Some methods not suitable for children? Motivation?
b How can you account for the discrepancy between high achievers and low achievers? _____ _____	

4 🔊 10.3 Read the follow-up questions added by the interviewer in the interview schedule. Listen to the interview again and answer the questions below. Then compare your answers with a partner.

What does Maya mean when she says …

1 her primary school teachers were not highly qualified?

_____

_____

2 asking students to work out the language rules on their own may not be feasible with complete beginners or small children?

_____

_____

3 there are two crucial factors that can account for the discrepancy in student achievement – that determine whether students who have the same classes and the same teachers are successful or not. These factors are aptitude and motivation?

_____

_____

POST-LISTENING

5 🔊 10.4 Listen to the excerpts from the interview (1–5). What information can you infer from Maya's statements? Choose the best answer (a–c).

MAKING INFERENCES

1 a Maya's school was quite wealthy.
  b Maya's school could not afford to hire a native speaker to teach English.
  c Volunteer organizations have improved education in Asia.
2 a The lessons were not well-thought out.
  b The lessons were very enjoyable.
  c The lessons were sometimes confusing.
3 a There were few differences between native and non-native speakers' lessons.
  b Universities in Malaysia have excellent teacher training programmes.
  c Training influences teaching style more than language background.
4 a Students are often unable to work out the rules themselves.
  b Students often expect English teachers to explain language rules.
  c Students enjoy detailed explanations from the teacher.
5 a Students who do not have a natural aptitude can still succeed.
  b Students who have a talent for language will never excel without motivation.
  c Motivation is one of many factors in learning a foreign language.

SKILLS

Connected speech: linking

In spoken English, words are usually linked together in connected speech. Sounds that combine easily are connected so that speech flows more easily. Awareness of this linking can make it easier to distinguish the words that are being said when listening.

The consonant sound at the end of a word often links with a vowel sound at the beginning of the next word.

They **weren't able** to translate their knowledge into interesting lessons.
t and *able* are linked so it could be heard as *table*.

The weak forms of *is* or *has* often link with surrounding words. Here, *is what* sounds like *swat*.

Motivation **is what** makes you read English in your free time.

---

6 🔊 10.5 Listen to the sentences from the interview for consonant–vowel linking and connect the letters. The number of links is given in brackets.

Check your answers with a partner.
1 I'd just like to pick up on what you were saying. (2)
2 I'd like to ask you if it's OK for me to record this interview, so I can use it in my research. (4)

7 🔊 10.6 Listen and complete the sentences with one word in each gap.

1 Another issue is that asking students to _____ _____ the language rules on their own may not be feasible with complete beginners or small children.
2 It _____ _____ my logical–mathematical intelligence.
3 It's _____ _____ the fun of learning for me.
4 For example, you need to understand what nouns and _____ _____ .
5 Let's _____ _____ to 'student achievement'.
6 Studies do show that students who have an interest in another language and its culture are more likely to _____ _____ _____ .

DISCUSSION

SYNTHESIZING

8 Work in small groups. Use ideas from Listening 1 and Listening 2 to answer the following questions.

1 Do you think that English is an easy or a difficult language to translate? What features of English are difficult or easy to translate?
2 What different factors motivate people to learn languages?
3 What aspects of learning a foreign language can be demotivating? Do machine translations help people to learn languages? Why / Why not?

SPEAKING

CRITICAL THINKING

At the end of this unit, you are going to do the speaking task below.

> Conduct an in-depth semi-structured interview with another student about learning English outside the classroom. You should find out what type of activities the student engages in outside the classroom to learn English. Which of these activities are the most useful and why?

Asking appropriate and productive questions

When preparing questions for a survey or an interview, it is important to ask questions that will give you useful information.

Yes/No questions: Avoid questions which only require the answer *yes* or *no*.
Have you been studying English long?
Instead, ask a *wh-* question.
How long have you been studying English?
If you use a yes/no question, make sure you ask follow-up questions.
Have you been studying English long?
How long have you been studying?

Leading questions: Avoid questions which assume something about your interviewee.
How many hours a day do you study English at home? (assumes the interviewee studies English outside of school hours, every day, at home)
Instead, ask a neutral question and then follow up.
Do you study English outside of class?
Where do you study? How many hours a week? / Why not?

Multiple questions: Avoid asking multiple questions at once.
Do you study English outside of class? If so, how many hours and where do you study?
Instead, ask your first question. Listen to the answer and then follow up.

Questions that are too technical: Avoid questions which include technical terminology.
Is your motivation to study English intrinsic or extrinsic?
Instead, ask a question that people who are not experts can understand.
What are your reasons for studying English?

Personal questions: Avoid questions which could make your interviewee uncomfortable.
What grade did you get in English this year?

Prompts: Not everything you in the interview has to be a question. You can use more open prompts, too.
Tell me a little bit about how you like to study.

1 Work with a partner. Read the interview questions. Tick ✔ the questions which are appropriate and productive. Put a ✗ next to the questions with problems. What kind of problem do these questions present?

1 ☐ How beneficial is using social media for learning English?
_____

2 ☐ Which aspects of English do you find most challenging: phonological, syntactic or semantic aspects? _____

3 ☐ Do use English outside the classroom? _____

4 ☐ Do you read, listen to, speak or write English outside school?
_____

5 ☐ Have you ever used an app to study English? Follow up to yes: Which ones _____

6 ☐ What helps you to remember new vocabulary? _____

7 ☐ Have you ever cheated on an English test? _____

8 ☐ Which TV programmes do you watch in English? _____

2 Work with a partner. Rewrite or replace the questions with problems in Exercise 1. You may need to write follow-up questions to target a range of possible answers.

_____
_____
_____
_____
_____
_____
_____
_____
_____

CREATE

3 Work with a partner and brainstorm ideas for your interview.

4 Compare your ideas with another pair. Do your ideas address all four language skills (reading, writing, listening and speaking)? Add any new ideas.

5 Choose two main topics you want to explore in your interview. Prepare your interview schedule. Add your topics. Choose ten questions for your interview.

Interview schedule

Student name: _____

topics and subcategories	notes / follow-up questions
Topic 1: _____	
a _____	
b _____	
c _____	
d _____	
e _____	
Topic 2: _____	
a _____	
b _____	
c _____	
d _____	
e _____	

---

6 Work with a partner. Review each other's questions, using the information in the Explanation box on page 227. Make any changes to questions that aren't appropriate or productive.

EVALUATE

INTERRUPTING AND HANDLING QUESTIONS

SKILLS

As an interviewer, you may want to interrupt the person who you are interviewing – in order to ask follow-up questions or to redirect the conversation to a topic that you want to explore further. Use these expressions to interrupt in order to ask follow-up questions:

Could I just stop you there?
I'd just like to pick up on what you were saying about ...
If I could just come in here, ...
I'm sorry to interrupt, but are you saying that ... ?
I just wanted to clarify one thing. You said that ...

As an interviewee, use these expressions to explain your idea or to emphasize anything mentioned before:

That's right.
As I was saying ...
If I could just return to ...
To get back to the point I was making about ...
What I was trying to say was that ...

1 Work with a partner. Read the short excerpt from an interview with a student. Add interrupting expressions and follow-up questions that the interviewer might ask.

Interviewer: So, do you speak a lot of English outside class at the University?
Student: My dad is a native speaker of English and so I speak English with him at home.
Interviewer: (1)_____
Student: That's right. He got a job in Seoul and that's where he met my mum.
Interviewer: (2)_____
Student: No, I speak mostly Korean with her. Her English is not that good.
Interviewer: I see. (3)_____
Other than speaking to your dad, do you use English any other time outside your classes?
Student: I read English novels and I listen to podcasts and news broadcasts ...
Interviewer: (4)_____
Student: No, I actually mostly watch TV and movies in Korean.

2 Work with another partner. Practise the interrupting expressions in the Explanation box and ask follow-up questions. You can use the questions from the dialogue in Exercise 1 or some of the questions you wrote in Critical Thinking.

PLUS

PLUS

PRONUNCIATION FOR SPEAKING

SKILLS

Intonation when interrupting

When we interrupt, we usually make the interruption with rising intonation and complete our question or point with falling intonation pattern.

🔊 10.7 Listen to these examples:

If I could just come in here | and ask you about your teachers.

I'd just like to pick up on what you were saying | about them not being qualified.

3 🔊 10.8 Listen to the interruptions. Use arrows to mark where the intonation rises and when it starts to fall.

1 Could I just stop you there and ask about your high school experience?

2 I'd just like to pick up on what you were saying about using the internet to learn English.

3 If I could just come in here and ask about your family background.

4 I'm sorry to interrupt. I just wanted to clarify one thing.

5 Let me stop you there. When did you say you started learning English?

SPEAKING TASK

> Conduct an in-depth semi-structured interview with another student about learning English outside the classroom. You should find out what type of activities the student engages in outside the classroom to learn English. Which of these activities are the most useful and why?

PREPARE

1 Review your interview schedule in the Critical thinking section on page 229. In the notes section, add questions to elicit any additional information that you want to find out about the student.

2 Refer to the Task checklist as you prepare for your interviews.

TASK CHECKLIST	✔
Write down any follow-up questions as you were listening.	
Ask follow-up questions that emerged during the interview.	
Listen and take notes in your interview schedule.	
Use a variety of expressions to interrupt and to ask for clarification.	
Use rising and falling intonation to indicate interruption.	
Use a variety of gerund and infinitive clauses when answering questions.	
Use phrasal verbs to vary your language when answering questions.	

PRACTISE

3 Work with a partner. Read the roles below. Decide who the interviewer will be and who the interviewee will be. Complete the task. Then change roles.

Interviewer: Use one or two questions from your interview schedule and ...
- practise expressions to interrupt and to ask for clarification.
- practise writing follow-up questions as you listen.

Interviewee: Answer the interviewer's questions and ...
- practise expressions used to clarify your ideas and to refer to what you have already said.
- practise using gerund and infinitive phrases as you describe your experience.

DISCUSS

4 Conduct your first interview.

5 Change roles and conduct your second interview.

OBJECTIVES REVIEW

1 Check your learning objectives for this unit. Write *3, 2* or *1* for each objective.

3 = very well   2 = well   1 = not so well

I can ...

watch and understand a video about language diversity.   _____

note down follow-up questions while listening.   _____

ask appropriate and productive questions.   _____

use complex gerunds and infinitives.   _____

interrupt and handle questions.   _____

conduct an in-depth semi-structured interview.   _____

2 Use the *Unlock* Digital Workbook for more practice with this unit's learning objectives.

WORDLIST

aptitude (n)	excel (v)	pick up on something (phr v)
coherent (adj) ⊙	explicit (adj) ⊙	radically (adj) ⊙
come across (as something) (phr v)	frown upon (phr v)	remotely (adv)
	frustrating (adj)	statistical (adj) ⊙
come out with something (phr v)	get at something (phr v)	talk somebody into / out of something (phr v)
	get something across (phr v)	
complexities (n pl) ⊙	grasp (n) ⊙	vague (adj) ⊙
determine (v) ⊙	incomprehensible (adj)	
discrepancy (n) ⊙	lacking in (adj)	

⊙ = high-frequency words in the Cambridge Academic Corpus

GLOSSARY

◉ = high-frequency words in the Cambridge Academic Corpus

Vocabulary	Pronunciation	Part of speech	Definition
UNIT 1			
abundant ◉	/əˈbʌndənt/	(adj)	more than enough; existing in large amounts
accelerate	/əkˈseləreɪt/	(v)	to speed up; to happen more quickly
be to blame for	/ˌbiː tə ˈbleɪm fɔː/	(v phr)	to be the reason for something that happens
be responsible for	/biː rɪˈspɒnsəbəl ˌfɔː/	(v phr)	to be the person who caused something to happen, especially something bad
burden ◉	/ˈbɜːdən/	(n)	a difficult or unpleasant responsibility
combat ◉	/ˈkɒmbæt/	(v)	to try to stop or prevent something
conversion ◉	/kənˈvɜːʃən/	(n)	the process of changing from one thing to another
credit (somebody) with	/ˈkredɪt ˌwɪð/	(phr v)	to consider someone as having been responsible for an achievement
dispose of	/dɪˈspəʊz ˌɒv/	(phr v)	to throw away
divert	/daɪˈvɜːt/	(v)	to use something for a different purpose
face up to (responsibilities)	/ˈfeɪs ˌʌp tuː/	(phr v)	to admit that a difficult situation exists, and take responsibility for resolving it
fall (squarely) on the shoulders of	/ˌfɔːl (ˈskweəli) ɒn ðəˈʃəʊldəz əv/	(v phr, idiom)	If responsibility falls on someone's shoulders, that person must take the blame, take action to resolve the situation, etc.
fertile ◉	/ˈfɜːtaɪl/	(adj)	rich; able to produce good-quality crops
have (somebody) to thank for	/hæv tə ˈθæŋk ˌfɔː/	(v phr)	If you have someone to thank for something, that person is responsible and is to be praised or blamed for it.
hold (somebody) accountable / to account	/ˈhəʊld əˌkaʊntəbəl / tuːw əˌkaʊnt/	(v phr)	to force somebody to admit what they did wrong and make it right or accept a punishment
loosen	/ˈluːsən/	(v)	to make something less firm or tight
nutrients ◉	/ˈnjuːtriənts/	(n pl)	substances that a plant or animal needs to live and grow
point the finger at	/ˈpɔɪnt ðə ˌfɪŋɡər ət/	(v phr), idiom	to accuse or blame somebody
sanctions ◉	/ˈsæŋkʃən/	(n pl)	punishments
shameful	/ˈʃeɪmfəl/	(adj)	morally wrong
shirk the blame / your responsibilities	/ʃɜːk ðə bleɪm / jɔː rɪspɒnsɪˈbɪlətiz/	(v)	to avoid people saying you are responsible for something that went wrong or duties responsibilities
sidestep responsibility	/ˈsaɪdstep rɪspɒnsɪˈbɪləti/	(v)	to avoid responsibilities
starvation	/stɑːˈveɪʃən/	(n)	death or terrible suffering due to a lack of food
step up (and do something)	/ˌstep ˈʌp/	(v phr)	to take action when there is a need or opportunity for it
take credit for	/ˌteɪk ˈkredɪt fɔː/	(v phr)	to accept praise and approval for an achievement
unprecedented	/ʌnˈpresɪdentɪd/	(adj)	having never happened in the past
viable ◉	/ˈvaɪəbəl/	(adj)	able to succeed
yield ◉	/jiːld/	(n)	the amount that is produced of something, such as a crop

Vocabulary	Pronunciation	Part of speech	Definition
UNIT 2			
backlash	/'bæklæʃ/	(n)	a strong and negative reaction among a group of people
circumvent	/ˌsɜːkəm'vent/	(v)	to find a way of avoiding something, especially a law or rule
customize	/'kʌstəmaɪz/	(v)	to make or change something to fit a user's needs
devise	/dɪ'vaɪz/	(v)	to create a plan or system using intelligence and creativity
downside	/'daʊnsaɪd/	(n)	disadvantage
drastically	/'dræstɪkəli/	(adv)	severely; with very noticeable effect
fabric ⊙	/'fæbrɪk/	(n)	cloth; material for making clothing
finite ⊙	/'faɪnaɪt/	(adj)	limited; set and fixed
foundation ⊙	/faʊn'deɪʃən/	(n)	the thing on which other things are based
innovation ⊙	/ˌɪnə'veɪʃən/	(n)	the development of new products, designs, or ideas
issue ⊙	/'ɪʃuː/	(v)	to say or send out something official
junk	/dʒʌŋk/	(n)	things of no use or value
mass production	/ˌmæs' prə'dʌkʃən/	(n)	the process of producing large numbers of one thing in a factory
obstacle ⊙	/'ɒbstəkəl/	(n)	something that prevents progress
rejection ⊙	/rɪ'dʒekʃən/	(n)	the failure of the body to accept a new body part that has been put in during surgery
resent	/rɪ'zent/	(v)	to feel angry because you have been forced to accept something that you do not like
UNIT 3			
clear your cookies	/ˌklɪə jə 'kʊkiz/	(v phr)	to remove all the small pieces of information stored on your computer about internet documents that you have looked at
combat crime	/ˌkɒmbæt 'kraɪm/	(v phr)	to try to stop crime from happening or increasing
compel	/kəm'pel/	(v)	to force someone to do something
disable	/dɪ'seɪbəl/	(v)	to stop something from working
disable cookies	/ˌdɪseɪbəl 'kʊkiz/	(v phr)	to prevent your computer from storing small pieces of information about internet documents that you have looked at
enable cookies	/ˌɪneɪbəl 'kʊkiz/	(v phr)	to allow your computer to store small pieces of information about internet documents that you have looked at
encryption	/ɪn'krɪpʃən/	(n)	the process of protecting data by changing it into code
identity theft	/aɪ'dentəti ˌθeft/	(n)	the illegal use of another person's personal details, for example in order to steal money from their bank account
in the interest of	/ɪn ðə'ɪntrəst ˌɒv/	(phr)	for the purpose of
insight ⊙	/'ɪnsaɪt/	(n)	new understanding of a complicated problem or situation
law-abiding	/'lɔːəbaɪdɪŋ/	(adj)	someone who is law-abiding obeys the law
law enforcement	/'lɔː ɪnˌfɔːsmənt/	(n)	the department of people who enforce laws, investigate crimes and make arrests, i.e. the police
legitimate ⊙	/lə'dʒɪtəmət/	(adj)	allowed by law

Vocabulary	Pronunciation	Part of speech	Definition
livelihood	/ˈlaɪvlihʊd/	(n)	the money people need to live on
move on	/ˌmuːv ˈɒn/	(phr v)	to start a new activity
offline	/ɒfˈlaɪn/	(adv)	not connected to the internet
organized crime	/ˌɔːɡənaɪzd ˈkraɪm/	(n phr)	criminal organizations that plan and commit crimes, or the crimes that are committed by such organizations
personalize	/ˈpɜːsənəlaɪz/	(v)	to make something suitable for a particular person
public safety	/ˌpʌblɪk ˈseɪfti/	(n phr)	the welfare and protection of the general public
retailer	/ˈriːteɪlə/	(n)	a business that sells to the public
secure network	/ˌsɪˈkjʊə ˈnetwɜːk/	(n phr)	a number of computers that are connected together so that they can share information in a way that keeps personal information protected
search engine	/ˈsɜːtʃ ˌendʒɪn/	(n)	a computer programme that finds information on the internet by looking for words that you have typed in
search terms	/ˈsɜːtʃ ˌtɜːmz/	(n pl)	words that are typed into a search engine in order to get information from the internet
surf the internet / the web / the net	/ˌsɜːf ðə ˈɪntənet / ðə ˈweb / ðə ˈnet/	(v phr)	to spend time visiting a lot of different websites
take steps	/teɪk steps/	(v phr)	to begin to act towards achieving a particular goal
target 🅞	/ˈtɑːɡɪt/	(v)	to direct something at somebody
trace 🅞	/treɪs/	(v)	to find the origin of something
trade-off	/ˈtreɪdˌɒf/	(n)	a situation in which you accept something bad in order to have something good
warrant 🅞	/ˈwɒrənt/	(n)	an official document that allows the police to take action

UNIT 4

Vocabulary	Pronunciation	Part of speech	Definition
abandon 🅞	/əˈbændən/	(v)	to leave a place, thing or person, usually for ever
analyze 🅞	/ˈænəlaɪz/	(v)	to study or examine something in detail, in order to discover more about it
buzzword	/ˈbʌzwɜːd/	(n)	a popular word or expression that is sometimes overused in a field
concisely	/kənˈsaɪsli/	(adv)	expressing information in a way that is short, without using unnecessary words
considerable 🅞	/kənˈsɪdərəbəl/	(adj)	large or of noticeable importance
corporation 🅞	/ˌkɔːpərˈeɪʃən/	(n)	a large company or group of companies that is controlled together as a single organization
disruptive 🅞	/dɪsˈrʌptɪv/	(adj)	changing the traditional way that an industry operates
donor 🅞	/ˈdəʊnə/	(n)	someone who gives money or goods to a person or organization that needs them
dump	/dʌmp/	(v)	put something somewhere without caring where
elaborate 🅞	/iˈlæbərət/	(adj)	detailed
emerge 🅞	/ɪˈmɜːdʒ/	(v)	to appear by coming out of something or out from behind or under something
enterprise 🅞	/ˈentəpraɪz/	(n)	a business or organization
option 🅞	/ˈɒpʃən/	(n)	one thing that can be chosen from a set of possibilities, or the freedom to make a choice
overload	/ˈəʊvələʊd/	(n)	too much of something

Vocabulary	Pronunciation	Part of speech	Definition
oversight	/ˈəʊvəsaɪt/	(n)	responsibility for a job or activity and for ensuring it is being done correctly
overview ⊙	/ˈəʊvəvjuː/	(n)	a short description giving the most important facts about something
primary ⊙	/ˈpraɪməri/	(adj)	more important than anything else; main
scope ⊙	/skəʊp/	(n)	the range of a subject covered by a book, programme, discussion, class, etc.
status ⊙	/ˈsteɪtəs/	(n)	the official or legal position of a person or organization
trace ⊙	/treɪs/	(n)	a sign that something has happened or existed
transaction ⊙	/trænˈzækʃən/	(n)	an activity that involves the exchange of money
venture	/ˈventʃə/	(n)	a new business
wary	/ˈweəri/	(adj)	careful in the face of possible danger
worthy ⊙	/ˈwɜːði/	(adj)	deserving respect, admiration or support

UNIT 5

Vocabulary	Pronunciation	Part of speech	Definition
aggression ⊙	/əˈgreʃən/	(n)	spoken or physical behaviour that is threatening or involves harm to someone or something
aggressive ⊙	/əˈgresɪv/	(adj)	behaving in an angry and violent way towards another person
application ⊙	/ˌæplɪˈkeɪʃən/	(n)	a way in which something can be used
approachability	/əˈprəʊtʃəbɪləti/	(n)	how willing someone is to be approached
approachable	/əˈprəʊtʃəbəl/	(adj)	friendly and easy to talk to
attractive ⊙	/əˈtræktɪv/	(adj)	very pleasing in appearance or sound; causing interest or pleasure
attractiveness	/əˈtræktɪvnəs/	(n)	the quality of being attractive
competence ⊙	/ˈkɒmpɪtəns/	(n)	the ability to do something well
competent ⊙	/ˈkɒmpɪtənt/	(adj)	skilled; able to do things well
cue ⊙	/kjuː/	(n)	a signpost; something that causes a response
definitively	/dɪˈfɪnɪtɪvli/	(adv)	completely; without doubt
deteriorate	/dɪˈtɪəriəreɪt/	(v)	to worsen
dominance ⊙	/ˈdɒmɪnəns/	(n)	the quality of liking to take control in a group and being a natural leader
dominant ⊙	/ˈdɒmɪnənt/	(adj)	liking to take control in a group and being a natural leader
exposure ⊙	/ɪkˈspəʊʒə/	(n)	experiencing something by being in a particular place or situation
impair	/ɪmˈpeə/	(v)	to damage
intensively	/ɪnˈtensɪvli/	(adv)	involving extreme concentration or effort
landmark	/ˈlændmɑːk/	(n)	a place or structure that is easy to recognize
likeability	/laɪkəbɪləti/	(n)	the quality of being readily or easily liked
likeable	/ˈlaɪkəbəl/	(adj)	a likeable person is pleasant and easy to like
navigate	/ˈnævɪgeɪt/	(v)	to find the way from one place to another
reconstruct	/ˌriːkənˈstrʌkt/	(v)	to create a description of a past event
relate to	/rɪˈleɪttʊ/	(phr v)	to understand something by connecting it with your own experiences
reliance on	/rɪˈlaɪəns ɒn/	(n)	the situation in which you always use or need the help of a particular thing

Vocabulary	Pronunciation	Part of speech	Definition
speculate	/'spekjəleɪt/	(v)	to guess when there is not enough information to be certain
thoughtful	/'θɔːtfəl/	(adj)	carefully considering things; quiet because you are thinking about something
thoughtfulness	/'θɔːtfəlnəs/	(n)	the state of being absorbed in your thoughts; consideration for other people

UNIT 6

Vocabulary	Pronunciation	Part of speech	Definition
accomplishment	/ə'kʌmplɪʃmənt/	(n)	something done successfully
analytical 🔾	/ˌænə'lɪtɪkəl/	(adj)	careful and systematic
be landed with	/biː 'lændɪd ˌwɪð/	(phr v)	to be forced to take responsibility for something or somebody unpleasant
cap	/kæp/	(n)	a limit on the amount of money that can be charged or spent
collaboration 🔾	/kəˌlæbə'reɪʃən/	(n)	cooperative effort
daunting	/'dɔːntɪŋ/	(adj)	making you feel less confident of achieving something; frightening
discrimination 🔾	/dɪˌskrɪmɪ'neɪʃən/	(n)	unfair treatment, especially based on sex, ethnic origin, age or religion
distinct 🔾	/dɪ'stɪŋkt/	(adj)	clearly separate and different
dreaded	/'dredɪd/	(adj)	unwelcome because of being frightening
format 🔾	/'fɔːmæt/	(n)	organization
probationary period	/ˌprə'beɪʃənəri 'pɪəriəd/	(n phr)	the time during which a new employee is monitored to ensure they are suitable for their role and can easily be removed if unsuitable
ramble	/'ræmbəl/	(v)	to speak in a boring and confused way
rehearsed	/rɪ'hɜːsd/	(adj)	practised and unnatural
reiterate	/ri'ɪtəreɪt/	(v)	to repeat
start out	/stɑːt aʊt/	(phr v)	to begin the part of your life when you work (in a job or particular industry)
vision 🔾	/'vɪʒən/	(n)	idea for how something could develop in the future

UNIT 7

Vocabulary	Pronunciation	Part of speech	Definition
aghast	/ə'gɑːst/	(adj)	suddenly filled with strong feelings of shock and worry
allergy	/'ælədʒi/	(n)	an abnormal physical reaction, such as a rash or breathing problems, when exposed to a particular substance, for example animal hair or pollen
appalled	/ə'pɔːld/	(adj)	having strong feelings of shock or of disapproval
appalling	/ə'pɔːlɪŋ/	(adj)	shocking and very bad
atrocious	/ə'trəʊʃəs/	(adj)	of very bad quality
compromise 🔾	/'kɒmprəmaɪz/	(v)	to harm or weaken something
concentration 🔾	/ˌkɒnsən'treɪʃən/	(n)	a large number or amount of something in the same place
contaminate 🔾	/kən'tæmɪneɪt/	(v)	to make something dirty, polluted or poisoned
correlation 🔾	/ˌkɒrə'leɪʃən/	(n)	a connection between two or more things
deplorable	/dɪ'plɔːrəbəl/	(adj)	shocking and very bad
dismayed	/dɪ'smeɪd/	(adj)	unhappy and disappointed
disparity 🔾	/dɪ'spærəti/	(n)	a lack of equality
dreadful	/'dredfəl/	(adj)	very bad, of very low quality, or shocking and very sad

Vocabulary	Pronunciation	Part of speech	Definition
guidelines ⊙	/ˈgaɪdlaɪnz/	(n pl)	formal advice (usually written) about how to do something
horrified	/ˈhɒrɪfaɪd/	(adj)	very shocked
hygiene ⊙	/ˈhaɪdʒiːn/	(n)	cleanliness; keeping yourself and your environment clean
incidence ⊙	/ˈɪnsɪdəns/	(n)	the rate at which something happens
intervene	/ˌɪntəˈviːn/	(v)	to enter a situation to stop it from getting worse
minimal ⊙	/ˈmɪnɪməl/	(adj)	very small in amount
obesity	/əʊˈbiːsəti/	(n)	the state of being extremely fat, in a way that is dangerous for health
outraged	/ˈaʊtreɪdʒd/	(adj)	a feeling of anger and shock
outrageous	/aʊtˈreɪdʒəs/	(adj)	shocking and morally unacceptable
property ⊙	/ˈprɒpəti/	(n)	a quality in substance or material, especially one that means that it can be used in a particular way
severity ⊙	/sɪˈverəti/	(n)	seriousness; how bad something is
shocked	/ʃɒkt/	(adj)	feeling very upset or surprised
shocking	/ˈʃɒkɪŋ/	(adj)	making you feel very upset or surprised

UNIT 8

Vocabulary	Pronunciation	Part of speech	Definition
bully	/ˈbʊli/	(v, n)	to intentionally frighten someone who is smaller or weaker, or someone who acts in this way
consensus ⊙	/kənˈsensəs/	(n)	a generally accepted opinion or decision
constructive ⊙	/kənˈstrʌktɪv/	(adj)	helpful, positive
counteract	/ˌkaʊntərˈækt/	(v)	to reduce the negative effect of something
defuse	/ˌdiːˈfjuːz/	(v)	to make a situation calmer or less dangerous
dynamics ⊙	/daɪˈnæmɪks/	(n pl)	forces that produce change in a system or group
hybrid ⊙	/ˈhaɪbrɪd/	(n)	something that is a combination of two or more things
legacy ⊙	/ˈlegəsi/	(n)	something you do that becomes part of history and remains after you are gone
outcome ⊙	/ˈaʊtkʌm/	(n)	result
ownership ⊙	/ˈəʊnəʃɪp/	(n)	attitude of accepting responsibility for something
perception ⊙	/pəˈsepʃən/	(n)	a belief or opinion based on observation
prevail	/prɪˈveɪl/	(v)	to eventually become the controlling force
resentment	/rɪˈzent/	(n)	anger at being forced to accept something
reservations	/ˌrezəˈveɪʃən/	(n pl)	doubts
resolve ⊙	/rɪˈzɒlv/	(v)	to solve or end a problem or difficulty
stake ⊙	/steɪk/	(n)	a personal interest or investment

UNIT 9

Vocabulary	Pronunciation	Part of speech	Definition
at stake	/ˌæt ˈsteɪk/	(phr)	in a situation where something valuable may be lost
compassion	/kəmˈpæʃən/	(n)	a strong feeling of sympathy for someone or something suffering and a wish to help them
confronted with	/ˈkənˈfrʌntd ˌwɪð/	(phr v)	to be in a difficult situation or to be shown something which may cause difficulties
constitute ⊙	/ˈkɒnstɪtʃuːt/	(v)	to make up a proportion of something
dexterity	/dekˈsterəti/	(n)	the ability to perform an action or actions skilfully with your hands

Vocabulary	Pronunciation	Part of speech	Definition
disposable income	/dɪˌspəʊzəbəl ˈɪnkʌm/	(n)	the money that is left over after you have paid your bills that you can spend as you wish
elaborate ⊙	/iˈlæbərət/	(v)	to explain or give more detail about something that you have said
illegal ⊙	/ɪˈliːgəl/	(adj)	not allowed by law
illegible	/ɪˈledʒəbəl/	(adj)	(of writing or print) impossible or almost impossible to read because of being very untidy or not clear
illiterate	/ɪˈlɪtərət/	(adj)	unable to read and write
illogical	/ɪˈlɒdʒɪkəl/	(adj)	not reasonable, wise, or practical, usually because directed by the emotions rather than by careful thought
immobile	/ɪˈməʊbaɪl/	(adj)	not moving or not able to move
immoral	/ɪˈmɒrəl/	(adj)	morally wrong, or outside society's standards of acceptable, honest, and moral behaviour
imperfect ⊙	/ɪmˈpɜːfekt/	(adj)	damaged, containing problems, or not having something
impersonal	/ɪmˈpɜːsənəl/	(adj)	without human warmth; not friendly and without features that make people feel interested or involved
implausible	/ɪmˈplɔːzəbəl/	(adj)	difficult to believe, or unlikely
inconsiderate	/ɪnkənˈsɪdərət/	(adj)	not thinking or worrying about other people or their feelings
indispensable	/ɪndɪˈspensəbəl/	(adj)	Something or someone that is indispensable is so good or important that you could not manage without it, him, or her.
inefficient	/ɪnɪˈfɪʃənt/	(adj)	not organized, skilled, or able to work in a satisfactory way
insignificant ⊙	/ɪnsɪgˈnɪfɪkənt/	(adj)	small or not noticeable, and therefore not considered important
insufficient ⊙	/ɪnsəˈfɪʃənt/	(adj)	not enough
intuition ⊙	/ˌɪntʃuːˈɪʃən/	(n)	the ability to understand or know something immediately, based on your feelings rather than facts
irrational ⊙	/ɪˈræʃənəl/	(adj)	not using reason or clear thinking
irreplaceable	/ɪrɪˈpleɪsəbəl/	(adj)	too special, unusual, or valuable to replace with something or someone else
irreversible	/ɪrɪˈvɜːsɪbəl/	(adj)	not possible to change; impossible to return to a previous condition
irrevocable	/ɪˈrevəkəbəl/	(adj)	impossible to change
mimic	/ˈmɪmɪk/	(v)	in science, to copy or imitate another living thing or the way that they are or behave
mundane	/mʌnˈdeɪn/	(adj)	very ordinary and therefore not interesting
peer ⊙	/pɪə/	(n)	a person who is the same age or has the same social position as other people in a group
pervasive ⊙	/pəˈveɪsɪv/	(adj)	present and noticeable everywhere
rational ⊙	/ˈræʃənəl/	(adj)	based on facts and not affected by emotions or imagination
related	/rɪˈleɪtɪd/	(adj)	connected
reluctant ⊙	/rɪˈlʌktənt/	(adj)	not willing to do something and therefore slow to do it
unavoidable	/ʌnəˈvɔɪdəbəl/	(adj)	impossible to avoid
undesirable	/ʌndɪˈzaɪərəbəl/	(adj)	not wanted, approved of, or popular

Vocabulary	Pronunciation	Part of speech	Definition
unproductive	/ˌʌnprəˈdʌktɪv/	(adj)	not producing very much
unscrupulous	/ʌnˈskruːpjʊləs/	(adj)	behaving in a way that is dishonest or unfair in order to get what you want
unsustainable	/ˌʌnsəˈsteɪnəbəl/	(adj)	Something that is unsustainable cannot continue at the same rate.
verify ⦿	/ˈverɪfaɪ/	(v)	to prove something is true, or to do something to discover if it is true

UNIT 10

Vocabulary	Pronunciation	Part of speech	Definition
aptitude	/ˈæptɪtʃuːd/	(n)	a natural ability or skill
coherent ⦿	/kəʊˈhɪərənt/	(adj)	well-structured and logical, and therefore easy to understand
come across (as something)	/ˌkʌm əˈkrɒs/	(phr v)	to behave in a way that makes people believe that you have a particular characteristic
come out with (something)	/ˌkʌm ˈaʊt wɪð/	(phr v)	to say something unexpectedly or suddenly
complexities ⦿	/kəmˈpleksətiz/	(n pl)	the features that make something difficult to understand or explain
determine ⦿	/dɪˈtɜːmɪn/	(v)	to discover the facts or truth about something
discrepancy ⦿	/dɪˈskrepənsi/	(n)	a difference between two things that should be the same
excel	/ɪkˈsel/	(v)	to be extremely good at something
explicit ⦿	/ɪkˈsplɪsɪt/	(adj)	clear and exact
frown upon	/ˈfraʊn əˌpɒn/	(phr v)	to disapprove of something
frustrating	/frʌsˈtreɪtɪŋ/	(adj)	making you feel annoyed or less confident because you cannot achieve something
get at (something)	/ˈget ˌət/	(phr v)	to suggest or express something in a way that is not direct or clear
get (something) across	/ˌget ˈəˈkrɒs/	(phr v)	to communicate an idea or a message successfully
go on about (something)	/ˌgəʊ ˈɒn əbaʊt/	(phr v)	to talk in an annoying way about something for a long time
grasp ⦿	/grɑːsp/	(n)	understanding of a subject or issue
incomprehensible	/ɪnˌkɒmprɪˈhensəbəl/	(adj)	impossible to understand
lacking in	/ˈlækɪŋ ˌɪn/	(adj)	not having a quality
pick up on (something)	/ˌpɪk ˈʌp ɒn/	(phr v)	to understand something that is not communicated directly
radically ⦿	/ˈrædɪkəli/	(adj)	in a thorough way; completely
remotely	/rɪˈməʊtli/	(adv)	in a very slight way
statistical ⦿	/stəˈtɪstɪkəl/	(adj)	related to numbers and trends
talk somebody into / out of (something)	/ˌtɔːk sʌmbədi ˈɪntuː / ˈaʊt əv/	(phr v)	to persuade somebody to do / not to do something
vague ⦿	/veɪg/	(adj)	not clearly expressed, described, etc

UNIT 1

 Saving Indonesia's birds of paradise one village at a time

Commentator: A rare glimpse, and it's gone. Locally known as *cendrawasih*, spotting these birds of paradise in the Indonesian jungle is becoming increasingly difficult.

Local 1: The habitat of the *cendrawasih* bird is in danger because of human activities which are mostly destructive. There's illegal logging, and then there is the conversion from tropical rainforests to agricultural plantations.

Commentator: Indonesia is home to forty one birds of paradise species, thirty seven of which can be found in the jungles of Papua. They are treasured by most locals and tourists alike.

Local 2: The *cendrawasih* bird is very special because it is called the bird of paradise. Its colours are unique, and it's not like other birds. It's only found in one place, not everywhere.

Commentator: Although authorities have banned the sale of birds of paradise, an ever-growing illicit trade threatens exotic birds across the archipelago. Often found smuggled in horrific ways to other parts of Indonesia and South East Asia.

Local 3: We ensure that the forests won't be destroyed, and of course the *cendrawasih* will last. And we hope that in the future since most of the forest in Raja Ampat is protected. It is a protected area, we will really protect it.

Commentator: Papua boasts one third of Indonesia's remaining rainforests and environmentalists here are looking for solutions that will preserve the bird's habitat, but will also boost the local economy.

Local 1: Birdwatchers provide jobs for the local people. For example the women who are in this village, they can cook and the men can provide homestays.

Commentator: With nearly twenty tourists visiting this area alone each month, birdwatching may be the only chance of survival for this colourful, exotic species.

1.1

Presenter: The Green Revolution has been credited with saving several generations of the world's poorest people from **starvation**. The techniques of high-**yield** agriculture were developed between the 1930s and around 1970. They include the extensive use of chemical fertilizers to improve the quality of the soil, and pesticides to kill insects and control diseases. These techniques brought changes that were sufficiently dramatic to earn the title 'revolution'. They produced **abundant** crops, especially wheat, from relatively small plots of land, and with much less labour than had previously been required. The United Kingdom alone produced over 16 million tons of wheat in 2015. That's almost 250 kilograms of wheat per capita. There is no doubt that thousands, if not millions, have benefited from the bounty of the Green Revolution. Today, however, I want to talk to you about the next chapter – about some of the consequences of this type of intensive agriculture – and about how we, the next generation, can do a better job of conserving our most basic and most valuable resources.

 1.2

Presenter: So what is intensive farming, and what happens when we farm intensively? By 'intensive' I mean that we grow huge amounts of one crop in the same fields, year after year. As I mentioned, the upside is that we get lots of food in return for relatively little labour. Unfortunately, there is also a downside – damaging effects on the health of the planet and the population. I want to talk about some issues through the lens of sustainability, because, let's face it, it won't do much good to produce a lot of food if we're using up all of our natural resources or destroying the planet in the process. Let's start by talking about natural resources. What are the most important resources in agriculture? Soil and water. I'm a professor of Agricultural Science now, but I grew up on a traditional farm, so I have seen the situation from different perspectives. On our farm, we grew a few different types of crops. On most big farms today, however, farmers grow the same crops every year – they specialize. This kind of farming drains the soil of precious **nutrients**, requiring farmers to replace them with chemical fertilizers.

My colleagues and I are working with a group of farmers to test some more sustainable techniques. Instead of chemical fertilizers, these farmers are using animal waste. They're also rotating crops – that is, planting different crops from year to year – and planting cover crops. It was very difficult to persuade the farmers of the value of this last technique. A cover crop is planted for the sole purpose of improving the quality of the soil. There is nothing to harvest and sell at the end of the season. So you can imagine how this wouldn't be considered a **viable** option for some farmers – to plant a crop that would result in no revenue. Gradually, however, they began to see how much better their cash crops grew in a field that had been filled with a cover crop the year before.

Now, what are some other advantages of practices like crop rotation and the use of cover crops? Diversifying crops can reduce the number of pests, such as insects and small animals, thus decreasing the need for pesticides. Planting cover crops can help farmers with another constant challenge – erosion. Erosion occurs when wind and water lift off the top layer of soil and carry it away. Erosion typically accompanies the **conversion** of wild spaces with natural vegetation to agricultural land. The act of ploughing exposes and **loosens** the soil, making it vulnerable to the forces of wind and water. The UK's soil quality has already been damaged. We have lost 84% of our **fertile** topsoil since 1850. The government warns that, in the long term, this continuing erosion will affect **yield** and therefore food supply. There is also an environmental impact of erosion. Eroded soil gets carried off into rivers and streams, often causing serious damage to these waterways, which are important habitats for a wide range of species.

It's hard to talk about soil without talking about water. Agriculture uses 70% of the water used in the world today. Some of our most important crops require massive amounts of water. To quench their thirst, we've been drawing from underground reserves, some of which are now drying up. Clearly, this practice is *not* sustainable.

But there is another obvious source of water – rain, right? Unfortunately, many farmers just let rainwater run off into rivers, as I just mentioned, often carrying valuable soil with it. But it doesn't have to be like this. We can conserve water *and* reduce erosion by altering the design of fields. Another aspect of water conservation is the retention of the soil moisture, and here again, planting cover crops can make a huge difference. They trap surface water and prevent it from evaporating. So you see, everything in nature – the soil, the water, and the food we eat – is all interconnected. So why doesn't everybody in the world just switch to sustainable practices? Good question. One reason is that some of the costs of sustainable agriculture are higher than those of conventional agriculture, in particular, labour costs. Sustainable practices require more people to manage them. But from a global perspective, perhaps a more important issue is yield. It's long been believed that the crop yields of sustainable farming are no match for those of modern, intensive agricultural practices – and there is some truth to this. But, with improved technology and greater knowledge, studies show that it *is* possible to shrink the gap between the two systems. Nevertheless, farmers aren't going to risk changing their time-tested methods without strong and direct proof that their yields won't suffer because of it.

I'll finish my talk by reporting on a recent study that compares three different forms of farming. It compared conventional methods that use chemical fertilizers and pesticides with two more sustainable approaches – one that relies on animal waste for nutrients and another that relies on crop management – the use of crop rotation and cover crops. The findings support the claim that conventional methods have higher yields than sustainable methods, but the differences were not large. Furthermore, the conventional farmers spent more to achieve that greater yield, so their profits were actually lower. When you combine those results with the environmental damage that conventional farming can cause, you really begin to wonder why we continue with conventional farming practices at all. Well, there *are* some good reasons for this, and we'll explore them next time.

 1.3

1 I want to talk about some issues
2 Let's start by talking about natural resources
3 I'm a professor of Agricultural Science now
4 These farmers are using animal waste
5 They're also rotating crops
6 Diversifying crops can reduce the number of pests
7 It's hard to talk about soil
8 This practice is *not* sustainable

 1.4

Moderator: Join us tomorrow for *Our Planet*. I'll be hosting a panel discussion with representatives of four organizations with differing perspectives on climate change. Learn which parts of the world have the highest emission rates for CO_2 and other damaging greenhouse gases. Which parts of the world have the highest *per capita* emission rates? Who is to blame for damage to the environment caused by these emissions? And how should we hold these countries accountable? With economic sanctions? With boycotts? We'll hear opinions on these issues tomorrow at 2.00 pm. So join us.

 1.5

Moderator: Welcome, everybody, to our session on global responsibility and climate change. Today we have a panel of four speakers who come from a wide range of organizations and points of view. Please welcome Grace Chin from StepUp, Russell Sanchez from Fair Share, Dara Staples from Citizens for Global Justice and, finally, Vijay Gupta from the Fund for the Environmental Future. Each of our panellists is going to make an opening statement that explains his or her organization's perspective on climate change and related issues. Then we'll open up the discussion to our audience. So, one of the most controversial issues at the United Nations' talks on climate change in Paris was the respective roles and responsibilities of developed and developing countries in working to **combat** climate change. Panellists, can you address this issue for us? Our first speaker is Grace Chin. Grace?

Grace: Thank you. Climate change is an immediate threat to the entire planet, but it's not a new problem. On the contrary, CO_2 and other greenhouse gases have been accumulating for over a century, largely as a result of the human activity in developed countries. The emissions per capita figures are quite clear. The bulk of the responsibility for global warming falls squarely on the shoulders of the developed world. The United States has the highest per capita emissions of any major country in the world. So shouldn't the United States and other developed nations be the ones making changes, even if those changes *are* expensive? The United States is a country with enormous economic resources. It's not fair to put the **burden** of lowering emissions on countries when they're trying to fight their way out of poverty. For many of these countries, economic development, including the extraction of natural resources, must remain a priority, even if the process has a negative impact on the environment. They can't afford to change to more expensive alternative energy sources even if they're less polluting. It's the governments and citizens of the developed world who need to step up and accept responsibility for the health of the environment.

Moderator: Thank you, Grace. And now Russell Sanchez from Fair Share.

Russell: We at Fair Share recognize the difficulties that developing countries face, and we agree that the developed world needs to provide some assistance, for example, by buying carbon credits. However, we should keep in mind that the per capita figures that Grace cited are somewhat misleading. Many developing countries, such as India, have huge populations. So, actually, although their per capita figures may be lower, their overall emissions rates are very high. One recent study estimated that 20 to 25 percent of annual CO_2 emissions come from countries where farmers still burn forests and grasslands to prepare their land for farming. So, those forces are ***accelerating*** climate change.

We're also losing our best hope to *slow* this process. The loss of trees in the Amazon rainforest, often called 'the lungs of the world', has reduced by half the ability of the planet to absorb CO_2. Overall, it's the rapid industrialization of the developing world that is bringing **unprecedented** levels of CO_2 emissions. In the nineteenth century, we didn't know any better, but now we do. Developing countries have what we might call a 'latecomer's advantage'. They know the consequences of their actions. If they don't use that knowledge wisely, there have to be some repercussions – economic repercussions. Why not organize a global boycott of any products whose manufacture causes significant negative environmental effects? If we refuse to buy wood that comes from a forest that should still be standing, or beef that was raised on land that was once a rainforest, perhaps developing countries will begin to make wiser choices.

Moderator: Thank you, Russell. Now we turn to Dara Staples from Citizens for Global Justice.

Dara: The position that Russell's described is deeply unfair, but I'm afraid I find the position taken by Grace's organization almost equally troubling. There is simply no way that developing countries can be held to the same standard as countries in the developed world. They don't have adequate economic resources, and punishing them with a boycott or other economic **sanctions** will push some of them even deeper into poverty. However, I also question the wisdom of encouraging developing countries to continue on a path that could eventually lead to their own destruction. It is as much in their interest to slow climate change as it is in ours. If global warming continues at its current pace, Bangladesh, for example, a country of 150 million people, could be under water in the not-too-distant future. How useful will economic development and resource extraction be to the people of Bangladesh then? Russell talks of buying carbon credits – developing countries get economic support and rich nations get the right to increase their emissions. Buying carbon credits is just another form of exploitation in which the people of the developed world buy the right to cause environmental damage. It's not much better than the current **shameful** practice of **disposing of** their old computers – so-called *e-waste* – in countries that can't afford to refuse the money developed countries are willing to pay to dump them there. Developed nations need to provide real support to poor countries so that their development does not come at the expense of the environment!

Moderator: Thank you very much. And finally, Vijay Gupta, from Fund for the Environmental Future, what is your position?

Vijay: Some of what all you have said may be true, but what good is pointing fingers and blaming one another? It's not going to help us solve this problem. The planet is warming up faster than ever. The last two years have been the warmest on record. If we are to have any chance of slowing climate change, all countries, both developed and developing, need to allocate more funding to this effort, even if it means **diverting** money from other worthwhile projects. The bottom line is that global warming is not just continuing; it is accelerating. As several of the panellists have suggested, there is not much point in economic development if it puts the health of our planet in danger. If we allow even a single country to increase its emissions, the problem will only grow worse. This is not an issue we can put off until another international conference, or chip away at gradually. We need to take immediate, dramatic and unified action if we want to preserve our world for the next generation.

Moderator: Many thanks to all our participants. I am sure our listeners have a lot of questions, so let's open up the phone lines and ... .

 1.6

Ranger: We're facing numerous challenges here at Grand Canyon National Park. In 2015, we hosted five and a half million visitors. It's the second most popular park in the nation. All those visitors put a lot of pressure on the park, so we've had to spend most of our annual budget on maintaining services for them. But there are many other problems that need attention. Most of the water in the Colorado River, which carved out the canyon over thousands of years, has been diverted to other uses: to cities and nearby farms. The river's level continues to drop, which has seriously affected the habitat of many of the plants and animals that live in and around the river. Outside of the park, there are mining operations that threaten to pollute the groundwater flowing under the park, and nearby power plants produce air pollution that regularly blocks the view of our beautiful canyon. Above the park, we have tourists in helicopters enjoying the view, but at the same time, creating so much noise that it disturbs park animals. Non-native species, mostly brought in by the park's many visitors, are endangering the native species. We need another $6.2 billion to address these and other pressing issues.

 1.7

Steve: You're poisoning the groundwater by using those pesticides in your garden.

Mia: Not necessarily. If you use pesticides carefully, they're totally safe. At least, that's what I've read.

Steve: Actually, there is no way to use these products safely. They should not be used under any circumstances.

Mia: I would agree with you if there were any other options, but nothing works as well against the insects that ruin my flowers and vegetables.

Steve: I'm afraid that's not really the point. What does it matter if they work really well in your garden? It's irresponsible.

UNIT 2

▶ Designer bikes become showcase for social status

Commentator: Pedal chic is in the air, and luxury brand Hermès is one of the latest to turn cycling into a fashion statement. Eight months ago, Hermès launched 'Le Flâneur' and more recently, 'Le Flâneur Sportif'. With a carbon-fibre frame, a silent chain and classic style, this bike costs a cool €8,000, and Hermès is struggling to keep up with demand.

Hermès employee: Today we're in line with the objectives we'd set. There was a real gap in the market but now with our production in full swing we're really trying to meet.

Commentator: In Tokyo, designer bikes can sell for €15,000. One local artisan is using his experience in yachts manufacturing to create beautiful bicycles made from mahogany.

Bike designer: My ancestors taught me how to manufacture boats, and now I'm using that knowledge to make bikes. I think it's the first time the whole world recognizes Japanese talent in this area, that's why, even if it doesn't make me much money, I have to keep doing it.

Commentator: Back in Paris, bicycle sellers are finding another way of boosting sales by personalizing the accessories that every 'posh pedaller' needs – from leather saddle bags to hand-painted bells.

Bike seller: What we can find are these pretty bells painted by hand in Japan. These little leather purses, these keyrings in leather, a nice collection of lead cyclists painted by hand, like when we were children.

Commentator: Now like a car, a watch, or a pair of shoes, the humble bicycle is evolving into a showcase for wealth and social status.

 2.1

Speaker: A part inside your dishwasher has broken? No problem, just print a replacement. No shoes for the wedding? No problem, just print a pair. The technology behind 3-D printing, the process of creating a solid object from a digital model, has been around since the 1980s, but only recently have the costs fallen far enough, and the computer software improved enough, to make these scenarios more than a dream. I think some of the most dramatic uses of 3-D printing have been in biomedical research, where scientists have been working on 3-D-printed organs. In these projects, the 'ink' that the printers use is actually made of human cells. So in the case of 3-D-printed skin, a printer builds up layers of skin cells. You can imagine how this could help a patient with a burn, or a wound that hasn't been healing on its own. Other printers are creating bone, muscle, ears and even brain tissue. Doctors and researchers have been working on recreating human organs for years, but 3-D printing is really an advance. For one thing, the computer software that guides the printing process is extremely accurate, right down to the micron – an accomplishment that human hands cannot match. In addition, since the new organs are often created from the patient's own cells, there is a lower risk of **rejection**. This biological 3-D printing function is the one that I am the most excited about; but the research and testing still have a long way to go before we can automatically include this technology among a patient's options.

On a lighter note, 3-D printing has also entered the world of high fashion, where designers are actively using it in their collections. What really attracts designers is the possibility of **customizing** their designs. And consumers? Well, they're dreaming of the day when they can download a design from the internet and print it out at home. That day too, however, is some distance in the future, at least until we can come up with better 'ink'. Today, the material fed into 3-D printers is a type of plastic. It's stiffer than **fabric** and not very comfortable. The cost of printing is also too high to make this a practical form of production. So you're more likely to find 3-D fashions on the runway than in a department store. That said, the possibility that this innovation could shift the production of clothing to local centres, and away from large facilities – most of which are now in the developing world – could seriously disrupt the clothing industry and global markets. There is no doubt that this technology has had, and will continue to have, the greatest impact in the manufacturing sector, where it's referred to as 'additive manufacturing', or AM. In the past, the key to keeping costs low was **mass production**. The more units you produced, the lower your cost per unit. 3-D printing has the potential to turn this equation on its head. In AM, there are no drawbacks to printing small quantities; quite the opposite, actually. It also completely disrupts two key elements that are part of the **foundation** of manufacturing: assembly and the supply chain. Rick Smith, a 3-D entrepreneur, cites the case of a man who was able to print an aeroplane part that had previously consisted of 21 separate pieces, all of which were manufactured in different factories, and then shipped to one factory, where they were assembled. The man had no background in manufacturing, yet he was able to print the part as a single piece, on the spot, right where the part was needed. What's more, by printing it as one piece, he created a part that was five times stronger than the original part and 83% lighter, which reduced fuel costs by 15%. So even though the raw materials for the part were relatively expensive, the potential cost savings more than made up for them.

Consider the potential impact on manufacturing. No more need for an assembly plant means no more global supply chain. No more need to maintain stock levels or to ship goods. Everything could just be created on demand and on location. AM would reduce waste and shorten supply chains, reducing our environmental footprint in the process. It could also help us keep our stuff working for longer. If an appliance breaks today, the cost of repairing it is often as high as the cost of replacing it. With all of its efficiencies, AM printing could **drastically** lower repair costs, so we would need to replace equipment, even cars, less frequently. All of this sounds like a dream come true. So, what's the **downside**, you may ask? There always is one, of course. Although I mentioned the positive impact AM could have on the environment, it could also have the opposite effect. First of all, the plastic that is used in most 3-D printers has a long supply chain and most of it, though not all, is petroleum-based. Also, printing that is this easy could encourage our already casual attitude towards the disposal of possessions. Don't like your shoes? Throw them out and print a new pair. But that old pair will have to end up somewhere. So I worry that along with all its advantages, 3-D printing may bring an explosion of **junk**. There is also the potential for abuse. The technology might be so easy to use that you could just download instructions and print something dangerous – like a gun. Already criminals have printed parts for bank machines in order to withdraw money illegally. So yes, there'll be problems, but I want to end my talk by stressing that in spite of these concerns, I am optimistic and excited about the possibilities presented by this 3-D printing technology. Some have predicted that it will trigger the third industrial revolution. Is this an exaggeration? Perhaps, but then again, perhaps not.

 2.2

Speaker: It also completely disrupts two key elements that are part of the foundation of manufacturing: assembly and the supply chain. Rick Smith, a 3-D entrepreneur, cites the case of a man who was able to print an aeroplane part that had previously consisted of 21 separate pieces, all of which were manufactured in different factories, and then shipped to one factory, where they were assembled. The man had no background in manufacturing, yet he was able to print the part as a single piece, on the spot, right where the part was needed. What's more, by printing it as one piece, he created a part that was five times stronger than the original part and 83% lighter, which reduced fuel costs by 15%. So even though the raw materials for the part were relatively expensive, the potential cost savings more than made up for them.

Consider the potential impact on manufacturing. No more need for an assembly plant means no more global supply chain. No more need to maintain stock levels or to ship goods. Everything could just be created on demand and on location.

🔊 2.3

1 The technology behind 3-D printing, the process of creating a solid object from a digital model, has been around since the 1980s.

2 The computer software improved enough, to make these scenarios more than a dream.

3 I think some of the most dramatic uses of 3-D printing have been in biomedical research, where scientists have been working on 3-D-printed organs.

4 What really attracts designers is the possibility of customizing their designs.

5 The possibility that this innovation could shift the production of clothing to local centres, and away from large facilities – most of which are now in the developing world – could seriously disrupt the clothing industry and global markets.

6 It also completely disrupts two key elements that are part of the foundation of manufacturing.

7 Rick Smith, a 3-D entrepreneur, cites the case of a man who was able to print an aeroplane part that had previously consisted of 21 separate pieces, all of which were manufactured in different factories, and then shipped to one factory, where they were assembled.

🔊 2.4

Teacher: Welcome everybody, and thanks for coming to this special presentation event that marks the end of our semester. The topic that students explored in this project is planned obsolescence. The students formed four groups, and each group investigated and will report on a different aspect of this phenomenon. Each group is represented by one of its members. We'll start with group one and Robert, who is going to help us understand the concept in general. Robert?

Robert: I want to begin by defining what *planned obsolescence* means. This term describes a deliberate design policy. It means that a product is designed to become obsolete – to break, fail, become outdated, or go out of fashion – in a set – and usually relatively short – period of time.

As you might imagine, the purpose of planning a product's obsolescence is to make sure that consumers will have to buy new products on a regular basis. So planned obsolescence is a design, marketing, and financial policy all rolled into one. Now it's easy to think of this process as a plot **devised** by large corporations to take advantage of consumers. And there is certainly some evidence to support this point of view. However, it's also important to see the other side of the issue, especially within the tech sector, where things change very rapidly. It wouldn't make sense to build a piece of equipment to last for twenty years when the technology it uses will probably be replaced in a year or two. In this way, planned obsolescence may have the positive effect of encouraging **innovation**. You could also argue that there is a consumer benefit because making products stronger, more durable, would probably push prices out of reach for many

consumers. That said, most consumers **resent** planned obsolescence. Besides the financial burden of constantly having to buy new things, people also point to the enormous amount of waste it generates, waste that has to be put somewhere. I hope this gives you the general idea of the issues around planned obsolescence. The next two groups will provide us with some specific examples.

Angela: We're surrounded by products that are designed to become obsolete, especially anything that involves new technology. Some products are actually designed with a **finite** lifespan; others could last much longer, but their design makes it either impossible or impractical to extend their life. Not surprisingly, consumer electronics top this list. Let's start with phones. Some people run out to get the newest model as soon as it comes on the market, because they truly are early adopters, eager to own the newest gadgets. For many of us, however, upgrading isn't a choice but, rather, a matter of necessity. Phones are complex devices and companies have made it difficult for people to repair them on their own. Something as simple as replacing the battery is often the biggest obstacle to a longer product life. For some phones, the price of the new battery is very close to the price of a new phone, leading many customers to conclude that they might as well upgrade.

In other devices, software upgrades, **issued** automatically, and often with no warnings, may actually impair the performance of older models. Or you may find that the software company no longer supports your older version at all. You have to upgrade the hardware, and with a hardware upgrade, a software upgrade may become necessary, too. You have no choice but to keep trading up. But, as Celia will explain, technology products are really just the tip of the iceberg when it comes to product obsolescence. Celia?

Celia: Thank you. So, Angela's given you some examples of obsolescence in the tech sector, but we also encounter this phenomenon in the world of clothing, where it's referred to as 'fast fashion'. Fast fashion is a relatively recent trend in which designers and manufacturers try to move fashions from the runway to retail outlets as quickly as possible. It also involves responding immediately to consumer preferences. This is how it works. A clothing company spots a trend, say, white lacy blouses are selling quickly at their shops in London. An order is placed for hundreds of white lacy blouses, which appear on shelves two weeks later, encouraging the trend. A few months later, nobody is buying white lacy blouses, but many customers have bought ripped black jeans. So another order is placed, and suddenly ripped black jeans are everywhere.

Some companies have become so good at this that they can design, manufacture, and have clothing on shop shelves in just two or three weeks at a very low cost. The quality standards for the material in this clothing are low, and manufacturing is done in locations where labour costs are also low, resulting in cheap but low-quality products. Yet this hasn't slowed sales. On the contrary, the low prices and perhaps, ironically, even the low quality, encourage consumers to buy more and more. Their attitude seems to be: 'This will be out of fashion by next year, but it's so cheap, who cares if it falls apart in a couple of months? I'll just buy the next big thing.' Without a doubt, fast-fashion businesses generate enormous profits, but they also generate a lot of waste – so much that some people have begun to refer to their products as 'landfill fashion'.

Mark: We're going to end this presentation by discussing some of the consumer **backlash** to planned obsolescence. There is an ongoing battle between big tech companies and consumers who want to modify or repair their devices. Manufacturers try to prevent this by limiting access to parts and repair information, and by using digital locks. In some cases there are penalties for even trying to open up the back of a phone or a tablet: the warranty is no longer valid or the company will refuse to make any subsequent repairs. In response, a consumer-led movement has risen to share knowledge that allows people to **circumvent** these restrictions. The organization ifixit.org argues that consumers have the right to repair their own possessions and that manufacturers should give them access to the information that they need to do so. They share information about how to fix products and how to get around the **obstacles** that manufacturers place in the way of repairs. There are numerous similar websites and blogs that promote the idea of repairing, reusing, and recycling possessions. Other sites, such as buymeonce. com, recommend products that will last and permit repairs, and they also offer tips on maintaining your high-quality products so you can hold on to them for a long time. Their goal is to reduce waste of all kinds.

We've only had a short time today to present you with a lot of material. We have lots of other examples and links to organizations. We would be happy to share more of our research or answer any questions you have about this topic. Thank you.

 2.5

1   clothing industry
2   complex devices
3   backlash
4   design policy
5   digital locks
6   fast fashion
7   finite lifespan
8   runway
9   tech sector

 2.6

1   dishwasher
2   video game
3   games console
4   textbook
5   ink cartridges
6   gym shoes

UNIT 3

▶ Internet security expert on latest ransomware attack

John Sparks: It's been a busy 24 hours for the engineers at this computer lab in Moscow, here grappling with streams of malicious code from the latest ransomware attack. They work for cyber-security firm Kaspersky and they have given the virus a name: X-Peter. It's more virulent than the WannaCry attack last month, they say, with an estimated 100,000 computers infected.

Engineer: Well this attack is even more sophisticated than WannaCry, so it uses several techniques which allows it spreading more effectively in corporate network and globally, so I think er the same amount, maybe more companies will be attacked than WannaCry.

John Sparks: This virus is so potent, he adds, it only takes one terminal to take down a network.

Engineer: For this attack it's possible to find one vulnerable PCs – PC and to – to infect the rest computer in corporate network, so it means er even if company invested a lot of money and efforts to improve protection, but er if corporate network includes, say, 100,000 computers, so it's not – it's not easy to protect everything.

John Sparks: It certainly wreaked havoc and Ukraine has borne the brunt. The ransom demand's been popping up on bank machines and bureaucrats' desks across the nation.

Engineer: There is no any clues about IP addresses and the original vector of infection.

John Sparks: Kaspersky's engineers won't get much sleep as computer users wrestle with the latest threat.

 3.1

Host: In recent months, the news has been filled with a debate that sets the privacy of private individuals against the needs of law enforcement agencies in combatting crime. We've heard the views of senior figures in law enforcement, as well as those of technology companies and experts in the fields of law and technology. But what about the views of ordinary people, the people who are affected when either their privacy is threatened, or those whose **livelihoods** are threatened by criminals? To find out, we've invited six people to participate in this forum and share their thoughts. We'll take questions and comments from listeners at the end of the programme.

Before we bring in our guests, however, let's talk about the two questions that we're going to ask them. Our first question is: should communication companies be **compelled** to hand over information about the activities of private individuals to the police **in the interest of** fighting crime? This question addresses the millions of records that these companies have – names, contacts, IP addresses, etc. – so called metadata, but also actual content, for example, what people said in phone conversations or in text messages, and information they have stored on their devices, such as lists of contacts.

Our second question addresses a different but related issue: should technology companies be compelled to help law enforcement agencies break into the electronic devices of private individuals, again, in the interest of fighting crime?

So, we're asking whether tech companies should have to write computer code to create a 'back door', that is, a way to circumvent the **encryption** of information on the devices that they make.

 3.2

Host: Let's start with Joel, who works in the insurance industry. Joel, should companies have to hand over information about their customers?

Joel: Absolutely. The police should have as much information as possible in order to keep us safe. We need to keep one step ahead of serious criminals and organized crime.

Host: And should they be required to help the police break into private devices?

Joel: Well, I'm not so sure about that one. That may be crossing the line.

Host: Lauren, a high school teacher here in town, is next. Should companies have to hand over information about their customers? What do you think?

Lauren: Well, if I have a contract with a private company for phone service or web access or whatever, that's between me and the company. They shouldn't give out information about me to anyone. That's what I think, but, I'm not sure it matters. You know tech companies are *already* doing it. A recent report showed they've actually been doing it for years.

Host: Then I suppose your answer to the second question would be …

Lauren: Don't get me started. If we're worried about crime the *last* thing we should do is make these companies write code to circumvent the encryption. If there's a back door for the government, then you can be sure that all kinds of criminals – well, they'll find a way to get access to it too. Think of all the information you have on your digital devices – financial information, passwords, scans of your passport. A back door is an invitation to thieves and fraudsters to steal your identity. Encryption is the only thing that is protecting us.

Host: OK, we'll see whether our next guest agrees with you. This is Dave and he's a police officer. Dave, as somebody involved in fighting crime what are your thoughts?

Dave: Most people just don't understand. Law enforcement is made more difficult without access to this kind of information. I've had cases when I couldn't arrest a criminal because of some law about *his* privacy. If the criminals know more than we do, how can we protect good, law-abiding people? Isn't public safety more important than privacy?

Host: Is it important enough to make tech companies break into our devices?

Dave: No doubt in my mind. If we have to give up a little bit of freedom and privacy for the sake of protecting your average citizen, so be it. Information is power these days, and law enforcement doesn't have enough of it. Without access to communications we can only ever catch the low level players – and we can't prevent the crime – we get the information after the fact. The crime bosses who are planning the crimes, it takes months, years of work to bring one of them down – they don't commit the crimes themselves – so without evidence from surveillance that's admissible in court we don't have a hope of putting them away.

Host: Let's hear from somebody with some legal expertise. Karina is a lawyer. Karina?

Karina: To my mind, if the government wants my data, it should have to ask me for it or get a **warrant**. The law requires this. So, if there is a convincing need for the information, and if a judge gives the government permission, then yes, I think this is perfectly **legitimate**.

Host: And do you think we should ask tech companies for help in cracking private devices?

Karina: Absolutely not. What everybody needs to understand is that in your *first* question, you're asking about information that the communications company actually *has*. But in the *second* question, you're asking if the tech company should be forced to write new software to break into an encrypted phone and *get* information. That is an entirely different story. The information on that phone doesn't belong to the tech company; it belongs to a private individual. Another thing: if law enforcement agencies really wanted to get information off a particular device, you know they could find a way to do it.

Host: OK, Tony, your turn to weigh in. Tony is a small business owner.

Tony: I think we need to do everything we can to help the government and the police put a stop to organized crime, so my answer is yes, tech companies should hand over any information the government asks for. But breaking into people's phones? Well, I think that's kind of odd – not just odd – it's disturbing that our agencies can't already do this. Why do the police have to ask tech companies for help? I think the majority of these agencies have their own experts, don't they? Karina there, she said she thinks they do have the expertise … But I guess if they don't, then maybe the tech companies do have an obligation to help – if it's really a matter of serious crime going unpunished.

Host: Finally we come to Miku, a data analyst, who might be able to give us some **insight** from the tech side.

Miku: I think if the information is limited to metadata – you know – phone numbers, dates, times – that kind of thing, it's fine, but I wouldn't want them to hand over the actual content of text messages or things like that. And I definitely don't think we should be asking tech companies to break into people's devices. Look, the police are trying to make it look as if this is a **trade-off** between privacy and public safety. That might be true if we were talking about the physical world – like unlocking the door to your apartment. But the digital world isn't like that. Any technology expert can tell you that if a company gives the government the key to the back door of one phone, it's the same thing as giving up the key to thousands of other phones. Doing that would actually make all of us much *less* secure, not *more* secure.

Host: OK, we've heard the views of our guests here tonight. Now let's hear from you. Call the station to tell us what you think. OK, I see we have our first caller. Yes, caller, go ahead.

 3.3

See script on page 66

 3.4

Speaker: Welcome everybody, and thank you for coming to this talk in our series on technology and privacy. Our speaker today is Hana Tanaka, who is an expert in the field. She's going to explain how some of the technology works and then talk about sensible steps you can take to protect your privacy when you use the internet. Hana?

Hana Tanaka: Thank you. I want to start with a slide. It shows data from a survey, and indicates only about nine percent of respondents believe they have 'a lot of control' over their information. I think we can conclude that we have a problem. So, today, I want to add to that percentage by helping you gain a bit more control over your 'digital footprint'.

So, you've probably all had this experience: you're surfing the internet; maybe you're looking for some new camera equipment. There's a new lens you really want, but it's a bit expensive, so you decide to put it off for a while. Maybe you'll be able to afford it next month. You **move on**. Later, you're reading an online newspaper or blog and then, bam! An advert for that lens you want appears on your screen. Quite scary isn't it? I mean, how did they do that? How do they know what you were looking at on a completely different website? Well, that's what I want to talk about today. What you experienced is called 'behavioural targeting'. With every click, you create and expand an online profile of your desires, preferences and behaviour. Companies track your browsing activity and use it to send you advertisements that **target** you specifically. Their hope is that by understanding what you like and want, they can send you adverts which you're more likely to click, for products and services that you're more likely to buy. How did all this begin? Well, it actually started with you, the web user, in mind. Let's be honest, when a website tracks and remembers where you've been, it can be pretty useful, can't it? You start typing the name of a website you've visited before in the search bar and it automatically fills the rest of it in for you. Or, if you can't remember the name of the site, you can check your browsing history, and there it is. You don't want to fill in your information every time you visit a site? No problem. It's all saved for you when you come back. The primary tool that companies use to track and remember you is the *cookie*.

A cookie is a small text file, which is downloaded onto your browser when you visit a site. It saves information about what you do while you're on the site. Cookies were first developed when online **retailers** were looking for a way to make shopping easier for customers. You've probably all used an online shopping basket, haven't you? Well, cookies are what make that basket possible. Without cookies, the basket couldn't collect the items you select. The site would forget them as soon as you left to go to a new page. But with cookies, you can even think it over and come back the next day. The items are still in your basket. So cookies are clearly useful. In general, cookies have made it possible to **personalize** the user experience in a way that makes searching and using the internet more efficient and satisfying.

That's how cookies work within a single website. The scary part starts when they cross over to *other* websites. Advertising companies that have hundreds of clients can connect cookies all across the web. For example, if you click on an advert when you visit a website, then another cookie is sent to your browser by the advertiser. This is sometimes called *a third-party cookie*. Now, every time you visit another site that has advertisements from the same company, the cookies can be **traced** back to you. As you surf and shop your way around the internet, these cookies eventually build a profile of your preferences and interests. It shows when and where you clicked and how long you spent on each page, all of which is very valuable information for companies that want to sell you services and products, like that camera lens.

One final cookie issue that you should be aware of is that some cookies are transmitted over a secure network; that is, they're sent in a type of code. These are usually called *secure cookies*, and many retail sites use these. *Non-secure cookies*, in contrast, are vulnerable to theft. If somebody grabs one of these during transmission, it can be used for the purpose of identity theft. Some of the most popular sites on the web use non-secure cookies. I think more sites will probably move to secure cookies in the future, but for now, only about half of all websites use secure cookies.

So now you know a little bit about how it all works. Maybe you're thinking you should stop using the internet altogether! Don't despair! I'm going to give you some advice about a few easy ways to manage and protect your privacy without going **offline**. And a lot of people are **taking steps** to protect themselves. In a recent survey, 86% of the respondents had taken some steps to erase their 'digital footprint'. So it's clear that people are starting to take action to protect themselves.

Many of the tools you need are right there on your browser, or are offered by individual websites. You just need to actively choose to use them. For example, you may be asked for your permission to let the browser know where you are and where you're going. You may be asked to turn on or enable your cookies. We get so many long and often complicated messages that we often just click 'yes' or 'I agree' because it's too much trouble to do anything else. If that describes you, then you need to become a more educated internet user and make more informed decisions. You should say 'no' if you don't want that company to store information about you.

Most browsers have a setting that allows you to **disable** cookies, preventing sites from collecting information on your web activities. But you may not want to disable this feature all the time; in which case, you can simply delete your browsing history – for the past week, month, year – or from the beginning of time, giving you some level of control over what information can be collected and stored. Most browsers also have an option that allows you to surf *incognito*, which means no information is collected on your activity. But remember, this means you will also get none of the benefits of that stored information. Finally, there are alternative browsers, ones which don't collect or store any data about users and their activities. If you take some of these steps, you'll probably be OK – or at least less vulnerable.

However, these cookies are just the first weapon in an online retailer's arsenal. There are other, more sophisticated methods for recording user activity, including ones that are more difficult for users to manage and control. Some tools, such as so-called flash cookies, also store information about you, but they're stored *outside* of your browser. And *web beacons*, tiny invisible graphics on web pages, can tell the server you're on a specific page, and these are not removed when you clear your cookies or browsing history. No doubt, tech privacy experts will soon catch up with these developments and find ways to counter them as well.

To sum up, you can't control everything, but you can take charge of some aspects of your privacy and online identity. I hope that this talk's given you some useful information and tools. And remember, think before you click!

 3.5

1 How can we protect good, law-abiding people?
2 Isn't public safety more important than privacy?
3 Is it important enough to make tech companies break into our devices?
4 Do you think we should ask tech companies for help in cracking private devices?
5 Why do the police have to ask tech companies for help?

UNIT 4

▶ Ugandan tech start-up caters to local markets

Commentator: With a successful gaming app already under his belt, Jasper Nunu has joined the growing ranks of East Africa's whizz kids, helping to propel the region into the tech spotlight. Mutatu, a traditional two-player card game, has long been popular here in Uganda. With the rapid growth of the smartphone market, in Kenya alone, one in five people access the web through their phones. Entrepreneurs like Jasper are building apps that cater to the needs of local markets.

Jasper: Mutatu is a very popular two-card playing game in Uganda, it's one of the ... it's actually the most popular game in Uganda right now. So umm the idea came up back in campus when we were attending a conference, and a thought just hit us that why don't people have this game in their phones? Can we do this game?

Commentator: In 2011, Mutatu was a finalist in Google's Android Developer Challenge for Sub-Saharan Africa, providing them with publicity and mentoring, as well as having their app posted in Google Play Store and Google Cloud. Now, with more than 60,000 downloads, Mutatu's success is the latest sign of the region's high-tech hopes.

Interviewee 1:   I like having it on the phone because I can play it any time, and even when I'm alone, I don't need to have friends around or a group of people, I can just have it on my phone – play it any time, anywhere – and it's fun.

Commentator: From the laying of fibre-optic cables to popular mobile money systems, East Africa has experienced a dramatic tech-hub boom, spurred on by collaborative workspaces such as Nairobi's iHub and growing international investment. Africa has the highest concentration of young people anywhere on the planet, many of whom have at least some disposable income. And increasingly, investors are looking to break into these lucrative local markets.

Interviewee 2:   But if we can have a place whereby somebody can say when they're listing in the top five apps on their phone, will have at least one or two Kenyan or African apps on it, I feel like that will go long way and umm encourage other young people to begin to believe that there is more potential than what they see, and we're not just consumers of content but we're creators of it.

Commentator: If the future of computing lies in mobile, and the fastest growth in mobile comes from the developing world, many are beginning to look to African start-ups for a taste of things to come.

🔊 4.1

Professor: You may have heard the **buzzword** 'disruptive innovation,' which is when a new technology or business model fundamentally changes a market. The classic example is the personal computer, which was pioneered by IBM, a company that had previously dominated the market for large mainframe computers. The company's primary customers had been businesses. With IBM's new smaller model however, computers became accessible to an entirely new group of customers – individuals, which changed the market forever.

The internet has become the engine of disruptive innovation in dozens of markets, from travel to publishing to insurance. By creating a system of universal access, the internet effectively redefined many business **transactions**.

🔊 4.2

Professor: You may have heard the buzzword 'disruptive innovation,' which is when a new technology or business model fundamentally changes a market. The classic example is the personal computer, which was pioneered by IBM, a company that had previously dominated the market for large mainframe computers. The company's primary customers had been businesses. With IBM's new smaller model, however, computers became accessible to an entirely new group of customers – individuals, which changed the market forever.

The internet has become the engine of disruptive innovation in dozens of markets, from travel to publishing to insurance. By creating a system of universal access, the internet effectively redefined many business transactions. By universal access, I mean two things: firstly, suddenly anyone with a computer and a network connection could access all kinds of information – information that had previously only been available to professionals who acted as 'middlemen' in transactions between businesses and their customers. Massive amounts of information were **dumped** onto the web for individual consumers to see and use. And secondly, networks among individuals were now possible. Buyers and sellers no longer needed intermediaries. They could connect directly to one other. As a result, most people no longer bothered with these intermediaries – the middlemen. Why use a travel agent? Airfares and hotel rates could now all be found on the internet. The public also began to abandon insurance agents and even their banks, instead going directly to the internet to find products and services. Sellers also changed the way they did business. Musicians could sell their songs directly to the public. Authors didn't need publishers. Small manufacturers no longer needed big retailers to carry their products. They could sell directly to customers from their own websites.

This revolution introduced two new business models. Firstly, we have aggregators; these are businesses, such as Amazon, which bring together every product imaginable and make them available with one click. Customers no longer have to visit different websites, let alone different shops, to get everything they need. Travel sites, such as Expedia and Kayak, aggregate information on dozens of airlines and car rentals, and thousands of hotels, allowing customers to compare and make their choices from a single site.

This model is perhaps just a larger, more **elaborate** online version of the supermarket or department store, but in the second business model, referred to as peer-to-peer (or P2P) retail, there is more of a departure from the past. In peer-to-peer businesses, all traces of the middleman are truly gone. Customers don't even bother with a hotel at all. Instead, they rent a room from another private individual. They don't rent a car from a car rental company; they rent it from another person. These peer-to-peer transactions are facilitated by a new breed of start-up companies. To find a room to rent, there are companies like Airbnb. To get a lift, you can go through Uber. To buy a pair of jeans, a toaster, or even a car from another individual, the public can turn to online market sites like eBay.

The key element shared by these two models is new technology. The internet has allowed universal access, but in addition, it's allowed the automation of transactions, reducing what Bill Gates referred to as 'friction' in the market. With online transactions, there is no need for people, no need for interaction, which could slow things down. Just a series of clicks. In 1995, Gates predicted that online markets might allow for 'frictionless capitalism'; in other words, the smooth and easy exchange of goods and labour, with no middleman and no transaction costs. So, has his prediction come true? Well, yes and no. The elimination of the middleman has indeed reduced costs generally. And it is true that the number of these intermediaries has dropped significantly. There are far fewer travel agencies today than there were 25 years ago. But some problems emerged with the disappearance of the middleman – starting with a lack of trust. How do consumers know if an individual seller on eBay is honest, for example? It's not like the old days when they ordered products from a familiar and reliable shop. Furthermore, the massive amount of information a consumer encounters online may lead to indecision, in some cases, even decision-making paralysis. There is so much information available that consumers just don't know what to do with it. Part of the problem is sheer volume, and part of it is that all this raw information can be difficult for end users to interpret. How are ordinary consumers to make sense of this information **overload**?

In fact, what they need is ... a middleman to sift through it all – all the news, all the data, all the songs, all the prices, all the products. The buzzword for this sifting activity is 'curation'. Customers want somebody to help make intelligent choices in this sea of information, and curation can help them do this. This need has created an entirely new set of businesses. Paul English, who founded and later sold the online travel aggregator Kayak, is still in the travel business. His latest **venture** is a travel app that provides all of the information available on other sites, but with one difference. It also offers the services of travel agents – humans who will help customers make decisions. These new 'curators' have become experts at harnessing the power of the internet. And as far as re-establishing trust is concerned, **wary** eBay customers can now turn to what are often referred to as 'power sellers', – participants who act as intermediaries on the site, buying and selling large volumes of items. In the process, these power sellers build a reputation so that other participants generally trust them more than they trust individual small-scale sellers. A final casualty of the elimination of the middleman has been luxury. Some customers want more than curation, more than just a little guidance. They want a middleman who will actually *do* everything for them. The buzzword for what these customers want is a 'concierge', and yes, the internet can provide this too. Concierge apps like AnyWysh will make your travel arrangements, do your errands, and arrange deliveries.

And so disruptive innovation has brought us full circle. The internet and accompanying technology have successfully eliminated the middleman in a wide range of markets, only to have the public realize that middlemen actually add value to the transaction, value that they miss.

 4.3

The classic example / is the personal computer / which was pioneered by IBM / a company that had previously dominated the market / for large mainframe computers.

 4.4

Presenter: Welcome everybody. Please help yourself to a drink, find a seat, and we'll get started. Your management professor told me that you're all interested in becoming entrepreneurs for social good, and so she thought it might be a good idea for you to learn something about the non-profit sector. I'll start by talking a little bit about the basics of a non-profit organization, then offer a few tips for those of you who are seriously thinking of going in that direction. I hope this will give you a good **overview**. I also hope that by the end, some of you will be convinced to enter the non-profit world. It's a place where you can use your business skills to make the world a better place. I started in this business after a trip to Haiti, following the 2010 earthquake. I saw so much suffering and need there, especially among the children. I wanted to do something to give them more opportunity.

There are many different kinds of non-profit organizations, established for many different purposes, but we usually think of them as having **worthy** aims – they're established to achieve some sort of social good. This may seem obvious, but the most important aspect of a non-profit is its mission. You really need to be able to express clearly and **concisely** the purpose of your organization. With for-profit businesses, the mission is easy to describe. They're in the business of making money. Unlike a for-profit organization, however, all of the revenue, that is, all the donations, grants, etc., in a non-profit organization, must be returned to the organization. Most of the money should be used for the organization's programmes, although some of it, obviously, must be used to actually run the organization. I'll return to that point a little later, but I want to stop and talk about what we mean by 'programmes' because this is where, unfortunately, some organizations have abused their non-profit **status**.

An organization's programmes are the activities that provide direct benefits to the people whom the organization is trying to help, for example, teenagers receiving job training, disaster victims who need medical assistance, etc. However, organizations can, and sometimes do, include other activities in their programmes, but this is where you need to be very careful. One well-known example is the Central Asia Institute, a charity with the mission of building schools in Afghanistan. It was getting lots of donations until it was revealed that included among its 'programmes' were activities to promote the director's books and lectures. That caused a very damaging backlash against the organization.

Although we call these organizations *non-profits*, this term is somewhat misleading. It's absolutely essential that the money coming into a non-profit is greater than its expenses; otherwise, it won't be able to help anyone. In other words, the organization needs to make money. What a non-profit cannot do, however, is create and distribute equity. A company's equity basically means its value, for shareholders, or owners. But a non-profit has no shareholders and no owner. Perhaps the biggest organizational difference between a non-profit and a for-profit **enterprise** is that no single person controls it. Boards of directors, generally composed of at least five members, have **oversight** of the operation of the organization.

So that tells you about some of the nuts and bolts of running a non-profit, but I know that all of you are more interested in how you can get started on turning your dreams into reality. Well, you may think that the starting point is your fabulous idea, but the real starting point is money. Money is what makes the wheels of commerce turn, and the same can be said of non-profits. But you're not going to be selling anything – not technically – so where will the money come from? The answer can vary, depending on the organization, but non-profits rely heavily on fundraising, so you need to accept this as a fact of life, right from the start. A lot of money comes from individual **donors**. Some non-profits also receive funding from corporations and private foundations; others receive funding from the local, state, or federal government. Whatever the source, I cannot stress enough that fundraising is the lifeblood of a non-profit. The more money you raise, the closer you'll come to reaching your goals. Running a non-profit is a little bit like having a child that is always hungry!

I do want you to have a realistic perspective, but I also want you to hold on to your dreams and don't let go just because this is hard. Anyone can go into an established business. Some people can manage a successful start-up, but only a very special type of person can establish and manage a successful start-up for social good. And I believe that all of you are among those special people.

To help you on your road to success, I want to offer some of the lessons that others in this sector have already learned. So, let me give you a few words of advice.

Make sure you understand and can articulate your mission. For example, our mission here is to provide inspiration and administrative support for new non-profits that serve children in need. Once you are sure of your mission, protect it. You're here because you believe in a cause. Sometime in the future, you may be offered funding by a donor or by a foundation for something that falls outside the **scope** of your mission. You will be tempted to take it, especially if it's a lot of money, but don't do it. You'll end up trying to do too many things and doing none of them well. More importantly, you won't be doing what you set out to do.

Invest in administration and development. This may sound like strange advice, but non-profits, like for-profit companies, need to innovate, and they need to lead. They can't do those things on a starvation budget. This doesn't mean you should pay everybody on your staff a fat salary, but you do need to invest in the operational side of your organization if you want to be effective and you want to succeed in the long term.

I mentioned the need for innovation. Today's most successful new non-profits are changing the way this sector works. Instead of relying exclusively on the goodwill of donors, they're learning from the for-profit sector about how to harness market forces, but for social good. Authors and non-profit experts Crutchfield and Grant express it this way, 'Great non-profits find ways to work with markets and help business do well while doing good.'

I hope this introduction has been helpful to you as you make decisions about your future. My years working in the non-profit world have been the most-rewarding of my life. There is no better way to make your mark on the world, so I hope some of you will step up and join me!

UNIT 5

▶ New virtual reality game helping to fight against dementia

Man: So ... em ... we'll show you a checkpoint level ...

Narrator: Sea Hero Quest is the world's first virtual reality game designed to help researchers understand dementia. While players are immersed in a mission at sea, the game collects information on their ability to navigate through simple mazes.

Man: I mean this kind of really like sweet interaction with creatures which is a really nice layer on top ... I mean

Dr David Reynolds: In erm ... in many forms of dementia, particularly Alzheimer's disease er ... your spatial awareness your ability to navigate is one of the first things that goes and that's we know is because that's where some of the earliest damage occurs in your brain the bit of your brain that does your spatial navigation. So it links to what we're seeing at the kind of cell level of your brain cells struggling and then dying and then what's happening at a functional level impacts your real world ability to find the right aisle in the shopping err ... in the supermarket or something ...

Narrator: Around 47 million people in the world today are living with dementia, a figure expected to triple by 2050. It is most common in over 65s. However, scientists believe it begins to develop when people are much younger. Dementia causes sufferers to slowly lose certain mental abilities, and there is no known cure, but early diagnosis can slow its progress.

Improved early diagnosis techniques are urgently needed. To collect essential data, Alzheimer's Research UK teamed up with scientists and Deutsche Telekom to develop Sea Hero Quest. The game was first rolled out on mobile devices last year. Over 3 million people around the world played the game, giving scientists a huge amount of data about how people navigate.

Dr David Reynolds: Until we got Sea Hero Quest, the largest study looking at spatial navigation – so how you navigate around a complex environment – was about 600 people, we've now got 3,000,000 so that's orders of magnitude more information. And with that information we can understand much better what 'normal' looks like. Because, until you know what normal healthy people ... how well they perform, it's difficult to tell when somebody starts to have problems, particularly in the early stages, where those um ... problems they've got are perhaps very small and subtle compared to a healthy individual ...

Dr Christophe Holscher: So and maybe for the topic of dementia, the most relevant discovery in this large data set is that a qualitative change in how well people perform the navigation task in this game starts much earlier than what you'd expect. Traditional laboratory-based research normally focuses on observations that people at my age start to slowly decline and then it goes down. But what we can actually pinpoint in this large data set is that from the age of about 19 onwards there are measurable differences that you will just obtain in a traditional laboratory study ...

Narrator: With the launch of the free virtual reality version of the game, researchers hope to discover even more about dementia.

Dr Christophe Holscher: What the virtual reality game really adds is much more fine-grain detail because people are immersed in the world that they're navigating around –

just as we are in the real world. And that will give us a lot more insight, I think, than being playing it on a mobile phone using your thumbs to navigate about.

 5.1

Eva: OK, so has everybody read all the material?

Ramzi: Yep. So how do you think we should organize it? There's so much information.

Sara: Yeah, the assignment is to present research findings, but I think we should present what we think will be the most interesting to the rest of the class – something they can **relate to**.

Eva: I like that idea. Let's talk about what we found in our readings and then plan the presentation.

Ramzi: Sounds good. OK, if I had to draw one generalization from all the readings, it would be that humans are sensitive to a variety of different **cues**, and we respond to them really, really fast.

Eva: I got the same sense from what I read. So what about some of the cues?

Ramzi: Well, in a nutshell, it's physical appearance that's the most important cue in first impressions, especially the face. In the study I read, the scientists gave the participants just a tenth of a second to decide how likeable, **competent**, trustworthy, and aggressive they thought a person in a photograph was. It was pretty incredible; in just a few milliseconds, they were able to make these decisions, and even more amazing, their judgments were pretty consistent with the judgments of people who had unlimited time to make them. Of the four characteristics, the one that the scientists found was the most consistent was trustworthiness. They **speculated** that, basically, deciding quickly if you could trust somebody must have been a really important ability during early human evolution.

Eva: It probably still is! That's really interesting. I read another study on a similar topic, but it was a little more specific. It was just about attractiveness. Based on a few milliseconds of **exposure**, participants had to decide if they think they'd like the person in the picture, on a scale of one to four. The researchers looked at images of the participants' brains as they made these judgments and saw that a specific area of the brain was very active. Then, a few days later, the participants actually met the people in the photos. Overall, it turns out the judgments they made in a few milliseconds held true in real life. Most participants ended up liking the people they rated as fours and not really liking the people they rated as ones.

Sara: Yeah, I reviewed that study, too. There was another part that I thought was really intriguing. Some of the photos were of really attractive people and all the participants pretty much agreed they were fours. But there were some photos that only a few people found attractive. When the researchers examined the participants' brain activity as they were rating those photos, the activity was in a different area from the rating of the really attractive photos.

Ramzi: So what does that mean?

Sara: Well, the authors of the study had an interesting explanation, similar to the one you mentioned about an evolutionary advantage. They conclude that our first response is to go for somebody who is generally attractive, what they call 'a good catch'. In evolutionary terms, that would be a good mate, and everybody seemed to agree on who that would be. But the different preferences suggest we also make judgments about who'd be 'a good catch for me'. And judgments about that are made in a different part of the brain.

Eva: There were a lot of other cues, too – like voice, how people walk, if they look into your eyes when you talk. But I think maybe we should keep a narrow focus and just talk about faces. We only have fifteen minutes for our presentation. What do you think?

Ramzi: I think you're right. There's no way we can present everything we read about. But there was another really interesting study about faces that we could include.

Sara: The one with the computer-designed faces?

Ramzi: Yeah! It's really interesting, isn't it?

Sara: Totally.

Eva: Wait! I didn't read that one. What was it about?

Ramzi: OK. So this one psychologist had probably read all of the studies that we have, and he wanted to take the idea a step further.

Eva: What do you mean? Can you just summarize it?

Ramzi: All the other studies had used actual human faces, which made it really hard to tell exactly what the participants were reacting to when they made their judgments. So he took a set of 1,000 photos and showed them to a group of people. They had to make judgments on a range of traits. Then, he took 65 different measurements of the faces. The bottom line is that he was able to get consistent judgment in relation to particular features of the face on three traits – **dominance**, attractiveness and approachability – which I think basically means friendliness.

Eva: Sixty-five? Wow! What features did he measure?

Ramzi: Oh, the tilt of the head, the width and shape of the eyebrows, the gap between the lips, the shape of lips – stuff like that. Then, using artificial intelligence, his team created a set of computer-generated drawings of faces that demonstrated the range of difference in these traits – so, from very **approachable** to not at all approachable, etc. Then they had human participants judge the computer-generated faces. The researchers think they're pretty close to identifying the specific facial features that result in these first impressions.

Sara: I think this one would be a good one to present to the class because of the cool visuals. Some of the features are obvious, like the smile, but I was surprised how important other features were – like eyebrow shape.

Eva: Yeah, I never thought much about eyebrows. I guess we aren't really aware of some of the things we respond to, even in less than a second.

Ramzi: We should probably include some practical **applications** in our presentation. The authors of the study discussed how useful this will be in computer-generated graphics in games and films. It will give artists a good rule of thumb for how to create the faces of different kinds of characters.

Sara: Well, OK, so it's not exactly solving world hunger, but I guess that *is* a useful application. OK, this is a great start. I think we're in good shape. Should we think of a title?

Eva: How about this: 'How to judge a book by its cover'.

5.2

See script on page 110

5.3

See script on page 110

5.4

Professor: Perhaps you've had the experience of getting step-by-step directions from somebody or using your smartphone to find a place, and later, when trying to find your way a second time, you discover that you have no memory of the route you took.

Today, I want to discuss some research that's been carried out over the past ten years that sheds lights on this phenomenon – research about some interesting findings about the connection between our increasing **reliance on** navigation aids such as GPS and our cognitive health.

Psychologists have known for some time that we create mental maps to make sense of our world. In the 1970s, scientists discovered that the site of this map-making ability is the hippocampus. You can see its location deep inside the brain, in the temporal lobe, on this slide. Within the hippocampus, differentiated cells allow us to orient ourselves in relation to **landmarks** and to adjust our position as we move through space – sort of like our own internal GPS. The hippocampus plays a key role in spatial memory and navigation. These are among the first abilities to **deteriorate** as we age, sometimes ending in dementia. So, you can see why understanding how it works is a top priority for researchers today. Spatial memory is involved in more than just remembering where things are, however. It plays a crucial role in memory overall because it allows us to **reconstruct** experiences and events that are connected in our minds to physical spaces.

Humans **navigate** in one of two ways. The first is the spatial or landmark strategy. This strategy relies on the hippocampus and involves building a mental map that uses landmarks, such as buildings, parks, trees, etc., like on this slide. The second method is the response strategy, which is more or less memorization. Using this strategy, knowledge emerges as the result of repeated trips along the same route. This strategy does not require the construction of a mental map. Scientists have shown that these two strategies use different parts of the brain.

Eleanor Maguire, a psychologist at University College, London, became interested in the role of the hippocampus in navigation. She was particularly interested in the brains of people who use the first strategy **intensively**. For study participants, she chose a very specific population of landmark strategy users – London taxi drivers. London taxi drivers are famous for knowing the city's 250,000 streets incredibly well. They study for three or four years to prepare for the very demanding test they have to take for a taxi license. As she suspected, the MRI images of the drivers' brains as they planned their routes showed a high level of activity in the hippocampus. She also found that this part of their brain was unusually large and, furthermore, that the more experience a driver had, the larger the hippocampus. Look at these images of two different brains. The first shows a taxi driver's hippocampus. These results strongly suggested that the constant creation of mental maps had affected the drivers' brains. However, Maguire couldn't be sure that the

relationship was causal. An alternative explanation was that people with a large hippocampus were more likely to pass the demanding exam and become drivers. So, Maguire did a longitudinal follow-up study. She took MRI images of applicants for a taxi license before they began their studies for the test. All participants had hippocampi of relatively similar size at the start of the study. Four years later, Maguire studied these participants again. Some of the applicants had failed the test while others had passed and become drivers. The hippocampi of the second group – the ones who had become drivers – were much larger, which is clear in these before and after pictures. These participants also did much better on cognitive tests. So all this points to a causal relationship between the creation of mental maps and the increased size of the hippocampus.

Maguire's studies came at a time when digital devices with GPS were just emerging. As they became more popular, some researchers began to wonder whether the increasing use of these devices might **impair** our ability to create mental maps. In 2005, Gary Burnett at Nottingham University conducted a study in which half of the participants were given step-by-step instructions to their destinations, and the other half had to find their way using maps. When they were later asked to draw a map of the route they took, the drivers who had simply followed directions performed much worse than those who had navigated on their own, as you can see in this slide. These findings support the idea that the choice of navigation strategy impacts this type of memory.

Professor Veronique Bohbot at McGill University in Canada also pursued this line of inquiry. In her study, she compared a group of participants who were accustomed to navigating with spatial landmark strategy with another group who relied on GPS for navigation. The participants in the first group had more grey matter in their hippocampi and exhibited a higher level of activity in this part of the brain. Perhaps more important, this group also performed better on a cognitive test that often reveals the first sign of dementia as a person ages.

As with Maguire's first study, it isn't possible to say **definitively** that this connection between GPS use and lower test performance is a causal one. Similarly, we cannot yet say whether engaging in spatial navigation and the creation of mental maps can delay the effects of ageing on cognition. More research is needed. Nevertheless, Professor Bohbot says that these results are strong enough to suggest that if we limit our reliance on GPS, we'll strengthen our brain's navigational skills.

UNIT 6

▶ '100k opportunities' job fair in Chicago

Narrator: Chicago, Illinois is America's third largest city and a major world financial centre, but that doesn't mean that it is free from social problems; in five districts of the city 79 to 92 percent of teenagers and 49 to 70 percent of young adults are jobless, areas which also have the highest rates of violent crime. The 100,000 Opportunities Initiative has organized a job fair in Chicago to reach out to 'opportunity youth' – young people who find it difficult to get into employment and education because of their backgrounds. The organizers say that hundreds of young people will walk away with jobs this evening, or at the very least with promising job leads.

Speaker 1:   Employed teens are also more likely to enrol and graduate from college because they learn on the job persistence and dependability.

Speaker 2:   And now we're trying to put young people to work in our city, and I can't think of anything to embrace more.

Speaker 3:   We can accomplish something and give every one of the young men and women – and also I would say their parents who are in that room – the sense that there's a tomorrow waiting for them.

Speaker 4:   The biggest obstacle for more young people making good choices is just the lack of opportunity. And so often the negative behaviour is not a choice, a first … a first … a first resort, it's a choice of last resort.

Commentator: An impressive array of corporate and governmental leaders with recording artist and actor Common adding star power to what's being billed as the 100,000 opportunities job fair and forum.

Speaker 5:   And I think we have to ensure the fact that the future generation of this country, irregardless of colour, station in life, zip code, er, is filled with the promise er, of the past generation.

Commentator: More than 4,500 young people between the ages of 18 and 24 meet with recruiters from 30 major companies, all of it under one roof at Chicago's McCormick Place.

Journalist: So you're optimistic that you're going to get a job as a result?

Job seeker 1:   I know I'm gonna get one. I know I'm gonna get one. I got a good personality; I'm very outspoken … I'm very helpful.

Commentator: Among the eager faces in the crowd, 18-year-old Everett from the Southeast Side.

Everett: I just wanna work with a good company. Honestly, the pay doesn't matter as long as I enjoy it.

Commentator: Visiting with recruiters from a delivery company, Everett hopes to find a part-time job to help him pay for college.

FedEx recruiter: [One] we're always looking to hire people and two, it is a growing market for us. And I'll talk about ground and, specifically, we just opened a brand new hub, South Side, Chicago.

Commentator: But Everett also interviews with a department store.

Journalist: They've pretty much made up their minds, you think?

Everett: Yeah, most definitely. I think umm they look at me as a very ideal candidate and I'm thankful just to have that opportunity for this interview.

Commentator: Deciding that Everett is a perfect fit, the department store makes their offer. So, bottom line, did he get a job?

Department store recruiter: He did. He was offered a role at our Lincoln Park Rack. We're really excited. Actually, he had several people on the interviewing team that were really interested in him.

Commentator: In addition to interviews, there's job fairs and forums all designed to open a door of opportunity for Chicago young people.

 6.1

Careers advisor: Good afternoon everybody. This is a special session that the Career Service Office is offering for computer science students. We wanted to target this session at all of you in computer science and related degree programmes because, frankly, you'll probably have a lot more options when you finish your degree than other graduates. Of course, having options is a good thing, but options are often accompanied by a degree of confusion. Specifically, what we want to address here today are some of the pros and cons of three **distinct** ways that you can enter the job market, focusing on the situation in the United Kingdom. If you're considering taking a position abroad, keep in mind that some of the legal issues and government regulations that we're going to discuss may not apply to you.

The most traditional and common route is simply to take a position as an employee with an established company, and for many of you, this may be the most appropriate choice. You can immediately start using the skills and knowledge you've gained in your studies. However, you could also consider the option of using those skills without joining a company – as a consultant, or what is often referred to as an independent contractor, or freelance worker. Finally, especially for those of you graduating with more advanced degrees, there's the option of establishing your own business – a start-up company.

So, now that you know what the three options are, let's talk about some of the pros and cons of each, starting with the employee option. For those of you getting an undergraduate degree and who haven't had a lot of work experience, this option may be your best bet. It's certainly the easiest way to **start out**. Employees at most big companies have relatively good job security – though, of course, there is often a **probationary period** at the start of your employment. If you're an employee, you know how much your pay cheque will be at the end of the month. So it's predictable, reliable. And other than the cost of getting to and from work – and maybe a wardrobe upgrade, there are no business expenses for employees. Finally – and this is what I meant earlier when I said our topic would be the UK market – in this country, the government provides employees with some measure of protection. In theory, at least, you should have a safe workplace and be protected against **discrimination** and harassment.

As an independent contractor, you have no such protection, and your life will be far less predictable. You have to find your own jobs, so how much you make is very much dependent on how often and how hard you work. In general, independent contractors, or consultants, earn more money than employees – up to 40% more, but don't let that fool you. The companies who hire you as a consultant are willing to pay you more because they don't have the same costs that they have for an employee, such as retirement benefits and taxes. You also don't get any sick leave. If you don't work, you don't get paid. If you want more than a state pension, you have to buy it yourself. However, these are all business expenses if you own your own company and, as an independent contractor, you *are* your own company. There are other expenses as well. You have start-up costs, insurance, business taxes, and if a customer can't or won't pay your bill, you may **be landed with** those costs too. So that's a look at the downsides. The key benefit of being an independent contractor is that you have much more control over your work and your income. You're your own boss. There's no **cap** on your salary, no limit to your growth. Some people like this kind of independence, but for others, the responsibility and uncertainty are so **daunting** that they don't even consider it. As an independent contractor, you take the responsibility and the blame. There's nobody else above you.

Now, if you already have quite a bit of work experience, and if you already have an idea that you think can be developed into an innovative product or service, you may want to take the last route – the start-up. I'm sure you've heard all sorts of stories about start-ups – probably at both extremes – the entrepreneur who became a billionaire by the age of 30, or the group of friends who slept under their desks for days on end in an unsuccessful effort to launch their company. And both are probably true, but which one do *you* think is more common? Make no mistake, a start-up is risky and a lot of work. I don't want to scare you, but, as in the case of consultants, you're your own boss, with full responsibility for the success or failure of your company. In this case, however, you're even more independent in that not only do you decide how much to work, when to work, etc., you're also able to decide *what* that work will be, and that's a crucial difference. When you're a consultant, the companies that hire you tell you what they want you to do. In a start-up, *you* provide the **vision**. So before you go down this road, you should engage in some self-reflection and decide if you have the discipline that this life requires. Just having a great idea won't be enough to carry you through to a successful launch and beyond. But if you're successful, you can take credit for all aspects of that success, and that can be incredibly rewarding.

One last note about this option. I've been discussing it as if you're going into it alone, but frequently, several people – often university friends, just like you – begin start-up companies together. I want to emphasize how stressful starting a new company can be, especially in the early days. So, if you decide to do this, make sure you take care of your personal relationships at the same time that you're taking care of business. There are lots of other details to discuss, and I encourage all of you to make individual appointments with our office if you have questions or you have a specific opportunity you'd like to talk over.

 6.2

1 We wanted to target this session at all of you in computer science and related degree programmes because, frankly, you'll probably have a lot more options when you finish your degree than other graduates.

2 Finally, especially for those of you graduating with more advanced degrees, there's the option of establishing your own business – a start-up company.

3 In theory, at least, you should have a safe workplace and be protected against discrimination and harassment.

4 However, these are all business expenses if you own your own company and, as an independent contractor, you *are* your own company.

5 I'm sure you've heard all sorts of stories about start-ups – probably at both extremes – the entrepreneur who became a billionaire by the age of 30, or the group of friends who slept under their desks for days on end in an unsuccessful

effort to launch their company. And both are probably true, but which one do *you* think is more common?

6 Frequently, several people – often university friends, just like you – begin start-up companies together. I want to emphasize how stressful starting a new company can be, especially in the early days. So, if you decide to do this, make sure you take care of your personal relationships at the same time that you're taking care of business.

 6.3

See script on page 131

 6.4

Careers advisor: Welcome everybody. This is supposed to be an informal session, guided by any questions you have about the whole job interview process. Keep in mind that there are going to be aspects of this process that are specific to different fields and industries, but I'm going to try to give you an overview and some advice that is general enough that it can apply to many different experiences. So, I'm going to divide our session into before, during and after the job interview, with an emphasis on the first two stages, which are really the most important. So, let's open the floor to questions about the before stage. Yes?

Student 1:   You say it's really important, so what do I need to do before the interview?

Careers advisor: I can answer that in a single word – prepare. There is absolutely no substitute for being prepared. That means doing research on the company or organization that you're hoping might employ you. There is a lot of information available on most public and many private companies, as well as non-profit organizations, on the web. We also have a lot of resources here in the office that you can consult. You want to know as much as possible about what the company does, what it sells and how it works before you set foot in the interview room.

Student 2:   Do I need to do research on the person who is going to interview me?

Careers advisor: If your interview is with somebody you might be working with, by all means; you should find out what you can about that person. But often you'll be interviewed by people in Human Resources who are just in charge of the hiring process.

Student 1:   I've heard that there is a standard set of questions that always get asked. Is that true, and should I prepare answers for them?

Careers advisor: Yes and no. I think there are some questions that you can anticipate being asked – and I'll mention some of them in just a sec, but you shouldn't count on those being the only ones. And as for preparation, yes, I think you should know how you want to answer the questions you think might be asked, but you shouldn't prepare so much that your answers sound **rehearsed** or mechanical. If, for example, you write out and practise giving specific answers, you probably won't sound natural or sincere. My advice would be to develop what we call 'talking points', that is, information that you want to be sure gets out there. You can probably work your talking points into some of your answers, no matter what the questions.

Student 3:   So what kind of questions should we expect? Will they be really general, like – What are your most important **accomplishments**? – or really specific, like questions about a specific computer language?

Careers advisor: Good question, and again, both are possible. As part of your research, you should find out the **format** for the interview. Will there just be general questions like the one you mentioned, or will there be a written part, or even a test of your knowledge or **analytical** skills?

Student 3: Well, what if it's just general questions?

Careers advisor: OK, so the kinds of things you can expect to be asked about are your accomplishments, certainly. You may be asked about your goals – where you see yourself in five years or in ten years. You may be asked about your work style – whether you do well in teams or if you like working on your own, how you deal with conflict, how well you adapt to change – things like that. You may also be asked the **dreaded** 'weakness' question.

Student 2: The weakness question?

Careers advisor: What is your greatest weakness?

Student 2: What should we say?

Careers advisor: Well, don't say something that makes you look bad, like 'I'm always late.' But you also shouldn't say something smug like 'My standards are too high.' Believe me, they've heard that one before. Your best bet is to think of something you have struggled with but have been working on trying to improve. For example, you can say in the past you had some problems with time management but now you use an app that helps you stay on top of tasks. OK, let's switch gears and talk about how to behave during an interview.

Student 2: Yeah, I need some help with that. I get nervous just thinking about it.

Careers advisor: Well, one thing you can do to help you feel less nervous is a practice interview with one of the advisors in this office. We record the session and then review it with you to make suggestions for improvement. But let me just give you a few tips to get us started. Probably, if I could make only one suggestion it would be to listen.

Student 1: Why is that? I thought they wanted information from us, not the other way around.

Careers advisor: It's both; they want to know about your communication skills, and listening is an important component of communication. You want to make sure that you answer the question that is being asked, not the one you *think* or *hope* is being asked.

Student 1: Makes sense.

Careers advisor: And ... Try to be concise in your answers. Say just enough to answer the question. Don't **ramble**. Whenever possible, provide concrete examples. So, if you're asked about your work style, don't just say you're collaborative, prove it by giving an example of a successful **collaboration** that you were part of.

Student 2: What if I can't answer the question? That's my biggest worry.

Careers advisor: Just be honest. Don't make things up. If you don't have the skill or you have no relevant experience to draw upon, just say so. Better for them to know now than later. OK, one final thing. Make sure you have some questions for them, just in case you're given that opportunity at the end of the interview. It shows that you've done your homework and also demonstrates your enthusiasm for the job.

Student 3: I know you said the first two stages were the most important, but what about afterwards? Do I need to write and thank the interviewers?

Careers advisor: It can be an informal email, but yes, you should always follow up an interview with a brief message, thanking the interviewers for their time. Also **reiterate** your interest in the position and remind them why you'd be a good fit for the organization.

Student 3: OK, thanks.

Careers advisor: That's about all we have time for today. If you already have an interview scheduled, please make an appointment for a practice interview as soon as possible. Thanks for coming everybody.

 6.5

1 If your interview is with somebody you might be working with, by all means; you should find out what you can about that person. But often you'll be interviewed by people in human resources who are just in charge of the hiring process.

2 And as for preparation, yes, I think you should know how you want to answer the questions you think might be asked, but you shouldn't prepare so much that your answers sound rehearsed or mechanical. If, for example, you write out and practise giving specific answers, you probably won't sound natural or sincere.

3 You may be asked about your goals – where you see yourself in five years or in ten years.

4 Well, don't say something that makes you look bad, like 'I'm always late.' But you also shouldn't say something smug like 'My standards are too high.' Believe me, they've heard that one before.

5 Try to be concise in your answers. Say just enough to answer the question. Don't ramble.

UNIT 7

▶ Water pollution in West Virginia

Reporter: West Virginia state officials say the water is safe, but Matilda Murray doesn't believe them. What do you say to them?

Murray: No way. You guys can drink it. I'm absolutely not going to let my kids drink it, or me. I won't even let my cat have the water.

Reporter: More than a week after a chemical leak contaminated the water supply of 300,000 West Virginians, the water company and the state's health officials are still trying to convince people that the water no longer poses a threat, even though the effects of the coal-cleaning chemical known as MCHM are unknown. Here in coal country, the chemical leak has reignited a debate about whether the power of industry trumps health and environmental concerns, and whether the politicians have blocked changes. Senator Joe Manchin is the state's former governor.

Reporter: The signs were there. West Virginia did not act. Is that fair?

Sen. Manchin: It depends on what side you're looking if it's fair. Could we have done more? Should we have done more? Must we do more? Absolutely. Is other states in the same peril that we're in? Probably so and don't know it.

Reporter: Manchin is a key supporter of legislation that will require regular inspections of chemical storage facilities nationwide like the Freedom Industries plant responsible for the leak.

Sen. Manchin: This legislation will prevent this from ever happening again. What I can do is, take from the situation that we're dealing with today, and hopefully prevent it from ever happening. And that's what you should do – learn from what has happened.

Reporter: Matilda Murray wants to know why oversight hasn't been there from the beginning.

Murray: Why haven't they been inspecting their equipment? And now it's all leaking in our water.

Reporter: She says it will be months before she even considers letting any of her children near it. For CBS This Morning, Jeff Pegues, Charleston, West Virginia.

 7.1

Presenter: Good evening, everybody. In this day and age, everybody knows somebody who has asthma. Maybe it's you, your child, a sibling or a friend, but asthma touches everybody in some way. I want to give you an overview of what this disease is, what we know about it from both scientific and historical research, and the current thinking on how to manage it. Asthma is a chronic disease of the lungs; specifically, it affects the airways that carry air in and out of your lungs. These airways become irritated and swollen if you have asthma, often causing symptoms such as difficulty breathing as well as coughing, especially when you lie down. As I'll explain a little later, it turns out that asthma is probably not just one disease. So, for some people, the symptoms only appear when they're exposed to some sort of trigger in the environment. Other asthma sufferers experience some level of these symptoms all the time.

So here is the big mystery. In many countries, asthma rates are soaring. In the first decade of the twenty-first century, the number of cases climbed 25%. Today, 300 million people suffer from asthma globally. What's more, asthma is 50 times more common in urban centres like London and New York than in areas of rural Africa. The big question is why? Why this enormous and relatively sudden increase, and why the huge **disparity** between the developed and developing worlds? Let me begin by telling you that we don't have definitive answers to these questions. We don't know what causes asthma, nor do we know how to cure it. However, we do have some idea of what triggers symptoms, and we do have effective ways to manage these symptoms.

Now, a lot of what I'm talking about today is environmental health, and indeed, although genetics is the single most powerful predictor of the development of asthma, it cannot be the whole story. Our genes change far too slowly to explain the rapid increase of this disease. So scientists and medical researchers have turned to the environment for explanations. Frequently mentioned triggers include indoor and outdoor pollution. Indoor pollution includes dust, mould, tobacco smoke, pet hair and various chemicals used for cleaning. Outdoor pollution includes particulate matter – very small pieces of dirt, chemicals, and pollutants trapped in the air – and ground-level ozone, formed when pollution from cars and factories combine with heat and sunlight. Studies have found a **correlation** between proximity to both of these types of pollution and the development of asthma. These factors are also strongly associated with the **severity** of its symptoms. Nevertheless, there is conflicting historical data. For example, the rapid increase in air pollution in Chinese cities has been accompanied by a similar rise in asthma in that country – as much as 40% in the past 20 years. On the other hand, the reunification of Germany in 1990 provides a counter-example. East Germany suffered from far more serious pollution than West Germany at the time, yet asthma was a much bigger problem in the West than in the East. Ironically, as the former East Germany tackled its air pollution, its rate of asthma actually rose. About this time, another proposal was made, the so-called ***Hygiene*** *Hypothesis*, which goes something like this: when children are young, adults make an effort to keep the home and school environments as clean as possible. One might even go so far as to say that we try to keep these places free of germs, often with the use of anti-microbial products. In doing so, they may actually be interfering with the natural development of the immune system by depriving it of exposure to infectious microbes. Without this exposure early in life, the immune system is unprepared when it encounters these microbes later in life. Environmental triggers can cause the immune system to overreact with an allergic response – or for some people, an asthma attack. This was the hypothesis used to explain the German situation. Germ-conscious West Germany may have prevented children from being exposed to infections – exposure that might have protected them later in life.

The problem with this theory is that, although the explanation works pretty well for **allergies**, it doesn't always hold up as well for asthma, particularly its most chronic forms. Let me explain. Where asthma rates are rising dramatically today is in poor, urban areas, which are not particularly clean or germ-free. So, what are we to conclude? Both the pollution and the hygiene hypotheses may partially explain the increased **incidence** of asthma, but neither provides a complete explanation. Other factors seem to come into play as well, for example, diet. Specific foods, like eggs, milk and nuts, trigger asthma attacks in some people. How much you eat is also an issue; there is a high rate of **obesity** among asthma sufferers. It's interesting to note that all of these factors – increased air pollution, an increased focus on cleanliness, rising rates of obesity resulting from an unhealthy diet and sedentary lifestyle – might all be placed into the category of 'modern life'. Certainly, none of these factors is present in the rural communities of the developing world that show such low rates of the disease.

So there simply are no clear and simple answers regarding cause – yet. However, we do have a pretty good track record on managing asthma symptoms. Of course, any asthma sufferer should consult a doctor regarding options for medication, but here are just a few **guidelines** sufferers can follow to keep themselves safe and healthy: One – check daily air quality reports. On days when pollution levels are high, stay indoors as much as possible and don't engage in vigorous exercise.

Two – plan exercise and outdoor activities in the morning or early evening when pollution levels are lower.

Three – eat a nutritious diet and ensure you maintain a healthy weight.

Four – control the amount of dust in your home.

Five – avoid the use of cleaning sprays, scented candles and air fresheners.

Six – don't smoke.

And finally, seven – learn your own specific triggers so you can limit your exposure to them or avoid them.

These are just some general suggestions. Each person is different and to some extent, he or she will have to learn about their triggers and reactions by trial and error.

 7.2

Presenter: Now, a lot of what I'm talking about today is environmental health, and indeed, although genetics is the single most powerful predictor of the development of asthma, it cannot be the whole story. Our genes change far too slowly to explain the rapid increase of this disease. So scientists and medical researchers have turned to the environment for explanations.

Frequently mentioned triggers include indoor and outdoor pollution. Indoor pollution includes dust, mould, tobacco smoke, pet hair, and various chemicals used for cleaning. Outdoor pollution includes particulate matter – very small pieces of dirt, chemicals, and pollutants trapped in the air – and ground-level ozone, formed when pollution from cars and factories combine with heat and sunlight. Studies have found a correlation between proximity to both of these types of pollution and the development of asthma. These factors are also strongly associated with the severity of its symptoms. Nevertheless, there is conflicting historical data. For example, the rapid increase in air pollution in Chinese cities has been accompanied by a similar rise in asthma in that country – as much as 40% in the past 20 years. On the other hand, the reunification of Germany in 1990 provides a counter-example. East Germany suffered from far more serious pollution than West Germany at the time, yet asthma was a much bigger problem in the West than in the East. Ironically, as the former East Germany tackled its air pollution, its rate of asthma actually rose.

About this time, another proposal was made, the so-called Hygiene Hypothesis, which goes something like this: when children are young, adults make an effort to keep the home and school environments as clean as possible. One might even go so far as to say that we try to keep these places free of germs, often with the use of anti-microbial products. In doing so, we may actually be interfering with the natural development of the immune system by depriving it of exposure to infectious microbes. Without this exposure early in life, the immune system is unprepared when it encounters these microbes later in life. Environmental triggers can cause the immune system to overreact with an allergic response – or for some people, an asthma attack. This was the hypothesis used to explain the German situation. Germ-conscious West Germany may have prevented children from being exposed to infections – exposure that might have protected them later in life.

The problem with this theory is that, although the explanation works pretty well for allergies, it doesn't always hold up as well for asthma, particularly its most chronic forms. Let me explain. Where asthma rates are rising dramatically today is in poor, urban areas, which are not particularly clean or germ-free.

So, what are we to conclude? Both the pollution and hygiene hypotheses may partially explain the increased incidence of asthma, but neither provides a complete explanation. Other factors seem to come into play as well, for example, diet. Specific foods, like eggs, milk, and nuts, trigger asthma attacks in some people. How much you eat is also an issue; there is a high rate of obesity among asthma sufferers. It's interesting to note that all of these factors – increased air pollution, an increased focus on cleanliness, rising rates of obesity resulting from an unhealthy diet and sedentary lifestyle – might all be placed into the category of 'modern life'. Certainly, none of these factors is present in the rural communities of the developing world that show such low rates of the disease.

 7.3

1 So, for some people, the symptoms only appear when they're exposed to some sort of trigger in the environment. Other asthma sufferers experience some level of these symptoms all the time.

2 Asthma is 50 times more common in urban centres like London and New York than in areas of rural Africa.

3 We don't know what causes asthma, nor do we know how to cure it. However, we do have some idea of what triggers symptoms, and we do have effective ways to manage these symptoms.

7.4

1 East Germany suffered from far more serious pollution than West Germany at the time, yet asthma was a much bigger problem in the West than in the East.

2 Without this exposure early in life, the immune system is unprepared when it encounters these microbes later in life.

3 Both the pollution and the hygiene hypotheses may partially explain the increased incidence of asthma, but neither provides a complete explanation.

7.5

Moderator: This is the story of how things went wrong and how some people tried to fix the problem, and some people tried to hide it. It's the story of one place in the UK, Swansbeck, but the lessons are relevant for cities and towns everywhere. If we want to prevent this from happening in the future, we need to know what happened. We've invited some of the people who played a part in this story to discuss Swansbeck's troubles. Not everybody agreed to participate, but we'll try to give you a balanced perspective, nevertheless. We'll also take some questions from the audience. Let me introduce our panellists:

7.6

Moderator: Let me introduce our panellists: Dr Huda Khan, an environmental scientist who works for the government. She did a lot of the water quality testing in Swansbeck and has been very helpful to the people of Swansbeck. So has Dr Robert Hardwick, a paediatrician, who documented the health of Swansbeck's children. Michael Kirk, an assistant to the current mayor of Swansbeck. I should point out from the start that none of those responsible for the deplorable condition of Swansbeck's water during the crisis would agree to participate in our discussion. Mr Kirk and the current mayor are both new to their jobs. Dr Khan, could you start by explaining how all of this happened, from a scientific perspective?

Khan: Of course. In many of our towns and cities, the water and sewer systems were installed more than a hundred years ago, when lead pipes were standard. Lead was cheap and easy to work with, and nobody had any idea about its toxic **properties** at that time. Even when we did discover the damage that lead can cause, we weren't thinking that much about lead poisoning because if the pipes are in good condition, it was thought that the amount of lead that escaped into the water would be **minimal**. On top of that, we have government guidelines that every city must follow. Cities are required to test lead levels regularly. Such measures are critical to public health and when cities follow these guidelines, the system works quite well. The city thought the water was safe and so did I, at least in the beginning.

Moderator: So why was the situation in Swansbeck different? Why were the pipes there a problem?

Khan: About a year and a half ago, the city switched its water supply and began using water that was more acidic than the previous supply.

Moderator: That's a problem?

Khan: The problem is that the acidity in the water began to eat away at the pipes, allowing the lead to **contaminate** the water. Every city is required to have a plan to test water for acidity and, based on those tests, take measures to counter the damage the acidity can do to water pipes, especially lead pipes. And that's where the council was at fault. They had no such plan. It was an appalling lapse in judgment. As a result, the **concentration** of lead in the city's water rose well above acceptable levels. I have spent my career studying lead toxicity, but I have never seen anything like this before.

Moderator: So, Dr Hardwick, what did this mean for the people of Swansbeck? What happens when people drink water with high levels of lead?

Hardwick: Lead is incredibly toxic – to the nervous system, to the reproductive system, but most of all, it affects brain development. And for that reason, lead poisoning has the most damaging impact on children. Numerous studies that I've been involved with have demonstrated that children with high levels of lead in their systems often end up with cognitive impairments, learning disabilities, behavioural problems, and in some cases, these can be quite severe. Even a small increase in lead levels has been shown to have a negative impact on cognitive development. And the most heartbreaking part is that the damage is irreversible. This means people who have been exposed to lead as children may face a lifetime of problems, in school, at work, in everything they do. Their futures are deeply **compromised** because of this lead exposure.

Moderator: Thank you. I see we have a question from somebody in the audience.

Johnson: My name is Monica Johnson. I moved to Swansbeck because I thought it would be a nice place to raise our children, and until about a year and a half ago, it was. But then things changed. The water coming out of the taps was yellow, sometimes orange. It smelled terrible and tasted worse. After I took a shower or my kids had a bath, our skin turned red. My kids got terrible rashes and severe stomach pains. The situation was unbearable. After a few months, our hair started to fall out. I panicked. I knew something was wrong, but I didn't know what to do. I called the council but they kept claiming that nothing was wrong. I was outraged at their lack of concern. I finally found somebody I could trust, Dr Khan. She agreed to come test the water in our home.

Moderator: Mr Kirk? I know you were not in your job at the time, but can you tell us anything about what happened?

Kirk: Well, what I can tell you is that the council was not conducting the tests of water quality correctly – local testing was not carried out to national standards, results led people to believe the water wasn't as contaminated as it really was. The people Mrs Johnson spoke to at the council really did believe the water was safe. Since then, we've updated the procedures for testing water quality. With the new tests, the damage to the pipes is very clear. The council is deeply sorry for the problems this has caused your family.

Johnson: Problems?! Both of my children have learning disabilities. My six-year-old son has literacy problems. My eight-year-old has been in so many fights that he's been kicked out of two schools. So, what do you think? What kind of life do they have to look forward to?

Moderator: Dr Hardwick?

Hardwick: In fact, I began to notice some of these problems in a lot of the patients at the clinic. I recognized them as possible symptoms of lead poisoning, so I started doing blood tests, and I was appalled by what I found. You need to understand that no level of lead in the blood is considered safe, and five micrograms per decilitre is considered highly toxic, capable of causing serious and permanent damage. And I was finding levels *above* that. So I started researching hospital records and found a dramatic difference between the lead levels in children before and after the water supply was changed. What I found was shocking, I would say, even criminal.

Khan: Dr Hardwick's findings are consistent with the test results on water from the Johnsons' house and many other homes that I tested. I found lead levels seven times higher than the government's action level. The action level is the point at which the council is supposed to step in to take measures to address the problem. In fact, they did nothing until the national government finally **intervened**.

Moderator: Mr Kirk, can you tell us what measures the council is taking now? You said you've gone back to the original water supply.

Kirk: Yes, but the problem is that all those pipes are now damaged and need to be replaced, which is an incredibly expensive undertaking. The national government has given the council a grant to begin replacing them, but that will be a lengthy process. For now, we're supplying residents with bottled water. I know these are not permanent solutions, but fixing a problem this big is going to take more time.

 7.7

Host: Good morning, welcome to *Morning Matters,* where we listen to what's on your mind. Good morning. Tell us your name and what's on your mind!

Zara: My name's Zara. I live near Great Crossing. It's a nice little complex. There's a library, an indoor play space for kids, an after-school tutoring centre and a few shops and offices. My son goes to the tutoring centre. I've just heard that a FryKing restaurant may be opening there.

Host: The fast-food spot. Is there a problem? Doesn't your son like FryKing?

Zara: It's his favourite. The problem is that he's ten years old and 48 kg! Yesterday I got a flyer under my door about the growing public health problems of heart disease and diabetes. Fast food is killing our young people. Is there some way I can stop FryKing from moving in next door? If it opens, I'm going to take my son out of the tutoring centre and so will my neighbours.

Host: I'm not sure. Hold on. We have another caller. Are you responding to this issue?

Hamid: This is Hamid and I have an electronics store in the complex. My business has been suffering terribly. Everyone just orders online. With FryKing on the corner, more people will walk by my shop. I can't wait for them to open!

Host: I can see that this is complicated. I have another person waiting to talk. Hello, who am I speaking to?

Nadia: My name is Nadia. My family runs an insurance office in the complex. It's right above where FryKing would be. Everything in the office will smell of fried food. Clients won't want to visit my office. And Zara is right about how unhealthy it is. When I was a child, we ate healthy food. Now everybody eats burgers and fried fish. Everyone I know is on medication. We should have a health club in this space instead of a fast-food restaurant!

Host: Everyone seems to have an opinion about this. The manager of the office complex has just called in. Perhaps he can help us out.

Manager: Thank you. I have been listening to this very interesting conversation. I am a businessman and my job is to make the complex profitable. If FryKing increases business in the complex, that's a good thing, but if it drives people away, perhaps we need to reconsider our plan. We also care deeply about public health. So, I've just spoken to the owner and he would like to invite all of you to a meeting next week to hear your views.

🔊 7.8

1 Lead is incredibly toxic – to the nervous system, to the reproductive system, but most of all, it affects brain development.

2 And the most heartbreaking part is that the damage is irreversible.

3 My kids got terrible rashes and severe stomach pains.

4 The council is deeply sorry for the problems this has caused your family.

5 You need to understand that no level of lead in the blood is considered safe.

6 What I found was shocking, I would say, even criminal.

UNIT 8

▶ **Lufthansa signs cooperation deal with Etihad**

Narrator: The Abu Dhabi airline, Etihad Aviation Group and Germany's Lufthansa Airlines have entered into a new commercial partnership.

At a press conference in Abu Dhabi today, the chief executives signed a contract which included 100 million dollars' worth of global catering provision and an agreement which promises cooperation in the maintenance and improvement of aircraft.

Today's deal is believed to be just the start of the airline's partnership – with both CEOs clearly signposting that they planned to explore the possibility of further ways to work together. The initial venture indicates their aim to expand their future collaboration in a joint strategy for growth in the European aviation market.

Lufthansa CEO: ... coming up around the world, what better answer is there than aviation?

Narrator: Lufthansa's LSG Sky Chefs will become Etihad's biggest caterer outside of Abu Dhabi. They will be dishing up the goods in sixteen cities around the globe for Etihad's passenger aircrafts over the next four years. This 100-million-dollar deal covers major cities Europe, Asia and the Americas.

Of equal importance was an agreement signed between Etihad and Lufthansa Technik – a subsidiary of Lufthansa Airlines and a world leader in maintenance, repair, improvements and the interior design and fitting of passenger planes. Etihad Airways and its partners will benefit from these services, whilst Lufthansa agreed to look for opportunities to collaborate with Etihad Airways Engineering, who provide a portfolio of similar services.

Other areas of future partnerships could include freight operations, procurement and passenger services, with both airlines keen to advance their offering not only in the European market, but globally.

As the new partners reached for the skies together they shared flight codes, which went on sale today. Lufthansa's 'LH' code will be seen twice a day on Etihad Airways' passenger flights between Frankfurt and Munich in Germany and Abu Dhabi in the UAE – giving the German airline access to new so-called 'feeder markets' throughout the Indian Subcontinent.

Etihad's 'EY' code will be placed on non-stop intercontinental services run by Lufthansa between the important business hubs of Frankfurt and Rio de Janeiro in Brazil, and later Bogota in Columbia – extending the Abu Dhabi airline's global reach into the South American market.

🔊 8.1

Speaker: All of you have worked in groups at one time or another – at school, at work, in your community, or even on a jury – groups that have to make decisions. Knowing how to work effectively in groups is very important in all kinds of settings. And knowing something about group **dynamics** – that's the technical name for this – can be very useful. It will help you develop insights into your own behaviour and how that behaviour can affect the dynamics of the groups you participate in, especially when there is conflict.

In general, groups have an assigned task to complete – a report, a project, or an assessment – giving the group members a shared goal. Completing the assigned task requires making decisions. Of course, individual members of a group may also have their own goals, which may or may not be consistent with the group goal. And some individuals may not be interested in arriving at a decision or completing the project at all. So then what happens? What will you do if your group has a 'bad apple' – a person who consistently engages in some sort of negative or destructive behaviour?

Now 'bad apple' behaviour can take several forms. Some bad apples are slackers. Slackers express a lack of interest in the task. They may not actively oppose the actions or disagree with ideas of other members of the group; they simply refuse to contribute any effort or deal with the task. Their attitude can be summed up in one word: 'whatever'. Other bad apples express generally negative feelings about the group, its task, and its chances of success. These naysayers reject or criticize the ideas and opinions of others without proposing any **constructive** ideas of their own. Finally, some bad apples are simply **bullies**. They'll insist on doing things their way and only their way. Now you might think that in a group, especially in a large group, one person might not make that much of a difference, no matter how badly he or she behaves. The majority should **prevail**, right? But this is not how group dynamics work. Research suggests that it only takes one member of a group to act badly – one bad apple – to interfere with the group's dynamics and prevent it from functioning effectively. One bad apple actually does 'spoil the barrel'. In one study in which the researchers hired actors to play 'bad apples' in group decision-making tasks, groups with a bad apple member generally performed 30–40% worse than groups with no negative members. The researchers concluded that the group's worst member was the best predictor of the whole group's performance. This was true even when a group's other members were all intelligent, well-educated, otherwise effective people. But it's even worse than that. What these researchers found was that the behaviour of one bad apple can spread to the whole group. The other members began to adopt the same negative behaviour. If the bad apple was a slacker and, say, pulled out a smartphone and started texting during the discussion, other members began to follow suit. They stopped making any effort and began to withdraw from the group interaction. If the bad apple was overly critical of others or made pessimistic statements like, 'This will never work' or 'This is so stupid', other members also became critical or began to express similarly negative views. And if the bad apple bullied the other members, for the most part, they didn't try to resist. They just let the bad apple have their own way. And perhaps just as importantly, everybody had a negative response to the entire experience. Just one bad apple destroyed the group's positive dynamics. Specifically, the bad apple's behaviour resulted in **perceptions** of unfairness among members, reduced trust in the group, withdrawal from interaction, and generally negative emotions – anger, **resentment**, even fear.

So what can you do if you're stuck in a group with a participant who displays such negative behaviour? A few strategies have been shown to be effective in **counteracting** the 'bad apple effect'. The most obvious approach is to simply remove the individual from the group, but, as I'm sure you know, that's not always possible. A second option is to demand that the individual change his or her behaviour – which is probably only possible if somebody in the group has sufficient authority to make that happen, and that's a big *if*. But the study also found that sometimes a group just gets lucky. If the group has an exceptional individual who is able to engage all of the group members, including the bad apple, it may be possible to **defuse** conflict. This kind of skilled leader can keep the decision-making process moving forward no matter what. Unfortunately, there's no guarantee that there will be a skilled leader in a group. In fact, very few of the groups in the study had one. And if results of this study are reflective of group dynamics in more natural situations, it's safe to assume that the 'bad apple' effect is pretty widespread. But perhaps you already know that. The lead researcher in the study said he had become interested in the topic because of a personal experience, and as he spoke about the idea to colleagues and friends, he found that just about everybody had had a 'bad apple' experience – a situation in which one person made the atmosphere in an office, a class, or other group thoroughly unpleasant. It can be difficult to prevent bad apples from

ruining a group and its dynamics, but recognizing them early and understanding how they operate may help you defuse the conflicts they create, so that your group can achieve its goals. I hope that this presentation has helped you gain that understanding.

 8.2

In general, groups have an assigned task to complete – a report, a project, or an assessment – giving the group members a shared goal. Completing the assigned task requires making decisions. Of course, individual members of a group may also have their own goals, which may or may not be consistent with the group goal. And some individuals may not be interested in arriving at a decision or completing the project at all. So then what happens? What will you do if your group has a 'bad apple' – a person who consistently engages in some sort of negative or destructive behaviour?

Now 'bad apple' behaviour can take several forms. Some bad apples are slackers. Slackers express a lack of interest in the task. They may not actively oppose the actions or disagree with ideas of other members of the group; they simply refuse to contribute any effort or deal with the task. Their attitude can be summed up in one word: 'whatever'. Other bad apples express generally negative feelings about the group, its task, and its chances of success. These naysayers reject or criticize the ideas and opinions of others without proposing any constructive ideas of their own. Finally, some bad apples are simply bullies. They'll insist on doing things their way and only their way. Now you might think that in a group, especially in a large group, one person might not make that much of a difference, no matter how badly he or she behaves. The majority should prevail, right? But this is not how group dynamics work. Research suggests that it only takes one member of a group to act badly – one bad apple – to interfere with the group's dynamics and prevent it from functioning effectively. One bad apple actually does 'spoil the barrel'. In one study in which the researchers hired actors to play 'bad apples' in group decision-making tasks, groups with a bad apple member generally performed 30–40% worse than groups with no negative members. The researchers concluded that the group's worst member was the best predictor of the whole group's performance. This was true even when a group's other members were all intelligent, well-educated, otherwise effective people. But it's even worse than that. What these researchers found was that the behaviour of one bad apple can spread to the whole group. The other members began to adopt the same negative behaviour. If the bad apple was a slacker and, say, pulled out a smartphone and started texting during the discussion, other members began to follow suit. They stopped making any effort and began to withdraw from the group interaction. If the bad apple was overly critical of others or made pessimistic statements like, 'This will never work' or 'This is so stupid', other members also became critical or began to express similarly negative views. And if the bad apple bullied the other members, for the most part, they didn't try to resist. They just let the bad apple have their own way. And perhaps just as importantly, everybody had a negative response to the entire experience. Just one bad apple destroyed the group's positive dynamics. Specifically, the bad apple's behaviour resulted in perceptions of unfairness among members, reduced trust in the group, withdrawal from interaction, and generally negative emotions – anger, resentment, even fear.

 8.3

1 They'll insist on doing things their way and only their way.

2 Of course, individual members of a group may also have their own goals, which may or may not be consistent with the group goal.

3 The other members began to adopt the same negative behaviour.

4 'This will never work' or 'This is so stupid,' other members also became critical or began to express similarly negative views.

5 And perhaps just as importantly, everybody had a negative response to the entire experience.

 8.4

Teacher: OK, class, we've come to the end of our unit on decision-making, so I'd like to take some time today to review what we've learned. We took a difficult, real-life problem and approached it in two ways. So first, let's review the problem. Would somebody describe it for us briefly? Yes, go ahead.

Student 1: OK, well, there is a basic disagreement about how to use a piece of waterfront property. An old structure has just been demolished, and a billionaire entrepreneur wants to build a museum on the site. He plans to donate his spectacular art collection to the museum and provide a huge amount of money which will ensure its future. This would be a public museum; it would not belong to the businessman. I guess you could say it's his **legacy** to the city. On the other side, a group of city residents, Citizens for Open Spaces, wants to add the property to the existing waterfront parkland and keep the area open for public use.

Teacher: Thank you. So the class's job was to make a decision about how to use this land. We went through two different decision-making processes. The first one was pretty familiar. Can somebody else describe that? Uh-huh.

Student 2: Representatives from the two different sides presented us with their arguments. We discussed the two different options and then we took a vote. Citizens for Open Spaces won, 18 to 8.

Teacher: OK, so one side won, but a lot of people must have been unhappy with the result.

Student 2: True, but the majority won.

Teacher: OK. And then we moved on to a different process, addressing the same issue. How was this process different?

Student 3: It took a lot longer!

Teacher: That's for sure. What else? Can somebody describe the steps we went through in this **consensus**-building process?

Student 4: Well, we were all pretty familiar with the issues already, but the facilitator just described the two options again. She was clearly trying to be objective and not take sides.

Student 5: Yeah, that was one big difference. We had a facilitator, a person who sort of kept the process moving and helped us organize our ideas. She stressed the process has to start out with everybody in agreement about one thing.

Teacher: What's that?

Student 5: That they're willing to work together to reach a decision; that they want to solve the problem. Without that, the process cannot work.

Teacher: OK, great, so how did it start out?

Student 5: Everybody had a chance to talk. We all stated what our concerns were, especially things that we didn't like about one or the other of the options.

Student 2: And we also talked about how to **resolve** differences, not just about choosing between the two options. I mean, we came up with lots of different ideas.

Teacher: What do you mean?

Student 2: We broke down both options into components so that we could look at them separately.

Teacher: Can you give an example?

Student 3: I can. So one of the objections to the museum was the design. It'll block the view of the lake, and it doesn't really fit in with the surrounding park area.

Student 4: And it'll have a big ugly parking lot, too.

Teacher: So did this step make a difference?

Student 1: Yes, I think it really did. It helped everybody to clarify what exactly they did and didn't like about the two options, and it allowed alternate and **hybrid** proposals to emerge.

Teacher: So did everybody agree on one of those?

Student 4: Not straight away. But it gave us a place to start. We had to go back to the drawing board when some people expressed **reservations**.

Teacher: So then what did you do?

Student 4: We tinkered with all of the elements until we came up with a proposal that everybody could live with.

Teacher: That *everybody* could live with? How do you know that?

Student 2: That's one of the steps in the consensus-building process. The facilitator tested for agreement. She asked everybody if they could support the proposal – or at least that they wouldn't oppose it.

Teacher: So there was no vote?

Student 4: No, not really. She just kept checking for agreement with each new version of the proposal until she got consensus from the whole group.

Teacher: So everybody was in favour of the final proposal?

Student 3: Well, that may be a bit of an exaggeration, but I think everybody felt as if they had participated in the decision-making process and that their concerns had been addressed.

Teacher: So what was the final proposal?

Student 3: We decided to let the museum proposal move forward, but with a very different design. The building will be much shorter, and the design will be more organic and consistent with the natural setting. Also, the car park will be underground and out of sight.

Teacher: Anything else?

Student 1: Yeah, the museum's founder, the entrepreneur, agreed to donate some money to improve and expand the park next to the museum.

Teacher: Wow. So a very different **outcome** than with the first process. So how do you feel now about these two different ways of approaching decision-making?

Student 2: I think everybody was a lot happier with the second way. Well, let me rephrase that: in the consensus-building process, there were no winners and no losers. I'm sure in the voting process the winners were happy, but the losers were really unhappy. When the decision was made by consensus, everybody still had a **stake** in the project going forward. Nobody felt like their opinion was ignored or dismissed.

Student 5: Yes, it felt like even the people who initially opposed the museum might end up visiting it. With the first process, you had the feeling that the losers might resent the park and never get any enjoyment out of it. The conflict had never really been resolved.

Teacher: So a compromise?

Student 4: Not really. In a compromise, everybody has to give something up. And maybe that happened here, but we all created the new proposal together, so it didn't feel as if anyone was giving something up exactly. Everybody felt some sense of **ownership**. It just felt like a better decision all around.

Teacher: Well, this all sounds pretty positive. Is there a downside to this? Why aren't all decisions made this way?

Student 2: Well, it took forever to arrive at the final decision. In the first process, the decision was made in an hour. In the consensus process, we worked most of the day. I guess what I'm saying is that not everybody is going to have that kind of time.

Student 1: Also we're a pretty small group. I think it could be really challenging if you tried it with a big group of people.

Teacher: All very interesting and insightful comments. Well, I hope that this has been a learning experience for all of you and that you'll use some of what you've learned here in the future.

🔊 8.5

Speaker: Our first candidate is DINESCO.

DINESCO has been on the campus for more than 20 years, providing a range of catering services across the campus, including the current dining room in the Student Centre, which is open from 7 am to 11 pm. It serves hot meals, salads, sandwiches, snacks, desserts – everything you'd expect from a catering service.

DINESCO holds the campus catering service contract, so that means that the university pays an annual fee to DINESCO for their services. Students who live on campus can eat at the Student Centre facility as part of their dining contract. They can eat as much and whatever they want. Other students and members of the public have to pay for individual meals or snacks there. The cost is reasonable for those who use unlimited services, perhaps less so for those who pay for individual meals.

Many students and visitors have complained about the quality and choice of the food that DINESCO provides.

🔊 8.6

Speaker: The next candidate for the campus catering service contract is Sharzad.

Sharzad is a popular casual dining chain that has Middle Eastern roots. Many of our students know and enjoy Sharzad food. They serve breakfast, pita sandwiches, kebabs and salad. They also sell snacks such as yogurt, fruit, and crisps. Service is fast and the prices are moderate. Sharzad already operates a 24-hour restaurant in the Natural Sciences building, which is very popular with students and always crowded. The Student Centre restaurant would also be open 24 hours. It would be included in the student dining contract, but there would be limits on the amount of food that students could consume. Some students complain that there is not very much variety in the menu. Sharzad would pay the university a significant sum of money to rent the space in the Student Centre. 10% of these funds would go to support student activities.

🔊 8.7

Speaker: The final candidate for the campus catering service contract is Unihub.

Unihub is the name of a proposed café and casual dining spot that would be managed and operated by hospitality and catering students. Students would manage the business operations, the kitchen, and the dining room under the supervision of the university staff. Working at Unihub would serve as the required practical experience component of their degree.

This new facility would serve sandwiches, salads, pasta, and other informal food. It would be open for lunch and dinner. During late night hours, a small section of the restaurant would be open for takeaway food. Though it would be included in the student dining contract, it would only cover lunch and dinner. And the prices would be expected to be higher than at the current DINESCO facility.

In addition, the university would have to subsidize the operation; in other words, we'd need to contribute funds toward its operation because it wouldn't be expected to make a profit, at least not initially. The money would come from the student activities fund.

UNIT 9

 First anthropomimetic robot

Presenter: I've come to meet a scientist, who has built the world's first anthropomimetic robot – which means, it mimics the human body. Because he believes that our physical form actually helps shape the way we think – and, without a body, artificial intelligence cannot exist.

Scientist: What we're interested in is how the brain controls the body – and, having built the body, we've realized what a serious problem that is.

Presenter: This robot – called ECCE Robot – obviously has no blood, skin, or flesh. But, it has bones, joints, muscles and tendons that move exactly like ours. So, it's able to have human-like interactions with its world. Now, this is an extraordinary piece of engineering, but how does it help in actually getting insight into intelligence?

Scientist: We are interested in what is known as embodied intelligence. And this is the idea that your intelligence is not a sort of abstract, free intelligence; it's actually tied very much to having a body – and, in particular, to having a human body. Now in order to investigate this, what we had to do was build a robot that had as near to a human body as we could manage. Then we can begin investigating how the way it interacts with the world enables it to develop a particular sort of intelligence for, um, dealing with objects, er, and so on. And, once we get on that track, we'll be able